bruss

CW00322432

a guide

First published in 2001
Virgin Publishing Ltd, London w6 9HA
Copyright 2001 © Virgin Publishing Ltd, London

getting your bearings
[→4–5]

mapping brussels'
key areas

virgin brussels contents

getting your bearings

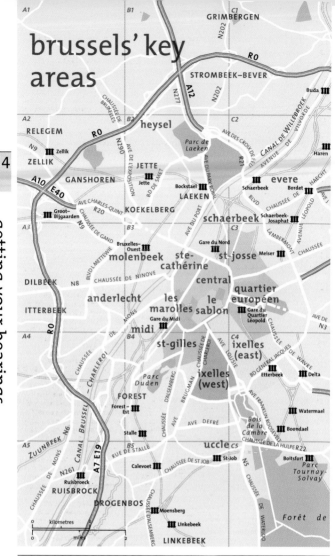

brussels' key areas

♟ directory

Anderlecht ♟A3–B3:
This run-down former industrial district, with a large Northwest African community, is famed for its football team and blamed for most of Brussels' crime problems. The glass-and-steel former abattoir now houses an excellent meat market, while the little-visited western parts of Anderlecht are refreshingly rural.

Central ♟B3 [→13–19]

Evere ♟C2:
Few visitors traipse out here unless they know someone who works for NATO, which hurriedly moved its HQ here when France briefly pulled

out of the alliance in the 1960s. It's a dismal compound resembling a prison-cum-barracks.

Jette ♟B2:
Northwest Brussels is mainly residential, but Jette is worth a visit for the Musée René Magritte [→68], the surprisingly bourgeois home of the arch Surrealist from 1930–1954, and for its light-house-style cultural centre.

Heysel (Heizel) ♟B2:
Home of the Atomium [→60], the notorious, once-eponymous football stadium (now renamed Stade Roi Boudouin), and Bruparck Village [→78] a sublimely

tacky leisure complex with fast-food joints housed in mock-baroque houses, a water park, the Kinepolis multiplex [→78], and the kitsch-tastic model monuments of Mini-Europe [→78].

Ixelles (East) (Elsene – Oost) ♟C4 [→38–41]

Ixelles (West) (Elsene – West) ♟B4 [→33–37]

Laeken (Laken) ♟B2:
Even though their castle is off-limits for the proles, you can't escape the influence of the Belgian royals in this verdant northern suburb: the Église Notre-Dame de Laeken houses the royal crypt,

grandioso

le sablon

The terraces of the cobbled place du Grand Sablon are *the* spot to observe the fur-clad and well-heeled in their natural habitat. Big-shot lawyers blow their salaries on penthouse pads in the 17th- and 18th-century houses lining the square, while those confined to ground level find designer boutiques, classy interiors stores, upscale antiques shops, and elegant restaurants and bars. If all the posing makes you paranoid, head to the Petit Sablon, an elegant garden edged with statues depicting the medieval guilds, or to the museums of the Mont des Arts. The Sunday antiques market, in front of the recently scrubbed Gothic Eglise Notre-Dame du Sablon, is the opposite of the Marolles flea market [→25] – ordered, expensive, and predictable – although Jeu de Balle regulars may find some of the stock, if not the prices, eerily familiar. You're more likely to find bargains in the hidden passageways off the main square, or in the streets leading down to the heart of town.

day

🎁 The area for antiques and posh shops, mainly on place du Grand Sablon and its surrounds. The focus is the Sablon Antiques Market on weekends.

👁 Palais de Justice [→61]; Palais Royal [→61]; Musées des Instruments de Musique [→69]; Eglise de Notre-Dame du Sablon [→71]; Synagogue Communaté Israélite de Bruxelles [→72]; Palais des Beaux-Arts [→74].

night

🍴 Superb and often expensive restaurants; bars are equally classy, if lacking in charm.

☆ For music and theatre, try the Palais des Beaux-Arts [→113], the Conservatoire and the Chapelle Royale [→114]. For a good flick head to the Musée du Cinéma [→112].

getting there

Ⓜ Gare Centrale; Parc; Arts-Loi; Trône; Porte de Namur; Louise

🚊 92, 93, 94

🚌 20, 34, 48, 71, 95, 96

le sablon

shopping

fashion

The Sablon is the hotspot of Brussels swank. That's why Giorgio Armani chose the cobblestoned place du Grand Sablon as the location for Brussels' **Emporio Armani**. It has the usual mix of suits that mean business,

plus street- and casual-wear with an up-market twist. Other high-style labels like Jil Sander, Jean Paul Gaultier, Issey Miyake and Prada are available at **Charlotte aux Pommes**, an intimate little boutique that draws well turned-

out women. Belgian label **César & Rosalie** does womenswear that's a bit more fun: think Esprit-like comfort filtered through Paul Smith style. **Isabelle Baines** attracts a similar crowd, who come here for her classic cardigans,

* = featured in the listings section [→84–110]

Celtica ♪B2
55 rue du Marché
aux Poulets
02.514.22.69

Le Cerceuil ♪B3
10–12 rue des Harengs
02.512.30.77

Chez Maman ♪A3
7 rue des Grands
Carmes
02.502.89.96

Le Cirio ♪B3
18 rue de la Bourse
02.512.13.95

Comme Chez Soi ♪A4
23 place Rouppe
02.512.29.21 ⊕–⊕⊕⊕⊕

Le Comptoir ♪B3–B4
24–26 place de la
Vieille Halle aux Blés
02.514.05.00

Le Corbeau ♪B2
18–20 rue St-Michel
02.219.52.46

Dali's Bar ♪B3
35 petite rue des
Bouchers
02.511.54.67

El Metekko ♪A3
256 blvd Anspach
02.512.46.48

El Pablo's Disco Bar ♪A3
60 rue du Marché
au Charbon
02.514.51.49

Elvis Pompilio ♪B3
18 rue du Lombard
02.511.11.88

L'Espérance ♪B1
1 rue Finistère
02.217.32.47

L'Express ♪B3
8 rue des Chapeliers
02.512.88.83 ⊕

Le Falstaff ♪B3
25 rue Henri Maus
02.511.87.89

FNAC ♪C1
City 2, 123 rue Neuve
02.275.11.11

La Galettière ♪B3
53 rue des Pierres
02.512.84.80

Gillis ♪B3
17 rue du Lombard
02.512.09.26

Goupil le Fol ♪B3
22 rue de la Violette
02.511.13.96

L'Homme Chrétien ♪B3
27 rue des Pierres
02.502.01.28

Il Paradiso ♪B3
34 rue Duquesnoy
02.512.52.32 ⊕

Inno ♪C1
111 rue Neuve
02.211.21.11

Intermezzo ♪B2
16 rue des Princes
02.218.03.11 ⊕

Jonathan
Bernard ♪B3
53 rue du Lombard
02.537.90.91

Kaat Tilley ♪B3
4 Galerie du Roi
02.514.07.63

Lauffer ♪B3
59 rue des Bouchers
02.511.15.92

Léonidas ♪B2
4 boulevard Anspach
02.218.03.63

Maison Dandoy ♪B3
31 rue au Beurre
02.513.10.57

Marjolaine ♪B3
7 rue de la Madeleine
02.513.20.54

Mary's ♪D2
15 rue Royale
02.217.45.00

Mokafé ♪B3
9 Galerie du Roi
02.511.78.70

Musicmania ♪B2
4 rue de la Fourche
02.217.53.69

Neuhaus ♪B4
Galerie de la Rein
02.512.63.59

Noire d'Ivoire ♪B3
25–27 rue de l'Hôpital
02.534.47.70

O'Reilly's ♪A3
1 place de la Bourse
02.552.04.80

Parnassos ♪B3
29 rue au Beurre
02.512.03.95 ⊕

Pizzeria Mirante ♪A3
13 Plattesteen
02.511.15.80 ⊕

Het Plaizier ♪B3
50 rue des Eperonniers
02.513.47.30

Planète
Chocolat ♪B3
24 rue du Lombard
02.511.07.55

Plattesteen ♪A3
41 rue du Marché
au Charbon
02.512.82.03 ⊕

Ricotta &
Parmesan ♪B3
31 rue de l'Ecuyer
02.502.80.82 ⊕

Rock Classic ♪A3
55 rue du Marché
au Charbon
02.512.15.47

Rosalie Pompon ♪B4
1 rue de l'Hôpital
02.512 35 93

Le Roy d'Espagne ♪B3
1 Grand' Place
02.513.08.07

Samourai ♪B3
28 rue du Fossé
aux Loups
02.217.56.39
⊕⊕–⊕⊕⊕⊕

Sea Grill ♪B2
47 rue du Fossé
aux Loups
02.219.28.28 ⊕

Shoe's victim.com
♪A3
105 blvd Anspach
02.502.81.00

Le Siècle ♪B2
41 rue de l'Ecuyer
02.513.45.65 ⊕

Sonik ♪A3
112 rue du Marché
au Charbon
02.511.99.85

Le Sparrow ♪B3
18 rue Duquesnoy
02.512.66.22

Sterling ♪B2
38 rue du Fossé
aux Loups
02.223.62.23

Studio Live ♪A3
17 rue du Poinçon
02.512.52.70

Le Sud ♪B2
43 rue de l'Ecuyer
02.513.37.65

Tast ♪B2
118 boulevard Anspach
02.502.10.99

La Taverne du
Passage ♪B3
30 Galerie de la Reine
02.512.37.32 ⊕

Tels Quels ♪A3
81 rue du Marché
au Charbon
02.512.32.34

Tintin ♪B3
13 rue de la Colline
02.514.51.52

't Kelderke ♪B3
15 Grand' Place
02.513.73.44 ⊕–⊕⊕

Totem ♪B3
6 rue des Grands
Carmes
02.513.11.52 ⊕⊕–⊕⊕⊕⊕

Virgin Megastore ♪B2
30 Anspach Centre
02.218.55.46

Waterstone's ♪B1
71–75 boulevard
Adolphe Max
02.219.27.08

Wilde ♪B3
79 boulevard Anspach
02.513.44.59

getting your bearings

St-Gilles (St-Gillis) ✯B3–B4 [→29–32]

Le Sablon (De Zavel) ✯B3 [→20–24]

Tervuren ✯E4:
Beloved of British expats because it's near the British School, this Dutch-speaking suburb has a pleasant wooded park and a cobbled central square. The Musée Royal de l'Afrique Centrale [→66] is the main attraction, although the local sausage shop has hordes of admirers.

Uccle (Ukkel) ✯B4–B5:
A green and pleasant land bordering on the Forêt de Soignes [→76]. Well-heeled residents live in the *villas* (detached houses) and the elegant Art Nouveau and fake neoclassical town houses on and around avenue Molière. The locals' discerning palates demand fine dining, while those oppressed by the not-so-discreet charm of the bourgeoisie can escape to tranquil Dieweg Cemetery, rambling Wolvendael Park [→77], or the more humble Quartier du Chat ('cat quarter').

Watermael-Boitsfort (Watermaal-Bosvoorde) ✯D5:
Low-key, laid-back and bohemian, this is an artsy district with plenty of green spaces, a few galleries, and several charming council cottages. Great for an early-evening stroll, with options galore if you've worked up an appetite.

Woluwe St-Pierre & Woluwe St-Lambert (St-Pieters-Woluwe & St-Lambrechts-Woluwe) ✯D3: The eastern suburbs of Brussels are favoured by Eurocrat families, more because they're handy for the office than because of any thrill factor. WSP is the cozier, with rolling Parc Woluwe [→76] and the whitewashed proto-Art Deco Palais Stoclet (now closed to the public because visitors kept stealing the exhibits).

Map legend:
- Ste-Catherine [→6–12]
- Central [→13–19]
- Le Sablon [→20–24]
- Les Marolles [→25–28]
- St-Gilles [→29–32]
- Ixelles (West) [→33–37]
- Ixelles (East) [→38–41]
- Quartier Européen [→42–44]
- St-Josse & Schaerbeek [→45–47]

while the public Laeken Park [→77] contains a Chinese pavilion and Japanese tower, both built for Léopold II.

Les Marolles (De Marollen) ✯B3 [→25–28]

Midi (Zuid) ✯B3:
Gare du Midi is the Eurostar terminus, its surroundings might make you wonder why you came. The office developments can't quite hide the district's down-at-heel nature, although the large migrant communities have led to cheap Greek, Spanish, and Portuguese restaurants. On Sundays, the drab streets are brought to life by a massive, souk-like market.

Molenbeek ✯A3–B3:
Like Anderlecht, this canal-side district has seen better days, but cheap rents and unused industrial spaces are drawing venues and cultural spaces into the area. The bizarre Art Deco Eglise de St-Jean Baptiste has a looping concrete ribcage that's part dinosaur, part underpass.

Quartier Européen (Europese Wijk) ✯C3 [→42–44]

Ste-Catherine (St-Katelijne) ✯B3 [→6–12]

St-Josse & Schaerbeek (St-Joost & Schaerbeek) ✯B2–C3 [→45–47]

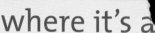

6

It's a familiar story: bustling trading area, work dries up, jobs dry up, properties get run-down, prices plummet, broke bohos move in and trendiness breaks out. Place Ste-Catherine was once the heart of the port district, with a spectacular glass-and-steel fish market (all that's left now is a fountain). As the canal's importance declined, the area went to seed. Nobody 'respectable' wanted to live there, until, in the 1980s, the low rents, *belle époque* architecture and central location proved irresistible for avant-garde designers, Flemish media types, and the gay community. Hip boutiques, bars, and restaurants came in their wake, and now the area's only problem is that it's too popular for its own good. Though the overcrowded place St-Géry and über-trendy rue Dansaert, with cutting-edge clothes and chichi cafés, feel almost too commercial, the Beursschouwburg and De Markten cultural centres draw an artsy crowd. Amid all the aching fashionability, you'll still find a few local hangouts.

day

⛺ Ste-Catherine is *the* area for top-of-the-range Belgian and international design. Clothes and shoes are the real draw.
◉ Eglise Ste-Catherine [→71]; Halles St-Géry [→74]; La Bourse [→60].

night

🐚 Places to see and be seen are all over – place St-Géry and rue Antoine Dansaert are the epicentre for restaurants and bars; but for trad *Belge* and seafood, try the place Ste-Catherine and its surrounds.
☆ Theatre, dance and music at Kaaitheater and Lunatheater [→115]; contemporary music at Beursschouwburg and Magasin 4 [→113]; L'Archiduc for jazz [→113].

getting there

Ⓜ Ste-Catherine; Bourse; Comte de Flandre; Yser; Ribaucourt; Etangs Noirs.
🚊 18, 23, 52, 55, 56, 81.
🚌 20, 47, 63, 89.

ste-catherine

shopping

fashion

Rue Antoine Dansaert is fashion central for downtown Brussels. This once-derelict street was taken over in the late 1980s by the alternative crowd: post-university types who listened to the Smiths and Joy Division, read too much William Burroughs and Jack Kerouac and thought dressing in black was the ultimate fashion statement – in other words, *très* Depeche Mode. Today it's mostly gentrified bohemia, but there's still enough style to take it out of the mainstream.

*Stijl ⬇ started it all. The first place to champion Belgian designers before the rest of the fashion world jumped on the bandwagon, this mega-

* = featured in the listings section [→84–110]

schoolgirl-sweet twin-sets and other knits that look like traditional wardrobe staples, until you look at the fine detailing. **Gaya** and **Momento**, meanwhile, do womenswear that is preppy-meets-career-gal-meets-art student chic: Paul Smith, JP Tod's, and French label Victoire are just some of the lines carried at these sister shops. If you're after something a bit more sleek, Edouard Vermeulen is your man. The local answer to Armani, his **Natan ⤴** label serves up ready-to-wear womens- and menswear at two different shops on rue du Namur. A top couturier, Vermeulen dresses Mathilde, Belgium's very own Princess Di. Think Gucci meets Marc Jacobs meets Yves Saint Laurent and you've got a handle on his style, and price range. Japanese designer **Kenzo** has a similar modus operandi, but he works from a wider palette: suits that mix classic with up-to-the-minute casual styles, as well as exotic holiday gear fit for your island getaway (upstairs for women, downstairs for men). And the woman above teenager sizes is well served by **Mariella Burani**'s flouncy skirts, *la Parisienne* blouses and ultra-feminine flowery dresses that whisper femme fatale.

le sablon

antiques

Whether browsing or buying, the place du Grand Sablon and its surrounds are treasure troves for Amex-brandishing antiques and art lovers. Even if you're not in the market for original Audubon prints or Fabergé eggs, the **Marché place du Grand Sablon** is worth a look. Going strong every weekend for the past 40 years, it's where stamps, coins, art, and other collectors' faves are sold in red-and-green tents. Aristocrats and regular civilians mingle, and it's as good for people-watching as it is for dealing. If you miss the market, don't worry. Galleries in the area offer booty from all corners of the world, from vintage French costume jewellery and Art Nouveau silver to Persian carpets and African art.

Near the Eglise Notre-Dame du Sablon, you can have your pick of vintage jewellery from the likes of Cartier and Boucheron at **Claude Noëlle** gallery. Or, if you prefer to splash out on your abode than yourself, there's the **Catherine Ghadimi** gallery, where Art Nouveau glass and carvings from the Orient are sold. Her namesake, **Ghadimi** Gallery, does vintage Persian carpets just south of the square. One of the best known of the lot is **Yannick David**, specializing in architectural drawings, miniatures, and 19th-century furniture.

The rue des Minimes runs the gamut from museum-quality tribal art and archaeological pieces at **M Koenig Ethnography** to Louis XV paintings and *belle époque* furniture and paintings at **Philippe Dufrasne**, with the **Boon Gallery**'s realistic portraits falling somewhere in between. Make way, and time, for megastore **Galerie des Minimes**, with over 500m/sq of floor space devoted to bric-à-brac, art, and antiques. And **Rabier Art Nègre** does totems and statues in wood from Central Africa, some resembling penises, giving a whole new phallic meaning to 'showing wood'.

The rue Ernest Allard is the other main drag for galleries, with *objets* a tad more swank. The **Cento Anni** gallery has florid Art Nouveau vases and figurines, **Dominique** does Art Deco furniture, lamps and knick-knacks, and **Zen Gallery** specializes in Asiatica: buddhas, vishnus, and other god-like figures.

But not all shops have sky-high prices. Collectors with a sense of humour and limited dosh can slink towards the city centre to the **Collector's Gallery**. Totally kitsch, and proud of it, the shop has a section dedicated to Barbie memorabilia, as well as vintage perfume bottles, classic toys, and other high-class junk from the early 1900s to the 1970s. Classier bits and pieces can be bagged at **Ma Maison de Papier**; with old books, vintage posters, and advertisements going back to the 1800s, it's like rummaging through an attic. More up-market still is **Les Vieux Sablons**. The antique maps, religious icons, books, and prints within this mini maze of shops are of consistently high quality. A good compromise for the fiscally challenged collector is **Senses Art Nouveau**. Reproductions of Art Nouveau trinkets and Klimt-inspired candelabras are done mostly in cost-conscious pewter.

chocolates

The place du Grand Sablon is Brussels' chocolate central. ***Godiva** has the name, but has it got the quality to live up to its rep? Well, having invented the truffle, and with customers able to choose the type of cocoa bean in their chocolates, it certainly seems so. ***Wittamer** ✓, doing freshly made chocs since 1910, is a favourite of many expat Belgians when visiting home. The shop puts as much into its packaging as it does into its pricey pralines: gold-leaf boxes, baskets, and lots of ribbons. Its namesake café serves wickedly divine pastries that are also wickedly expensive. ***Pierre Marcolini**, a recent winner of the Chocolatier of

the World award, is a relative newcomer on the chocolate scene (only four shops in Belgium). His semi-sculptural creations have a sinfully high cocoa content.

one-offs

Just off the place du Grand Sablon, get herbal teas for whatever ails you at **Claire Fontaine**. The country village-styled deli also has classy nibbles such as foie gras and artily-packaged marmalades and olive oils that make great hamper gifts. **Le Grand Cerf** doesn't do teas, but it has the same old-style, decadent dishes and food gifts. Fancy a Cuban cigar? **Davidoff** is the best place in Brussels to get them. Humidors, gold lighters, cigar boxes in materials like leather and crocodile, and other smoking accessories are sold in this upscale boutique – as well as all brands of cigarettes.

homewares

From the elegance of a country house to penthouse chic, Le Sablon has it all. Fans of modern Italian and Scandinavian design shouldn't miss out on a visit to **L'Objet du Désir**. Retro futuristic furniture and home furnishings by Alessi and others have Barbarella/ Space Odyssey/Jetsons vibe. More florid is **Marie-Rêve**, where rustic furniture and homewares are given a refined finish. It's the sole outlet of home furnishings by Belgian artist Isabelle de Borchgrave, who specializes in tapestries, fabrics and brocades that reek of luxe abandon. Luxuriously decadent bath oils, candles and other items to pamper yourself are also on sale. **Home Store** works home style from a different angle: goat-skin rubbish bins, wooden vases, sleek dishware, and contemporary tables. The shop has a *Wallpaper* magazine-style chill to match the sleek stock. Less pricey is **La Vaisselle à Kilo** (meaning 'dishes by the kilo'). Warehouse sale is the atmosphere, with a mix of Limoges, Royal Boch, and tableware for everyday use. Upstairs there's a better than average selection of authentic Belgian beer glasses. But for the best, and most traditional linen, try the ***Linen House**.

eating & drinking

restaurants

This is posh-ville and the restaurant terraces here are poseurs' paradise – looking good is as important as eating well. Good taste – in decor and menu – is the rule, not the exception, and restos often offer up as much a feast for the eyes as the palate. **Au Grand Mayeur** is an excellent example. This 17th-century building brings the romance of the Steppes to its dining room, with a nightly gypsy band and a menu of beef stroganoff, borscht, and blinis. A guilty pleasure – you know it ain't really authentic, but after a few vodkas, who cares?

Less over-the-top is *Lola. Black and white and red all over, the clean, sleek space feels like the set of an American soap, but the mix of Belgian and French cuisine (roast beef with rocket and buffalo mozzarella, rank lobster, smoked salmon and foie gras) is actually very good. *Au Vieux St-Martin is a designer update of an old-style brasserie, with the works of contemporary Belgian artists on the walls. The expensive food – rabbit cooked in *kriek* (cherry beer), blood sausage, scampi croquettes – is pure Belge, and done with great refinement.

Bare-brick-walled decor is so seven years ago, but *Tour d'y Voir is a 14th-century abbey – so it's forgiven. Flattering lighting, French cuisine and an ambience so intimate it feels illicit. Adventurous folk order the chef's surprise: you don't know what you're getting until it arrives on your table. Sort of like Russian roulette.

Make sure you reserve a good week in advance for **Ciao**: it's hard to get a table at this little Italian eatery. The food is classic Italian served in a clean, white-table-clothed setting. Those with a jones for Tex-Mex head to **Pablo's**. Fajitas, tortillas, and other favourites are served in the large, open, and very noisy dining room to an international crowd. Generous portions of food make up for the thimble-sized margaritas. Framed butterfly prints on clean white walls are a cute touch at *La Découverte, where there is one set menu nightly: take it or leave it. That might seem a tad arrogant, but it pulls it off for two reasons – the food is French and is always excellent. Also on the smallish side is **Wasabi**, the latest hot

resto serving sashimi, sushi, and other Japanese faves with a slight hint of fusion. The decor looks more like a magazine spread: prism-coloured walls here, zebra-print banquettes there, and a trolley on the bar leading back to the kitchen. It's very impressive and pretty inviting.

It's pretty pish-posh around the place du Grand Sablon, but head out a bit and it gets much quainter (and cheaper).

And if you still haven't found your niche (for lunch only), **Le Pain Quotidien** ↗ makes it easy: this faux rustic chain café has one huge central table that diners share and lots of diddies for daytime intimacy. Although the drinks and light meals are expensive, the price does filter out a certain element you might not want to cozy up to. An added bonus on sunny days is the large terrace out back.

bars, cafés & clubs

Yuppies kicking back, affluent tourists, preppies hanging loose, and Brussels' *beau monde* chilling out; this bourgeois mishmash sums up café culture in Le Sablon. EU *stagiaires* flock to **Le Perroquet** ↑, a corner bar with Art Nouveau decor that's a nice backdrop for drinking and flirting. The service is slow, but no matter: the motto here

is chill. You may come across jazz, café-theatre, salsa, Afro-beat, and deep discourses into philosophy, depending on what night you hit *Le Cercle. The crowd is *très* international, especially on Friday and Saturday nights. Find a spot on the terrace at **Un Grain de Sable**; this bar-resto has yellow-coloured walls that drive you nuts after a few drinks. The pricey – *plat du jour* changes daily. **Le Zavel** is much more inviting; it also does decently priced daily specials (and the *moules et frites* are top notch). The crowd is older, less into posing and more into relaxing – a firm fave.

Uptown **G. Club Cigare** ↖ prides itself on being an exclusive hang-out for pretty boys in tight T-shirts and too much of whatever the latest fragrance is. It's presided over by ageless fairy godmother Gervaise, an ebony nightlife institution who23 brings a little Studio 54 into the lives of everyone she touches. Less grown up is *Chez Richard, the place for thirtysomethings to be insane for a few hours.

♟ directory

Au Grand Mayeur ♟B2
43 place du Grand
Sablon
02.512.80.91 ⊛⊛–⊛⊛⊛

**Au Vieux
St-Martin** ♟B2
38 place du Grand
Sablon
02.512.64.76 ⊛⊛–⊛⊛⊛⊛

Boon Gallery ♟B2
24 rue des Minimes
02.503.24.94

**Catherine
Ghadimi** ♟B2
8 rue Bodenbroeck
02.511.74.49

Cento Anni ♟B2
31 place du Grand
Sablon
02.514.56.33

Le Cercle ♟B2
20–22 rue Ste-Anne
02.512.32.15

César & Rosalie ♟B2
50 rue de Rollebeek
02.514.58.64

**Charlotte aux
Pommes** ♟B2
29 rue de Rollebeek
02.512.34.59

Ciao ♟B2
28 rue Joseph Stevens
02.513.03.23 ⊛⊛–⊛⊛⊛

Claire Fontaine ♟B2
3 rue Ernest Allard
02.512.24.10

Claude Noëlle ♟B2
20 place du Grand
Sablon
02.511.41.72

Collector's Gallery ♟B2
17 rue Lebeau
02.511.46.13

Davidoff ♟B2
1 place du Grand
Sablon
02.512.94.22

La Découverte ♟A2
26 rue de l'Épée
02.513.43.11 ⊛

Dominique ♟B2
7 rue Ernest Allard
02.514.25.41

Emporio Armani ♟B2
37 place du Grand
Sablon
02.551.04.04

**Galerie des
Minimes** ♟B2
23 rue des Minimes
02.511.28.25

Gaya ♟C2
38 rue de Namur
02.512.23.76

G. Club Cigare ♟B2
39 rue du Pépin
02.511.63.22

Ghadimi Gallery ♟B2
1 rue des Minimes
02.512.98.41

Godiva ♟B2
48 place du Grand
Sablon
02.502.99.06

**Un Grain
de Sable** ♟B2
15–16 place du Grand
Sablon
02.514.05.83

Le Grand Cerf ♟B3
22 rue du Grand Cerf
02.511.44.83

Home Store ♟C2
65 rue de Namur
02.502.39.09

Isabelle Baines ♟B2
48 rue du Pépin
02.502.13.73

Kenzo ♟C2
44 rue de Namur
02.514.04.48

Lola ♟B2
33 place du Grand
Sablon
02.514.24.60 ⊛⊛

Linen House ♟B2
10 rue de Bodenbroeck
02.502.63.02

**Ma Maison de
Papier** ♟B1
6 Galerie de
Ruysbroek
02.512.22.49

Mariella Burani ♟C2
29 rue de Namur
02.514.08.85

Marie-Rêve ♟B2
27 rue de Rollebeek
02.514.36.39

**M Koenig
Ethnography** ♟B2
27 rue des Minimes
02.511.75.07

Momento ♟C2
47 rue de Namur
02.511.23.71

Natan ♟C2
68 rue de Namur
02.503.53.56 (men's)
78 rue de Namur
02.512.75.00
(women's)

L'Objet du Désir ♟B2
21 place du Grand
Sablon
02.512.42.43

Pablo's ♟C2
51 rue de Namur
02.502.41.35 ⊛

Le Pain Quotidien ♟B2
11 rue des Sablons
02.513.51.54

Le Perroquet ♟B2
31 rue Watteeu
02.512.99.22

Philippe Dufrasne ♟B2
15 rue des Minimes
02.503.36.01

Pierre Marcolini ♟B2
39 place du Grand
Sablon
02.514.12.06

Rabier Art Nègre ♟B2
8–10 rue des Minimes
02.512.86.74/
02.514.51.50

**Senses
Art Nouveau** ♟B1
31 rue Lebeau
02.502.15.30

Tour d'y Voir ♟B2
6 place du Grand
Sablon
02.511.40.43 ⊛⊛–⊛⊛⊛

**La Vaisselle
à Kilo** ♟B2
8a rue Bodenbroek
02.513.49.84

**Les Vieux
Sablons** ♟B2
9 place du Grand
Sablon
02.502.14.32

Wasabi ♟B2
12 rue Joseph Stevens
02.511.96.93

Wittamer ♟B2
6 & 12–13 place du
Grand Sablon
02.512.37.42

Yannick David ♟B2
27 rue Watteeu
02.513.37.48

Le Zavel ♟B2
7 place du Grand
Sablon
02.512.16.80

Zen Gallery ♟B2
23 rue Ernest Allard
02.511.95.10

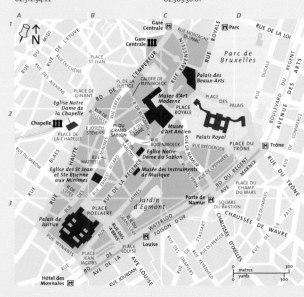

rock the kasbah

les marolles

Downhill from the swanky Sablon, Les Marolles couldn't be more different. Where the former is all snoot and show, this area is poor and gritty – and proud of it. It's a rowdy place of working-class heroes and politically active priests who have triumphed in the face of adversity; like when King Léopold kicked out thousands of locals to build his preposterous Palais de Justice in 1883 or during the Nazi oppression in WWII, when *Marolliens* sheltered hundreds of Jews. These days cheap rents and cute-but-chichi restaurants are luring the trendy, and techno temple The Fuse is helping to turn the area into Brussels' clubbing epicentre. Early-rising bargain-hunters find rummaging heaven at the flea market on place du Jeu de Balle and in the bric-a-brac shops of rues Haute and Blaes. Gentrification has made the area more fun for visitors, but those who inhabit its (still) rough edges – the dwindling population of *Marolliens*, the post-war Spanish migrants, and the more recent arrivals from North Africa – haven't seen much benefit.

day

🗓 The flea market on place du Jeu de Balle is the main pull here, and is especially busy on Sunday mornings. Lifestyle and gift stores are clustered along rue Blaes and rue Haute.

👁 Porte de Hal [→62] overshadows the low-rise buildings to the south of the area. There are a few good art galleries: Recyclart [→74], Orion Art Gallery [→75], and Sabine Watcher Fine Arts [→75].

night

🍷 Although there are many posh restos, eateries and bars tend to be quirky and offbeat, and their cuisine international.

☆ With Fuse and Bazaar here, Les Marolles is a key area for clubbing. Théâtre Les Tanneurs [→116] is well known for its innovative choreography, and Eglise des Minimes [→114] for choral music.

getting there

Ⓜ Porte de Hal; Hôtel des Monnaies; Lemonnier.
🚋 20, 48
🚌 91, 92, 94

les marolles

shopping

homewares & interiors

The two main drags are the parallel steets of rue Blaes and rue Haute. The former can be divided into two chunks: south of place du Jeu de Balle are shops selling fresh fruit, nuts, and junk food.

North of Jeu de Balle, rue Blaes is browsers' row, with antiques, bric-a-brac, and home decor stores aplenty. Rue Haute has many fine shops and restaurants where locals go for grub.

But the neighbourhood nexus is the place du Jeu de Balle, where the daily Flea Market takes place. Spread out on tables, tarpaulins, and blankets are much trash and treasure. So prepare to

* = featured in the listings section [→84–110]

do some serious sifting through piles of clothes, costume jewellery, dishes, furniture, and other miscellanea. The best bargains are had during the week, but haggling can knock a few francs off already decent prices. Many of the items resurface with much higher prices in Le Sablon.

Martha Stewart meets IKEA at **New De Wolf**, a one-stop shop for the home. Almost every genre of decor is available. The main shop spans a whole block, with a smaller store selling kitschier knick-knacks across the street. While New De Wolf does current, cost-conscious copies of older styles, **Rambagh Asian Home-style** balances old and new, with antique furniture and homewares from India and Korea. For those on a tight budget, this spacious two-floor shop also does knock-offs. A new branch has recently opened just across the road.

Need a lion statue for your grounds? Try **Espace 161** . This mini-mall of antiques and brocante dealers has Limoges dishware, carousel ponies, baby grand pianos, Murano glass, and other amazing curiosities. Stock changes constantly. Tucked into a nearby side street, **Palace** specializes in quirky furniture and vintage toys from the fabulous 1950s. Or try Art Deco specialists ***Fin des Siècles et Plus**' two Marolles locations: the smaller one selling portable items – toys, lamps, shaving kits – from the early 1900s; the other does furniture to fit out your penthouse with 1930s panache.

books & CDs

If you're looking for something rare or out of print, try the Boulevard Lemonnier: it's home to **Pêle Mêle \!**, two shops that prove one man's trash is another man's trashy reading, with old issues of *Elle*, *Marie-Claire*, and *Photo* as well as comics and bona fide literature. The shop also has a good used-CD section. For a better range, the rest of the street is dotted with shops specializing in all genres, from goth to industrial, from 80s synth-pop to disco and more.

gifts

Looking for a typical Belgian gift? You're out of luck in Les Marolles. But go international and options abound. **Bali-Africa** ✏ is almost too much of a good thing. Wooden and leather masks, drums, and other trinkets and totems from Angola to Zanzibar pack every inch of its three storeys. It has a helpful yellow line painted on the floor to guide you, otherwise you'd never get out alive. Gifts from afar are also **Nuhr Nebi**'s speciality. Dreadlocked Belgian Fabienne Goris hand-selects the oils, incense, kilims and other exotica on sale at her two shops from regular trips to Africa and Asia. French artist Muriel Bardinet draws from her years in Africa and the south of France in her shop-cum-studio **Dune**. The result: sleek *objets* in teak, sea-shells and other exotic materials. And if you want to treat yourself to something, **Côté Provence** has the goods: aromatic candles, knick-knacks and incense from Provence.

Photographer Nicolas Springael brings images of his travels to the framed prints and postcards sold at **L'Instant Présent**. The archives of photographs at **Rue Haute** are also worth a look – from classic European scenes in the mode of Cartier-Bresson to nudes by Avedon.

You might luck into something *typiquement Belge*, however, at **Mont-de-Piété**, where one man's debt is another man's deal. This auction has been selling objects pawned for quick cash since 1618. If it can be hocked, it can be bought here.

fashion

High-street shops have given the Marolles a miss, so secondhand duds are the neighbourhood's forte. ***Modes** is one of the area's best: 1930s flapper dressers, 1940s dressing gowns, headgear from top hats to bowlers, and other elegant vintage stuff. The selection is so good that it's a regular port of call for costumers from theatre companies throughout Europe. The threads are timeless, but the clothes are new at **Michiels**. This men's shop, specializing in made-to-measure suits, has been open since 1856 and the Belgian Royal Family are favoured customers. For women, sexy lingerie to get their groove on is sold at **Les Charmes d'Hélène**. Dior, Ferré, Féraud and other labels are 1950s sexpot fabulous, and are sure to get a rise out of the right man.

eating & drinking

restaurants

Finding a Belgian restaurant is hard in Les Marolles, but **Au Stekerlapatte** is an exception. It's a Brussels institution serving old-style Belgian cuisine to Eurocrowds – which means lots of beef, potatoes and lashings of cream. The smell of butter in the air will lead you there. Three local restaurants offer different takes on French cuisine. **Le Gourmandin** takes itself very seriously. And so it should: the food is as refined as its dining room is intimate, thanks to master chef Jean-Bernard van Hauw, renowned for his way with cod and monkfish. *L'Idiot du Village* ✔ has the royal seal of approval: Queen Paola has eaten Alain Gascoin's creative interpretations of French mainstays like rabbit and raisins, and tuna grilled with artichokes. Chef Pascal Fellemans also does a take on French cuisine at **Le Bermuchet**, for a young, trendy clientele. Specialities include ostrich, and the decidedly non-French spaghetti Bermuchet, with a sauce of ham, cream, and Fellemans' special secret spices. An even more eclectic menu is on offer at **Ici-Même**, where you don't need to plump for just one dish: its global tapas menu means the 480BF special of the house includes a taste of seven dishes from around the world.

Better known for its kaleidoscopic kitsch decor is **La Cour des Miracles**. The ground floor is a bar with a red baby grand piano, a dance floor, seashells, harps, and even a pool full of carp and bass with a chandelier hanging over it. The first floor has dining rooms serving Mediterranean, Middle Eastern and North African cuisine – fancy a little couscous with lamb? Veal kebabs? *Baklava?* And the second floor is a tearoom *à la* Aladdin: several candlelit areas with plush seating surrounded by dazzling throw cushions. Meanwhile, the floral mural on the wall at **Indigo** is as close as you can get to an LSD experience without actually taking it. Totally East Village Manhattan in vibe, it serves scrumptious quiches and wicked, wicked desserts.

Located in what was the Spanish quarter, **La Villa Rosa** has been *the* place for paella in Brussels for 50 years. Next door, **Mar Bravo** serves up a Portuguese version that benefits from the large jug of Porto accompanying it. *Les Larmes du Tigre** is the place to go for Thai cuisine. A ceiling of rice-paper parasols cover both smoking and non-smoking dining rooms, and the menu – which includes rice noodles in peanut sauce with chicken, seafood or beef – is a revelation. The Sunday buffet is especially popular, and reservations are a must.

Mad eclectica best describes Les Marolles; it's glamorous and gritty all at once.

bars & cafés

Marolles café culture revolves around the place du Jeu de Balle and the flea market; shoppers and browsers often stop off for a drink after a visit to the square. **Galerie 18** has a mix of bric-a-brac and antiques in a setting where everyone seems to be recovering from a hangover on the weekend. Less alternative is **De Skieven Architek**, with its murals of Brussels cityscapes and limited menu of sandwiches and soups. The big draws are the international newspapers and mags sold here, so you can catch up on what's going on round the world. Native *Bruxellois* tend to opt for **Café Chez Marcel**, a hole-in-the-wall joint for flea market salesmen to grab a beer. Marcel also serves the meanest onion soup you've ever tasted – just don't make any dates for afterwards. To the north *Porte Noir* tempts the buds with over 120 beers, and *La Fleur en Papier Doré* attracts art and history buffs. It was here that Magritte and his buddies supped.

les marolles

club-bars & clubs

Most clubs in the Marolles are multi-purpose: dancing is done at the weekends, with bar and restaurant action throughout the rest of the week. **Bazaar** ► is the joint of choice for much of Brussels' bohemia. A hot-air balloon made of brocade curtains hangs over the bar, old gilt mirrors reflecting subdued lighting show you to your best advantage, and comfy old armchairs give it a laid-back atmosphere. On weekends, disco, salsa, trip-hop, and other dance beats mix it up in the cellar. During the week, take in the light menu of couscous, tapas, and mint tea. But *Fuse is a club and nothing more. And what a club it is – Belgium's premier techno stomping ground has two dance floors to handle the thousand-plus crowds on Fridays (free before midnight) and Saturdays. Every third Sunday is turned over to La Démence, the city's uninhibited gay mega-party series, with house and garage as the soundtrack.

🔖 directory

Au Stekerlapatte 🎵C4
4 rue des Prêtres
02.512.86.81 ⊕–⊛

Bali-Africa 🎵B3
154–156 rue Blaes
02.514.47.92

Bazaar 🎵B3
63 rue des Capucins
02.511.26.00

Le Bermuchet 🎵C3
198 rue Haute
02.513.88.82 ⊕–⊛⊛

Café Chez Marcel 🎵B3
20 pl du Jeu de Balle
02.511.13.75

Les Charmes d'Hélène 🎵C3
123 rue Haute
02.511.13.32

Côté Provence 🎵C2
69 rue Haute
02.502.30.92

La Cour des Miracles 🎵B3
5 rue de l'Hectolitre
02.513.92.94 ⊛

De Skieven Architek 🎵B3
50 place du Jeu de Balle
02.514.43.69

Dune 🎵C3
234 rue Haute
02.511.17.21

Espace 161 🎵C3
161 rue Haute
02.502.31.64

Fin des Siècles et Plus 🎵C3
157 & 180 rue Haute
02.502.66.35

Fuse 🎵B4
208 rue Blaes
02.511.97.89

Galerie 18 🎵B3
18 rue du Chevreuil

La Fleur en Papier Doré 🎵C1
53 rue des Alexiens
02.511.16.59

Le Gourmandin 🎵C3
152 rue Haute
02.512.98.92 ⊛⊛

Ici-Même 🎵C3
204 rue Haute
02.502.54.24 ⊛

L'Idiot du Village 🎵C2
19 rue de Notre Seigneur
02.502.55.82
⊛⊛–⊛⊛⊛

Indigo 🎵B3
160 rue Blaes
02.511.38.97 ⊛

L'Instant Présent 🎵C3
136 rue Blaes
02.513.28.91

La Villa Rosa 🎵B4
395 rue Haute
02.537.33.21 ⊕–⊛⊛

Les Larmes du Tigre 🎵C3
21 rue de Wynants
02.512.18.77 ⊛⊛

Mar Bravo 🎵B4
397 rue Haute
02.538.04.14 ⊕–⊛⊛

Michiels 🎵C3
195 rue Haute
02.511.69.35

Modes 🎵B3
164 rue Blaes
02.503.54.00

Mont-de-Piété 🎵B3
19 rue St-Ghislain
02.512.13.85

New De Wolf 🎵C2
91 rue Haute &
46 rue Blaes
02.511.10.18/
02.503.38.36

Nuhr Nebi 🎵C2
23 rue Blaes &
55 rue Haute
02.514.04.29/
02.411.45.44

Palace 🎵B3
16 rue des Renards
02.512.52.17

Pêle Mêle 🎵B1
55 blvd Lemmonier
02.548.78.00

Porte Noire 🎵C1
16 rue des Alexiens
02.511.78.37

Rambagh Asian Homestyle 🎵C2
64 rue Haute
02.514.58.27

Rue Haute 🎵C3
203 rue Haute
02.513.96.09

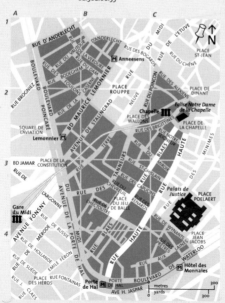

faded splendour

It's got a reputation for being run-down, and tourists tend to pretty much keep their noses out, but St-Gilles' most loyal inhabitants wouldn't dream of living anywhere else. Once one of the city's richest communes, as proved by the extravagant Hôtel de Ville, it has an unbelievable number of glorious *belle époque*, Art Deco, and Art Nouveau houses, the city's best-stocked beer bar (Moeder Lambic), a thriving gallery culture, and plenty of ethnic eateries, from rough-diamond couscous joints to top-end Portuguese establishments. In the richer east, the swish restaurants of chaussée de Charleroi offer a more sophisticated take on international cuisine; in the poorer west, which has a large North African population, Brussels' largest market sprawls around the Gare du Midi on Sundays; in between, there's a cozy bohemian scene that's long been acting as a magnet for aesthetes and artists alike.

day

🛍 Shops are local but with an international flavour. Chaussée de Waterloo is the high street of the area.

👁 St-Gilles Hôtel de Ville [→63]; commercial art at Salon d'Art & de Coiffure, Pascal Polar, Espace Photographique Contretype (in the Art Nouveau Hôtel Hannon) [→74], and Art Kiosk [→75].

night

🍽 Chic restaurants on chaussée de Charleroi; cheap ethnic joints near Gare du Midi; neighbourhood bars around parvis St-Gilles and the Barrière.

☆ Massive music and dance venue Forest-National is just to the south [→113].

getting there

Ⓜ Porte de Hal; Hôtel des Monnaies; Parvis St-Gilles; Horta; Louise.

🚋 18, 81, 82, 91, 92

🚌 48, 54

st-gilles

st-gilles

shopping

Up-and-coming professionals, bohemians, and ethnic communities live and shop, cheek by jowl, in St-Gilles' faded splendour. Thanks to the ethnic mix – Spanish, North African, Portuguese, and Greek – the food shops are to die for. Best are the marinated lamb steaks and *merguez* sausages from the halal butchers around place de Bethléem and along rues Théodore Verhaegen and de Mérode. The *Marché du Midi, next to Gare du Midi, on Sunday mornings (7am– 1pm) is a true celebration of Mediterranean riches, with stalls selling salt cod, preserved lemons, cured meats, fresh pasta, and Italian cheeses. Along the same lines, but with a North African spin, is the morning market (not Mondays) on *parvis St-Gilles. The finest bakers in an area of many are La Miche de Pain (fab baked-sugar

* = featured in the listings section [→84–110]

pies, custard tartlets, and wholemeal loaves). Top look-ins are hip kitchenware store **Dille en Kamille**, which also does scrumptious organic food ; and style-conscious café-cum-brunch place **La Crémerie de la Vache**, which sells patisseries, bottled olive oils, and Mariage Frères teas. Connoisseurs of the coffee kind find their fix at **Brûlerie Française**, which blends, grinds, and sells a wicked choice of whole coffee beans.

More chichi shops are located on the fringes of St-Gilles, by avenue Louise and around the Hôtel de Ville [→63], where hair guru Frédéric Blondel's flamboyant salon **Santi's** is a shrine to the area's Art Nouveau heritage. He attracts a gay clubland scene and women after tea, sympathy, a cool cut, or the clubby labels displayed at the front of the shop. *·**Table d'Hôtes** is reminiscent of past glory days with its antiques from the 1920s – an eclectic stash of crockery, *objets d'art*, Art Deco scent bottles, and lamps. Glitzy old dress and jewellery hire store, **Amandine** ✒, is good for posh functions. For today's ethnic decor at knock-down prices, however, head for **La Caravane Passe**, in the heart of the North African community. It sells *tagines*, silver teapots for mint tea, and colourful scatter cushions to bring Morocco to you.

Jaded megastore shoppers will find comfort in the old-fashioned stores around the Barrière, where the main arteries of St-Gilles meet and haberdashers and ironmongers still thrive. Recommended is cutlery and penknife specialist **La Coutellerie**, which sells the type of utensils that the Conran Shop would charge double the price for, such as grooming kits and herb cutters.

Bande dessinée (comic strip) fans should make a beeline for *·**Ziggourat**, whose monthly exhibitions make shopping there all the more enticing. If this inspires you to put brush to canvas, German artists' supplies shop **Schleiper**, where you can buy portfolios, top-notch stationery, and expensive prints and brushes, is a must for amateurs and pros alike.

eating & drinking

restaurants

Few establishments reward the eyes on first sight more than the kasbah-styled **Les Salons de L'Atalaïde** ✓, with its Italian-influenced French menu. Opulent drapes, murals, and candlelights scale down the baroque grandeur of this former auction hall to an intimate level. Among the highlights on the menu are the Irish entrecôte with Roquefort sauce and the fillet steak with marrow bone.

For a touch more snob value, impress your date with the upscale decor at *·**Le Living Room**. The bold menu is varied and includes fried red mullet with anchovy paste, as well as sashimi and sushi. Equally lush, but rather more peaceful, is the *·**Chelsea**, which serves high-quality French cuisine and offers garden dining for balmy, summer evenings, a wide-ranging menu, and an excellent wine list. Elegant surroundings, outstanding, beautifully arranged food, and fine wines are also top priorities at **Inada**, an expensive but exquisite French restaurant named after its Japanese chef/proprietor, who often emerges from the kitchen at the end of a hard night's cooking to mingle and chat with his guests. Delicate Eastern influences grace both the light spacious interior and the menu. High in quality and innovation, the Phillipe Starck-designed **Les Capucines** is all dark wood and blue lighting. The fine cuisine is French in flavour and hot on sauces that are unmatched anywhere else in town. The place attracts business people, rich ladies, as well as foodies. The old adage 'you get what you pay for' is all too true here in the evenings, but catch a table for lunch and it's far better value.

Lower prices and simple fuss-free Franco-Belgian fare are on offer at **Le Temps Délire**, with classic brasserie fare including *moules et frites*. Jazz and blues concerts are held here on Saturday nights. A popular, informal lunchtime place is **À Toi Mauricette (ATM)**, a bright, contemporary space where you can munch on inventive, Mediterranean-style salads (the dressings are divine) and light snacks.

St-Gilles' mixed bag of ethnicities translates in many styles of eateries, with the roost firmly ruled by Mediterranean joints. For country Italian cooking, head to **Perbacco**, a relaxed, no-frills canteen-style resto where the menu changes daily.

Restaurant Thassos, meanwhile, is a cheap and cheerful Greek joint which specializes in *petits os* (spare ribs) for 200BF. Iberian tastes are satisfied at **Le Forcado**, a well-established, up-market Portuguese restaurant serving traditional cuisine like great salt cod. Intimate **El Madrileño** is a family-run Spanish eaterie that specializes in paella, *petit cochon de lait*, and *jamón serrano*, plenty of which hangs from the bar. Excellent tortilla too. It lures a mixed crowd of locals and Commission workers.

The best North African restaurants in the area are along rue de Moscou. **Aux Mille & Une Nuits**, a Tunisian couscous joint with a fantastically kitsch Arabian Nights interior, is *the* place for a young and vibrant Congolese and North African crowd. Nearby is **Beni Znassen**, one of Brussels' most authentic Moroccan restaurants. Started around 25 years ago as a local café, it used to give away free couscous on Friday nights. With the unstoppable growth of its reputation, the place slowly transformed into a restaurant. But it's still cheap, which is why this St-Gilles institution remains a favourite haunt of students, artists, and the local Moroccan community.

> Hidden behind the imposing doorways of St-Gilles are restaurants with lavish interiors and eclectic cuisine.

bars & cafés

St-Gilles' bars span the full spectrum from traditional Belgian beer sampling to internationally themed spots around rue Jean Stas and rue Berckmans. Real beer drinkers head straight to *Moeder Lambic*, which serves over 800 different brews (most of them Belgian, with a few exotic imports). But don't expect a comfy seat inside – it's small (the beer gets more space than the customers), pretty chaotic, and comfort plays second fiddle to the sipping brews. Punters are mainly boys on a boisterous night out. More tranquil is **La Porteuse d'Eau**, a beautiful Art Nouveau-styled café/bar with a light, airy atmosphere. Enjoy a quiet beer with the locals or sample one of their scrumptious patisseries with some tasty, strong coffee.

A flurry of international bars has opened in St-Gilles over recent years. For the exotic, head to **Tierra del Fuego**, a popular, colonial-styled Latin American bar/café. It serves some of the best *caipirinhas* in town, but there's also a good selection of rums, tequilas, and South American grub. **SiSiSi** attracts a trendy multi-national twentysomething crowd who come for the cheap beer and to watch the *St-Gilleois* at work and play. For American football, darts, and snooker, try **JJ's**, an American cocktail bar with Tex-Mex food on the menu. But beware – it's a bit of a meat market in the evenings. Popular Irish bar **MacSweeney's** is a safe bet for anglophones, especially those suffering withdrawal from Sky Sports. The terraces are particularly pleasant in the summer.

Local trendies have taken to listening to

funky beats at the hip ***Brasserie Verschueren**, whose recent renovation has restored it to its original, homely 1930s style. **Brasserie de l'Union** is a legendary bar that draws a bit of a dodgy, underbelly-of-the-city crowd, as well as rowdy bohos. **Le Comiqu'Art**, meanwhile, serves Belgian food and good brews to the starving audiences of the local comic/theatre often on offer here.

🔑 directory

À Toi Mauricette (ATM) *♁D3*
29 chaussée de Charleroi
02.534.70.18
⊕⊕–⊕⊕⊕

Aux Mille & Une Nuits *♁C2*
7 rue de Moscou
02.537.41.27 ⊕⊕⊕

Beni Znassen *♁B2*
81 rue de l'Église
02.534.11.94
⊕⊕–⊕⊕⊕

Brasserie de l'Union *♁B2*
55 parvis St-Gilles
02.538.15.79

Brasserie Verschueren *♁B2*
11–13 parvis St-Gilles
02.539.40.68

Brûlerie Française *♁C4*
280 chaussée de Waterloo
02.537.48.06

Les Capucines *♁C2*
22 rue Jourdan
02.538.69.24 ⊕⊕⊕

La Caravane Passe *♁C3*
2 rue de Tamines
02.538.05.90

Chelsea *♁D2*
85 chaussée de Charleroi
02.544.19.77 ⊕⊕–⊕⊕⊕

Le Comiqu'Art *♁C2*
1 rue de la Victoire
02.537.22.75

La Coutellerie *♁C2*
187 rue de l'Hôtel des Monnaies
02.538.86.39

Le Crémerie de la Vache *♁D1*
6 rue Jean Stas
02.538.28.18

Dille en Kamille *♁D1*
16 rue Jean Stas
02.538.81.25

El Madrileño *♁B3*
50 chaussée de Waterloo
02.537.69.82
⊕⊕–⊕⊕⊕

Le Forcado *♁D4*
192 chaussée de Charleroi
02.537.92.20 ⊕⊕⊕

Inada *♁D2*
73 rue de la Source
02.538.01.13 ⊕⊕⊕

JJ's *♁C2*
28 rue Jourdan
02.538.78.28

Le Living Room *♁D2*
50 chaussée de Charleroi
02.534.44.34
⊕⊕–⊕⊕⊕

MacSweeney's *♁D1*
24 rue Jean Stas
02.534.47.41

Marché du Midi *♁Xx*
place de la Constitution

La Miche de Pain *♁D4*
2a avenue Brugmann
02.345.87.60

Moeder Lambic *♁C4*
68 rue de Savoie
02.539.14.19

Perbacco *♁D2*
179 chaussée de Charleroi
02.537.67.99 ⊕⊕⊕

La Porteuse d'Eau *♁B2*
48a avenue Jean Volders
02.537.66.46

Restaurant Thassos *♁A2*
118 chaussée de Forest
02.537.26.53 ⊕⊕

Les Salons de L'Atalaïde *♁D2*
89 chaussée de Charleroi
02.537.21.54 ⊕⊕⊕

Santi's *♁B3*
22 ave Paul Dejaer
02.534.64.22

Schleiper *♁D3*
149–151 chaussée de Charleroi
02.541.05.41

SiSiSi *♁D3*
174 chaussée de Charleroi
02.534.14.00

Table d'Hôtes *♁B4*
16 avenue Demeur
02.534.70.25

Le Temps Délire *♁D2*
175–177 chaussée de Charleroi
02.538.12.10 ⊕⊕⊕

Tierra del Fuego *♁D2*
14 rue Berckmans
02.537.42.72 ⊕⊕⊕

Ziggourat *♁D2*
34 rue Dejoncker
02.538.40.37

32

st-gilles

uptown, upbeat

Coming from central Brussels, western Ixelles can be disappointing at first sight. The lashings of concrete house such international names as Gucci, Hermès et al, who attract a fur-clad clientele of local ladies and Eurocrats. Beyond the hustle and bustle, however, lies one of the city's most elegant neighbourhoods, with heaps of intimate restos and chic one-off boutiques; even the Irish bars have a touch of class. The main public spaces have a laid-back, villagey feel, with bistros, cafés, and bookshops dotting place Brugmann, cozy parvis de la Trinité, and leafy place Châtelain. Traditionally the haunt of artists and intellectuals – Victor Horta and sculptor Constantin Meunier both lived here – western Ixelles is now a magnet for media types, while its 19th-century town houses, with wrought-iron balconies and large front doors, have been snapped up by the seriously rich.

day

🏬 Designer central; big-name flagships line boulevard de Waterloo and avenue Louise. The place Châtelain market is a big draw.

👁 Musée Horta [→67]; Musée Constantin Meunier [→67]; Bois de la Cambre [→76].

night

🍴 High-quality, high-priced restaurants; this is where the southern bourgeois set eat out. Bars are good, but pretty low-key.

☆ Music of both the live and DJ variety is pretty rare, save some bar-based acts.

getting there

Ⓜ Louise; Porte de Namur; Toison d'Or.
🚊 23, 81, 82, 90, 91, 92, 93, 94
🚌 38, 54, 60

ixelles (west)

shopping

place Louise district

The Guccis and Hermès of this world find the turn-of-last-century's grand mansions on boulevard de Waterloo des res enough for their Brussels boutiques. **Delvaux**, Belgium's answer to Louis Vuitton, holds its own with hand-turned leather luggage and accessories. The converted coach house out back is home to Belgian household linen queen *Martine Doly. She

designs and sells a divine line of hand-finished linen and organza drapes, night-dresses and jim-jams. **Versace** is just a few doors down. Other notables are **Régina Rubens'** Parisian sophisticate clothes for thirtysomething women, Italian counterpart **Ventilo**, and a sizeable **Ralph Lauren**.

Facing the boulevard is the less-elegant avenue

de la Toison d'Or. It fronts the Galeries Louise, Ixelles, and de la Toison d'Or, ensuring a steady stream of browsers. High-spot here is the designer-label mecca of **Francis Ferent** for women's, men's, and kids' togs, accessories, and home decor by the likes of **Miu Miu, DKNY** et al. Take a break with some Belgian truffle ice cream at **Häagen-Dazs** before

* = featured in the listings section [→84–110]

tackling avenue Louise. **Cartier**, at No.1, leads the line-up of international flagships, big Belgian names, and top chain-stores. Hot spots needing no intro are clothes labels **Cacharel, Hugo Boss, Adolpho Dominguez**, high-street fashion star **Zara**, and trad kids' shops **Jacardi** and **Bonpoint**. The country's only true department store, **Inno**, is better after a revamp, but doesn't rank well against its European peers.

womenswear & accessories

food

ixelles (west)

The international ready-to-wear scene in this area is awesome. Cutting-edge Irish fashion can be had at **Harmony**, with natty separates by John Rocha and Paul Costelloe alongside hand-crocheted numbers in luxury yarns by Lainey Keogh. Bombay and Goan store **Camelot** chose Brussels as its first out-of-India branch, with work by the cream of India's avant-garde, such as Alpana Bawa and Abraham & Thakore. At designer **Ming Tsy**'s one-off shop, there are slinky embroidered cocktail numbers, simple shifts, and a cool line in accessories and stationery – handmade papers from Tsy's native Taiwan.

Cashmere collectables woven in Mauritius are piled high in **Kirane**. Timeless staples like twin-sets, scarves, and jerseys come in tens of colours. Less conservative are multi-coloured jumpers and scarves by Belgian Valérie Barkowski for her Mia Zia label, made by Marrakesh artisans and sold at her shop **Da Zia**. Erotica accessories – crotchless knickers, peephole bras, and less-revealing lingerie by Marlies Dekkers can be had at **Undressed**.

Gorgeous contemporary space **Cachemire** is a homage to Italian design, where the rails are filled with classic separates with a twist. Shoes by Carshoe and the equally expensive Heschung are downstairs. Justice is done to Belgium by haute couturier **Gerald Watelet**'s ready-to-wear line Simply Couture, with lots of hand-finished details. If you are caught on the hop without a suitable frock – or jewels – for a high-society bash, don't despair. **Amandine** hires out stunning ballgowns, chic cocktail dresses and wedding robes at a moment's notice. Britpack women's fashion is brought to Ixelles by **Smadja Femme**: Whistles, Ghost, Paul Smith, Joseph, and then some. Kids aren't left out in the cold either – Paul Smith for babes to teens is on offer at friendly one-off boutique **Claude Hontoir**.

Wild mushrooms, game, cheeses, and fruit and veg couldn't be fresher at the ***Place du Châtelain Market** (2–7.30pm Wed). If cooking is out, there's a master chef at classy *traiteur* **L'Atelier Gourmand**. This deli's cordon bleu takeaways can't be faulted, but expect to pay through the nose. Up-market convenience store **Le Déjeuner sur l'Herbe** has a great selection of wines, gourmet tins, organic veg, and takeaways. For dessert, try top-notch patisserie **St-Aulaye**'s yummy fruit tarts and pastries. And for the cheese course, regional specialities are in tip-top condition at **Fromageon** or **Fromagerie Vinothèque**. Round off the feast with coffee, which doesn't come much better than at **Degroof**. Whole or ground arabica beans can be bought by the kilo, as can fine teas. Healthfood shop **La Tsampa** keeps the same hours as its restaurant out back. Pulses, beansprouts, wholemeal bread, organic fruit, and essentials for healthy living are sold here. Lastly, if truffles make you tick, don't miss **L'Atelier de la Truffe Noire**, which sells truffle-seeped new-laid eggs, truffles by the 100g, and cutters and storage containers for this highly prized fungi; the café does an excellent (if expensive) line in lux sarnies and cooked breakfasts. It shares the same owner as Michelin-star resto La Truffe Noire. For the best Portuguese pastries, try **Le Petit Forcado**.

menswear

Trad men's outfitter **Degand** combines bespoke tailoring with luxury gifts for the man who has it all – wooden desk accessories by David Linley, silver cigar trimmers, and deluxe board games. Style and Italian panache rule at **Ermenegildo Zegna**'s Brussels flagship, where suits and leatherwear are sold. Fashion-conscious professionals head for **Smadja Homme**, which sells Comme des Garçons, Paul Smith, and Joseph. Outdoor types can try **Entre Terre Ciel** – state-of-the-art camping equipment is upstairs, hi-performance clothes below.

lifestyle stores

Edouard Vermeulen, of the **Natan** ready-to-wear stores, has his haute couture nerve centre here. Upstairs is a lifestyle emporium of furniture and objects for the home, hand-picked by trendsetter Sophie Campion. **Antithèse** is another must, with wonderful furniture and smaller homeware items designed by Christophe Delcourt, Marie-Claude Bérard, and Xavier Lust. For lining the walls of minimalist interiors go to **Baltazar**, where signed lithographs and original artworks by living Belgian artists like Benoît Jacques are for sale.

Lend an oriental touch to the home at **Compagnie de l'Orient et de la Chine**, which sells crockery and soft furnishings. A similar minimalist approach is taken at *Cinabre, with Japanese-style ceramics, lacquered dishes, and glassware by Belgium's Harry Dean. Aficionados of stainless-steel kitchen utensils will be sorted – at a price – at **Fahrenheit**. If kitsch clutter pleases, go to **MagicLand**, where, alongside wacky clubwear, there are lots of trinkets, pink faux-fur, and novelty items for the home. **Graphie Sud** sells women's clothes, accessories, and an enlightened choice of homeware for modern living.

Antiques-lovers should head for place Brugmann, an area made for Sunday browsing, when everything is open. **Scènes de Ménage** sells an eclectic mix of old and new bed quilts, fine linen, cutlery, and glassware. *Faisons un Rêve has Art Deco jewellery, lots of Bakelite *objets*, and choice ceramics. Bargains are commonplace at nearby **Bleue comme... une orange**, which peddles mirrors, dinner and tea services, vases, and anything for the home that takes the owner's fancy. For Art Nouveau and Art Deco furniture, head to *Essences de Siècle.

Essential finishing touches can be snapped up at **Annick Goutal**, a Parisian perfumier with sublime floral home fragrances and scented candles. Or treat yourself to a bouquet of flowers at **Catleya** ↘, where florist Brigitte Fux is in the same league as Britain's Packer & Prycke. For further inspiration, browse in bookshop **Peinture Fraîche**, which has an international selection of coffee-table tomes on architecture, art, and design. Glossy interiors mags and multilingual newspapers are sold at **Librairie Candide** and **Librairie de Rome**.

bargains

Near to, and along, rue du Bailli – a boho area – is a cluster of second-hand and end-of-line shops. Leader of the pack is **Dod**, which sells last season's designer gear for men and women and lingerie at bargain prices. **Les Enfants d'Edouard** is best known for barely worn big-name men's and women's labels. Nearby charity shop **Les Petits Riens** is a mecca for bargain clothes and furniture. **Nijinski** is where Brussels' international crowd sell their books. This is *the* place for bargain English-language lit.

eating & drinking

restaurants

The streets around elegant place Châtelain are teeming with excellent eateries which attract moneyed locals and gourmet out-of-towners in equal numbers. *La Quincaillerie ✔ is probably the best-known restaurant in the area thanks to the sumptuous wrought-iron decor and legendary seafood. Some believe the brasserie rests on its laurels, while fleecing customers in the process. Make up your own mind – if you can afford to. Better value, though still pricey, is *Le Fils de Jules. This Starck-and Art Deco-influenced eatery serves delicious Basque and *Landais* dishes. The warm foie gras is the size of a bookend and the grilled squid dish big enough to keep an ink factory in business. Cozy and candlelit *L'Amadeus is located in Rodin's former workshop. Spare ribs are about the best thing on an otherwise predictable menu, but the wine list is impressive and the atmosphere lively.

If Italian food is more your bag, the **Convivio** is a popular trattoria famed for its inexpensive antipasti and sizzling grilled fish. Unfortunately, the two sisters who run it are equally famed for their erratic service. **Cosi** is an altogether more traditional Italian ristorante. The food isn't cheap, but the extensive range of grilled vegetable entrées and adventurous pasta dishes is of top quality. It also has a cheaper and sister restaurant – Pizza Cosi – several doors down the street.

This area of Ixelles is also a good place for vegetarians. *La Tsampa, in particular, has an astonishing selection of imaginative dishes (from Tibetan ravioli to Japanese pot-au-feu). There's also an organic foodstore up-front. *EAT is equally appealing to veggies and carnivores; the salad composé never fails to impress. It's not open in the evenings, but is the perfect place for a light lunch and a chit-chat. Definitely not for herbivores is Le Pavillon, a cozy bistro where just about anything that moves is served up with a tasty sauce. The wine list is resolutely French at this cheap and cheerful *bon viveurs'* haunt, but thankfully the beers are brewed locally.

Brussels is not famed for its Chinese restaurants, but there are two excellent places here. **Ô Chinoise-Riz** is a dark and atmospheric eaterie packed with Chinese folk tucking into sizzling platters of seafood and punters worrying about the unfeasibly large knives wielded by the chefs. *La Cantonnaise is less cozy – it doubles as a take-away – but the Chinese/Vietnamese über-cheap food is a delight. Along avenue Louise, the restaurants tend to cater for well-to-do passers-by on their way to bourgeois suburban residences. Housed in a beautiful old *maison de maître*, *La Fin de Siècle is a typical example. The clientele is well-heeled and a table quite difficult to get. But the Italian food is top-notch, the baroque decor suitably OTT, and the garden a treat in summer. Further up the avenue, *La Porte des Indes is easily the poshest Indian restaurant in town. The dishes are from the French, not British, former colonies and the emphasis is quite firmly on seafood. *Les Brasseries Georges is a Parisian-style bistro in one of the leafiest areas of western Ixelles. If you're after an evening of pure self-indulgence, it's worth the trek through the woods, though, because the surf and turf takes some beating.

> Gentrification may have brought high prices and trendy eateries, but this area remains one of the best places to eat out in Brussels.

bars & cafés

Smarter and more yuppified than the ethnically diverse eastern Ixelles, the streets around place Châtelain are not the city's best for drinking. But there are some spots for a nice bevvy. *The Bank is the best of these. Although there's Guinness on tap and the Cranberries on air, there aren't any nicotine-stained ceilings here. Instead, you'll find gaudy artworks, a relaxed vibe and scores of safety-deposit boxes on the walls (it's a former bank building). **MacSweeneys** is a typical Irish pub and, with its big screens, is an excellent place to watch sport on rainy afternoons. So is **Monkey Business**, a more raucous anglophone expat drinking den off avenue Louise. Although trying a bit too hard to be an all-American sports bar, the scrumptious Tex-Mex fare more than compensates. For a quieter drink, head to **Le Châtelain** on the square of the same name. Don't be put off by the local yuppies; the steaks are the best in town and the place

is jumping after the Thursday-night street market in the place.

♗ directory

L'Amadeus ♗B2
13 rue Veydt
02.538.34.27
🍷⊖–🍷 🍷

Amandine ♗B2
150 rue Defacqz
02.539.17.93

Annick Goutal ♗B2
52 avenue Louise
02.514.56.64

Antithèse ♗B2
17 rue du Mail
02.539.03.93

L'Atelier Gourmand ♗B3
470 rue Vanderkindere
02.344.51.90

L'Atelier de la Truffe Noire ♗B2
300 avenue Louise
02.640.54.55

Baltazar ♗B2
100 rue de Stassart
02.512.85.13

The Bank ♗B2
79 rue du Bailli
02.537.52.65

Bleue comme… une orange ♗B2
69 rue Alphonse Renard
02.344.92.23

Les Brasseries Georges ♗B2
259 avenue Winston Churchill
02.647.21.00
🍷🍷⊖–🍷 🍷

Cachemire ♗B2
rue Franz Merjay

Camelot ♗B2
47–48 rue Châtelain
02.647.22.27

La Cantonnaise ♗B2
110 rue Tenbosch
02.344.70.42 🍷⊖–🍷 🍷

Catleya ♗B2
118 avenue Lepoutre
02.344.63.64

Le Châtelain ♗B3
17 place du Châtelain
02.538.67.94

Cinabre ♗B3
5 rue Washington
02.345.26.95

Claude Hontoir ♗B4
14 place Brugmann
02.346.59.47

Compagnie de l'Orient & de la Chine ♗B3
1a place Stephanie
01.511.43.82

Convivio ♗B3
6 rue de l'Aqueduc
02.539.32.99
🍷🍷⊖–🍷 🍷

Cosi ♗B3
95 rue Américaine
02.534.85.86 🍷🍷🍷

Da Zia ♗B3
61 rue Darwin

Degroof ♗B4
427 rue Vanderkindere
02.343.54.36

Degand ♗B2
415 avenue Louise
02.649.00.73

Le Déjeuner sur l'Herbe ♗B4
6 ave Louis Lepoutre
02.346.17.59

Dod ♗B2
89–91 rue du Bailli
02.219.43.52

EAT ♗B2
103 rue de l'Aqueduc
02.537.22.90 🍷

Les Enfants d'Édouard ♗B2
175 avenue Louise
02.640.42.45

Ermenegildo Zegna ♗B2
30 blvd de Waterloo
02.511.41.57

Entre Terre Ciel ♗B2
20 place Stéphanie
02.502.42.41

Essences de Siècle ♗A3
133 rue Franz Merjay
02.345.37.39

Fahrenheit ♗B2
130b avenue Louise
02.644.28.00

Faisons un Rêve ♗B4
avenue Lepoutre
02.347.34.29

Le Fils de Jules ♗B3
35 rue du Page
02.534.00.57 🍷🍷

La Fin de Siècle ♗B2
423 avenue Louise
02.648.80.41 🍷⊖–🍷 🍷

Fromagerie Vinothèque ♗B2
106 rue du Bailli
02.537.66.53

Fromageon ♗B4
309 rue Vanderkindere
02.344.26.12

Gérard Watelet ♗B2
268 avenue Louise
02.647.35.50

Graphie Sud ♗B4
15 avenue Georges Brugmann
02.344.31.92

Harmony ♗B2
405/415 ave Louise
02.648.84.32

Kirane ♗B2
67b avenue Louise
02.539.16.02

Librairie Candide ♗B2
1–2 place Brugmann
02.344.81.94

Librairie de Rome ♗B2
50b avenue Louise
02.511.79.37

MacSweeneys ♗B2
24 rue Jean Stas
02.534.47.41

MagicLand ♗B2
41 rue du Bailli
050.62.88.06

Martine Doly ♗C4
27 Chaussée de Waterloo
02.512.46.28

Ming Tsy ♗B3
rue du Page
02.424.29.68

Monkey Business ♗B2
30 rue Defacqz
02.538.69.34

Natan ♗B2
158 avenue Louise
02.647.10.01

Nijinski ♗B3
15–17 rue du Page
02.539.20.28

Ô Chinoise-Riz ♗B3
94 rue de l'Aqueduc
02.534.91.08 🍷⊖–🍷 🍷

Le Pavillon ♗B2
64 rue Defacqz
02.538.02.15 🍷⊖–🍷 🍷

Peinture Fraîche ♗B2
10 rue du Tabellion
02.537.11.05

Le Petit Forcado ♗B3
2 rue Américaine
02.537.92.20

Les Petits Riens ♗B3
101 rue Américaine
02.537.30.26

La Porte des Indes ♗B2
455 avenue Louise
02.647.86.51
🍷⊖–🍷 🍷

La Quincaillerie ♗B2
45 rue du Page
02.538.25.53
🍷⊖–🍷 🍷

St-Aulaye ♗B2–B3
4 rue Jean Chapelié
02.345.77.85

Scènes de Ménage ♗B3
4 place Brugmann
02.344.32.95

Smadja Femme B2
16 place Brugmann
02.347.66.70

Smadja Homme ♗B3
21 avenue Lepoutre
02.513.50.13

La Tsampa ♗B3
109 rue de Livourne
02.647.03.67 🍷⊖–🍷 🍷

Undressed ♗B3
rue de l'Aqueduc
02.544.08.44

37

ixelles (west)

the melting pot

The *Bruxellois* love to describe themselves as *zinneke* (meaning mongrel or bastard) and eastern Ixelles is as *zinneke* as it gets. You can taste the difference as you leave the dreary Toison d'Or and plunge into the Matongé, a vibrant jumble of cafés, restaurants and fabric shops that's home to the city's central African community (a by-product of colonialism the colonisers didn't expect). A short walk, and a world away, place St-Boniface is a fast-developing trendster hangout favoured by the city's young international set. To the west lies chaussée d'Ixelles, the area's main artery; a workaday high street at the northern end, it gains character as it rolls south. The Art Nouveau residences around the willow-lined Ixelles ponds are the exclusive domain of the local bourgeoisie, while further south, chaussée de Boondael's lively taverns and myriad ethnic eateries attract a never-ending stream of students from the nearby uni.

day

🛍 The Matongé's great for African food & fabric; the high street, chaussée d'Ixelles; the food & plants market on place Flagey.

👁 Église St-Boniface [→71]; Musée d'Ixelles [→74]; Fondation pour l'Architecture [→74]; Art Nouveau on rue de la Vallée & rue de Belle Vue [→73].

night

🍴 Restaurants are ethnic and there are some authentic gems to sample; the bars are lively and always busy.

☆ Live jazz at Dolma [→113]; puppetry at the Théâtre du Peruchet [→115]; and arthouse cinemas Vendôme & Styx [→112].

getting there

Ⓜ Louise; Porte de Namur; Trône.
🚊 81, 82, 93, 94
🚌 38, 54, 59, 60, 71, 95, 96

ixelles (east)

shopping

clothes & accessories

This area is variety at its best – there are ethnic food stores in the Matongé, a daily market on place Flagey, and boho shops dotted all around. The humdrum chaussée d'Ixelles, a traffic-congested shopping artery snaking down to place Flagey, is no great shakes, though: it's essentially side-by-side discount electrical stores, fast-food outlets, and low-priced chainstores. It gets less mainstream as it heads south, where notable one-off boutiques include **Lorenzo Lebon**, who sells his sleek, hand-crafted trendy leather handbags. Vintage clothes and accessories are sold at **Look 50**, known for its range of secondhand Levi's. It's a bit of a fleapit, but the place is full of bargain-hunters oozing street cred. Clothes by Carhartt and Dickies and 1970s props are worth checking out nextdoor at **Pax**, while **Cocoon** is unmissable for recent end-of-line bargains by Belgian designer Olivier Strelli, as well as quirky accessories by local designers. Bang up-to-date, Valérie Janssens' natty hats and bead jewellery are for sale in the eye-catching **Tarlatane**, and **Nina Meert**'s shop for chic evening clothes, bridalwear, and accessories reflects the upbeat tone of rue St-Boniface.

food

Activity in the Matongé is focused on the ethnic food shops, making the area buzz from early morning until sundown. **Exotic Foods** is good for Congolese dried river fish, frozen greens from Burundi, and *moambé* (a peanut chicken stew); next door, **African Asian Foods** is *the* place for fresh fruit. The district's cool ethnic-food mix is enhanced by a smattering of no-frills Japanese shops selling specialities like good, fresh fish destined for sushi and tashimi. Sushi to go is on offer at **Tagawa Superstore**, which also does a great line in rice, fresh fish, and exotic tinned and packet foods. For a blast from the Med, be prepared to queue at family-run Moroccan store **Agadir II**, where fresh fish is piled high, or **Himi**, which sells pre-marinated halal lamb brochettes and fillets. Ready-to-eat take away food couldn't be better at *Mary's, run by Irish cook Mary Fehily, the sideline to her high-society catering business. Try her seafood lasagnes, traditional moussakas, or salads with a twist. And cheese-lovers shouldn't miss the array of delights at **Fromagerie Maison Baguette-Gaspard**, complete with fab marbletop shop fittings. It's tiny, has been here forever, and the owner, a master cheese-seller, knows all there is to know about Belgium's specialities, including the delish medium-hard Maredsous. She also sells fantastic goat's milk cheeses made by Trappist monks in Orval and Chimay.

speciality

Apart from food stores, the Matongé's other big business is fabric. The trendiest shop in the area is **Bethel Boutique**. It stays open late and sells lengths of *wax* (bright batik prints) and funky high-heeled shoes. European style is on offer at **The Gallery**, where German collector Konrad Kern sells contemporary furniture and objects by the Milanese Memphis group, Bakelite necklaces from the 1950s, and pieces by Italian contemporary furniture designer Andrea Branzini. For a leisurely browse, go to one of two **Arlequin** shops, which have been peddling used CDs and vinyl for years. One sells rock, funk, African and reggae imports; the other classical, videos, jazz and good old *chanson*. Photographers love **Campion's** two shops: one deals in secondhand lenses and cameras from the 1930s, the other sells good-value brand-new equipment.

eating & drinking

restaurants

Trad Belgian isn't the usual bag here – African, Middle Eastern and Japanese cuisines top the bill in this mix-and-match area. The proliferation of central African eateries in the Matongé earned it the nickname Upper Kinshasa. **Ile de Gorré**, on place St-Boniface, is one of the best. There are also half a dozen African cafés on the rue de la Longue Vie serving up trad favourites like *moambé* (chicken in spicy peanut sauce). There's a strong African flavour to the cooking at **Les Jardins de Bagatelle** (which includes crocodile and antelope), but this sumptuously decorated restaurant is a cut above (in price and cuisine). Equally decadent, but much less pricey, is **Art Sauvage** ✓, a magical Moroccan restaurant; *tajines*, couscous, and *pastilla* are authentic and the rich red interior brings a splash of warmth. With its Arabian-Nights decor, *El Yasmine is a great traditional North African joint, and you won't find a fresher mint tea or tastier Tunisian salad this side of the Sahara. A few doors down is Egyptian eatery *Les Pyramides – order a tableful of Egyptian and Lebanese dishes, such as *tabouleh* or falafel, sit back and, if it's the week-

end, watch the belly-dancer shake her stuff. The **Ouzerie** is another place where it's best to order meze. The food in this inexpensive Greek joint is excellent, the service impeccable and the sound of Greek voices reassuring. Don't expect plate-smashing or cheesy music though – owner Stefanos Svanias is way too classy for that.

Place St-Boniface is one of the trendiest spots in Brussels, and new places are springing up all the time. The best is **Le Ilème Elément**, a modern Thai restaurant with metallic tables, esoteric murals and sharp lighting. The Thai chefs make authentic, delicious food, and, unusually for a Thai place, inexpensive. Across the square is a newish Italian joint called **Mano a Mano**. It's always packed, but once you've tasted their crisp pizzas and adventurous pastas, you'll know why. More trad, but pricier, is another Italian, **La Crèche des Artistes**. Although it's tiny inside, don't be surprised if there's a fleet of Mercs outside: the chef has quite a fan club among moneyed food buffs. He deserves it because the food is ace. If it's modern French/Belgian cooking you're after, try **Vins Vins**. The menu is adventurous – check out the marinated salmon *ceviche* for starters – and there's a chatty neighbourhood feel. Or book a table for you and your dog (yes, they cater for pooches too) at *Canterbury, a busy modern brasserie with good food and high prices. *De la Vigne à l'Assiette is another local joint whose reputation has spread far and wide. The name means 'from the vine to the plate', and the food is always as fresh as the pale-lemon colour scheme. Pricey, but worth splashing out for the

adventurous combinations of modern French cuisine on offer. Simple and unfussy, *L112 fuses the best of French and the Far East in dishes such as steamed fresh vegetables perfumed with coriander, served up to an affluent thirtysomething crowd.

If you're ready for an assault on the taste buds, and don't mind forking out for it, carry on down the road to *Chez Marie. Although part of the ultra-trendy Kasbah and Bonsoir Clara stable (it was started up by the same guy), this local restaurant is smaller and more intimate than its downtown siblings. The largely French cuisine is meticulously prepared, and the wine list one of the finest in the city. Japanese food is all the rage, and for the best in sushi and sashimi, head to *Yamayu Santatsu. For something more filling, try **Yamato**. It's always packed with Japanese businessmen and students, but it's worth the wait for the enormous bowls of pork and noodle

soup, and the delicious ravioli-like *gyoshi*. The best in a row of Vietnamese joints on chaussée de Boondael is **Poussières d'Etoile**, with its innovative (and cheap) menu. Veggie options in Brussels are few and far between. *Dolma is an exception; the vegetarian buffet at this Tibetan health-food joint is excellent. It's very chilled, with brushed yellow walls, photos of Tibetan monasteries, and piano music in the hall. If you prefer a more carnivorous eastern experience, pitch up at Pakistani **Anarkali** and jostle for a table. You can eat as much chicken *bhuna* and lamb tandoori as you like for less than 500BF. They'll also throw in a dessert and coffee for those who have the room.

bars

The bars here reflect the ethnic mix of this lively uptown 'hood. African drinking dens dominate the area around Porte de Namur, while around place Flagey, Portuguese is the most commonly heard language. In between are many fine bars – a just reward for the trek from downtown. The elegant place St-Boniface is dominated by *L'Ultime Atome ✓. One of the city's most buzzy cafés, it's packed with expat yuppies and local *artistes* who come here for solid French food and a staggering array of beers and spirits. A similar vibe is on offer at *L'Amour Fou. This local mainstay is a great place to chat, chill-out, and

admire the art. It serves cheap and cheerful food all day. Further down chaussée d'Ixelles is one of the area's most eccentric bars, Le Pantin. Beatniks, pub philosophers, and chess-players swarm to this eccentric joint like barflies. If jazz is more up your street, head to Sounds, a venue-cum-bar with live music (Wed–Sat). It's oh-so-cool, with purple velvet and black and white photos of all the greats. **Volle Gas** also used to be a jazz bar and still has occasional live acts. But it's gone more up-market and now bills itself as a soft-lit bistro. As befits this area, there are dozens of bars pumping out reggae and serving up African dishes. On a summer's night hang out on the pedestrianized part of rue de la Longue Vie. **L'Horloge du Sud** is one of few places where Euros and Africans mix in equal numbers. Try the fab African food if you're peckish. The University area hosts cheap and cheerful bars, always rammed, but usually great fun. *L'Atelier is legendary more hidden (and intimate), **Le Brassin** is a cozy spot to tuck into hearty Belgian food. It's a bit rough around the edges, but the regulars who hum along to Jacques Brel and drink fine beer don't seem to mind.

♪ directory

41

ixelles (east)

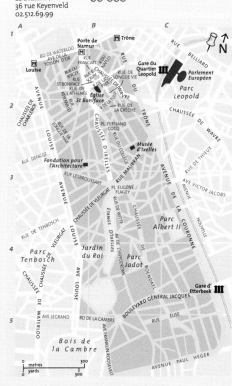

euro vision

On weekends, when the offices lie empty and most restaurants are closed, this concrete embodiment of a European superstate could induce Europhobia. On weekdays, however, the streets buzz with a Babelesque linguistic hubbub. This is the daytime hangout of lobbyists, translators, and all who feed off the Commission. Gossip hums through the air in the pubs, snack bars, and expense-account restaurants. National-themed shops mean homesick Eurocrats can pay over the odds for Nordic furniture and baked beans, while at night, the Irish bars are packed until the early hours with gregarious young professionals and *stagiaires*. For a less manufactured scene, head for the fantastical Art Nouveau buildings of squares Marie Louise and Ambiorix, unwind in pretty Parc Léopold, the former playground of the city's bourgeoisie, or check out the latest international hangouts on revitalized place du Luxembourg.

day

🛍 Not for the serious shopper, this area is a haven of EU imports and tacky souvenirs.

👁 Parlement Européen [→62]; Résidence Palace [→62]; Musée Wiertz [→68]; Art Nouveau [→72]. Parc du Cinquantenaire's museums [→65–66] and the Arc de Triomphe are nearby [→60].

night

🍸 On weekdays, it's expense-account heaven, suits schmoozing suits. Irish bars abound, with family-less young Euros drinking and dancing into the night.

☆ Théâtre Varia [→116]; outdoor summer cinema in Cinquantenaire Parc [→112].

getting there

Ⓜ Trône; Arts-Loi for the west; Maelbeek; Schuman.

🚌 20, 21, 22, 29, 34, 38, 59, 60, 63, 80, 95, 96

quartier européen

shopping

shopping

The EU quarter may not be the city's retail hot spot, but there are a few shops worth their weight. You can pick up Euro-souvenirs at virtually any newsstand in the Rond Point/Schuman area but, for the best variety, head to **Eurotempo**, where the familiar 12 gold stars are on everything from pens to gold watches. If you're

after something not designed by a Euro committee, try the comfy wool sweaters from Ireland at **Kenlis** or the vast selection of teas from **The English Shop**. Jack **O'Shea**, an Irish butcher, does a brisk trade with organic pork and hams, especially on high days and holidays. **Nordica**, meanwhile, sells hand-

made ornaments and dainty household decorations from Scandinavia.

Head to **Grani-Flora** ⁑ for a colourful selection of flowers; or spoil yourself at **Maison Chevalier**, near the European Parliament. Here you'll find luxurious all-natural bath products and other scented goodies.

* = featured in the listings section [→84–110]

eating & drinking

restaurants

It's difficult to go wrong restaurant-wise in this area – so influential is the Euro-custom that anything not up to scratch simply has to close its doors. With its string of restaurant frontages on each side, the tree-lined rue Archimède is vaguely reminiscent of Greenwich Village, though much less hip. Atmospheric and busy both day and night, all the restaurants are in classic Brussels townhouses, most with terraces in the original gardens. **Balthazar** has kept the feel of a house but with an ultra-modern look. The food is French fused with Pacific; a traditional base spiced up by look and flavour, such as scampi risotto with *galangal* or calf's liver with ginger and soya. More trad is **Le Dieu des Caprices**, one of Brussels' classics; a typical Italian menu in a very Italian setting. Move round the Med to **Le Jardin d'Espagne**, with its tapas bar in the basement, frequented by Commission types of all nationalities. You'll find **L'Atelier** through an unassuming set of coach doors: the restaurant is in an old artist's studio with a pretty courtyard used for alfresco dining in summer. Inside or out,

Belgian-French food is served with flair and confidence. Two newer chic brasseries take a large share of Eurocrat covers: **Cosmopolite**, all bleached wood and halogen, offers designer salads and classics with a twist, including foie gras with shrimps. **Brasserie Michel-Ange** is an informal place to tuck into *moules-frites* and Belgian beer, with a front terrace in the summer.

On the other side of the area, place Luxembourg hosts another clutch of restaurants. **Chez Moi** is classy, modern and efficient, with friendly staff and honest authentic French country cooking. Next door, walk into the theatre set that is **Sotto**

Ripa and enjoy modern Italian food amongst the dripping candles and outrageous drapes. A further hub of local restos is on place Jourdan, an atmospheric square of Belgian patisseries, eateries, and bars too numerous to mention. Among them is **⁎Maison d'Antoine ↲**, Brussels' most famous *friterie*, whose chips are double-fried and the sauces double-dolloped. Tucked into a quiet residential street, **Mi Tango**, run by Walter from Argentina, is the area's best-kept secret. Lunchtimes are buzzy, and candlelit tables in the evenings are often booked out owing to the great-value pasta, sangria, and Riojas.

Euroland isn't all business – tucked between the towers of power are lively hubs of restaurants and bars.

bars & cafés

Irish pubs dominate the drinking scene: all swinging, all lively, they're not places for a quiet night out. Some, like the **James Joyce ↗** and **The Hairy Canary** (a Victorian-style boozer), are as traditional as they come, and seem to have been *en place* forever. Good, honest food is served in both. Newer kids on the block include **O'Dwyer's**, more of a bar than a pub, with its long room leading through to the garden. With the vast International Press

Centre in the heart of the area, many bars are filled with quaffing journos and BBC reporters, such as the **Old Hack**, a small, simply furnished bar with understated decor and a big following. Even bigger is **Kitty O'Shea's**, packed at all times and serving wholesome pub grub. In the same area is **The Ceilidh**, a bit quieter, but again with its own following who come here for the live sport on satellite TV. Sitting on a corner, its

Sin scéal eile

tables spread onto the street in summer, is •**Wild Geese** – big, brash, and blousy, it's a real crowd puller. With its live music and late openings, a young crew of international *stagiaires* use it as their local. For a more traditional feel, **Chez Bernard** is a classic Brussels bar, all dark wood and mirrors, with a good choice of beers and bar snacks. Perfect for that pre-dinner sip or post-*digestif*. For something more new millennium, **L'Arlequin** is a trendy, glass-fronted café-restaurant, with reasonably priced drinks and good modern brasserie-style food.

quartier européen

♟ directory

L'Arlequin ♟C3
45 rue Froissart
02.280.41.11

L'Atelier ♟C2
28 rue Franklin
02.734.91.40 ⓦⓦⓦ

Balthazar ♟C2
63 rue Archimède
02.742.06.00 ⓦⓦⓦ

Brasserie Michel-Ange ♟D2
85 ave Michel-Ange
02.733.82.16 ⓦ

The Ceilidh ♟B2
37 rue du Taciturne
02.280.49.37

Chez Bernard ♟C4
47 place Jourdan
02.230.22.38

Chez Moi ♟A3
66 rue du
Luxembourg
02.280.26.66 ⓦⓦⓦ

Cosmopolite ♟D2
36 avenue de
Cortenburg
02.230.20.95 ⓦ–ⓦⓦ

Le Dieu des Caprices ♟C2
51 rue Stévin
02.736.41.16 ⓦⓦⓦ

The English Shop ♟C2
186 rue Stévin
02.735.11.38

Eurotempo ♟C2
14 rue Archimède
02.230.04.11

Grani-Flora ♟C2
30 square
Marguerite
02.734.49.90

The Hairy Canary ♟C2
12 rue Archimède
02.280.05.09

Jack O'Shea ♟C2
30 rue Le Titien
02.732.53.51

James Joyce ♟C2
34 rue Archimède
02.230.98.94

Le Jardin d'Espagne ♟C2
65 rue Archimède
02.736.34.49 ⓦⓦⓦ

Kitty O'Shea's ♟C2
42 boulevard de
Charlemagne
02.230.78.75

Kenlis ♟C2
48 rue Archimède
02.230.69.11

Maison d'Antoine ♟C4
1 place Jourdan
02.230.54.56 ⓦ

Maison Chevalier ♟A3
7 rue Marie de
Bourgogne
02.513.03.14

Mi Tango ♟B2
31 rue de Spa
075.25.27.20 ⓦⓦ

Nordica ♟B3
220 rue Belliard
02.230.13.05

O'Dwyer's ♟C2
55 rue Archimède
02.735.10.09

Old Hack ♟C2
176 rue Joseph II
02.230.07.95

Sotto Ripa ♟A3
60 rue du
Luxembourg
02.230.01.18 ⓦⓦⓦ

Wild Geese ♟B2
2 avenue Livingstone
02.230.19.90

northern lights

These once rich areas, now home to the city's Turkish community, are too often tarred with the 'crime and grime' brush. True, both have seen better days, but their streets are still boisterous and bustling, especially the main thoroughfares, chaussée de Louvain and chaussée de Haecht. More than half the population of tiny St-Josse is non-Belgian, including a sizeable expat crowd drawn by comfy townhouse conversions and proximity to Euroland. Halles de Schaerbeek and Le Botanique provide top-class evening entertainment in this area that has been home to Puccini and *chanson* legend Jacques Brel. Schaerbeek, the larger of the communes, has emerged from the grip of a right-wing mayor who whipped up tension between long-time residents and the migrant population; its elegant 19th-century houses and Art Nouveau gems rub shoulders with Moroccan spice shops and Turkish bakeries.

day

▢ Shopping here is local and specialist, although there are some dirt-cheap clothing stores.

◉ The canals are a short walk away [→77]. Among the local landmarks are Tour et Taxis [→62], the Eglise Ste-Marie [→61], and Le Botanique [→60].

night

♫ There are plenty of good, cheap Turkish and North African joints to snack in. Bars are very local, apart from Flemish institution Ultieme Hallucinatie.

☆ Le Botanique and Halles de Schaerbeek always have things going on – theatre, dance, art exhibitions, and music [→113].

getting there

Ⓜ Botanique
🚌 90, 92, 93, 94
🚋 55, 61, 66

st-josse & schaerbeek

shopping

food

Only a few streets are worth checking out for shopping in St-Josse: rue Verbist is the place for fresh fruit and veg; chaussée de Haecht has Turkish videos and gimcrackery; and rue du Brabant brings a taste of the Turkish bazaar to Brussels, with rows of shops selling exotic-

looking things you can only guess at the function of. Both **Merci-Cash** and **MC Négoces** sell dried fruits, tea, and spices, as well as cous-cous pots, velvet paint-ings, silk flowers, and other assorted kitsch. Best buy: the mosque alarm clock. For a sugar rush Belgian-style, with

over 80 different vari-eties of pralines, the tiny **Manon** ranks as one of the best chocolate shops in Brussels. For cheeses, head down to place St-Josse, where small **À La Petite Vache** keeps *fromage* lovers happy. A Brussels institution, it has one of the very best selections in the city.

* = featured in the listings section [→84–110]

fashion & accessories

Upmarket designer fashion at fell-off-the-back-of-a-lorry prices is **Dod**'s speciality. Most clothes at its five branches are end-of-the-line collections or recent stock bought from stores gone bankrupt. Among the goodies on sale here are Dolce & Gabbana's sexy, feminine dresses, DKNY's classic T's, as well as designs by Calvin Klein and Tommy Hilfiger. Complete the look with top-notch footwear by the likes of Airwalk, JP Tod's, and others. **Yoca**, its companion shop up the road, offers many of the same labels to fashion- and money-conscious blokes. Both stores are highly recommended. Just across the street, **DeGrif** has a much smaller selection of footwear, but prices are cheap enough to make it worth a look. It's luck of the draw as far as selection goes (turnover is fast), but Patrick Cox, Charles Jourdan, and Pied-à-Terre have all been known to feature in their women's lines. With clothes strewn all over the place, exploded laundrette is the best way to describe what **Le Dépôt** looks like. But hunt it down for even cheaper fashions than Dod and Yoca – this is their warehouse for clothes from seasons of the recent past.

comic strips

*Le Deuxième Souffle is *bande dessinée* central; a comic-book shop for lovers of the so-called eighth art. All the stock is in French.

eating & drinking

restaurants

For value-for-money dining, you can't beat the chaussée de Haecht. Mostly Turkish, the street has sit-down restaurants (a few featuring belly dancers some nights) and a plethora of chip-and-kebab joints. The thriftiest way to munch is to get Turkish pizza-on-the-go, often for as little as 140BF. For dinner-proper, try upscale **À Table**, which has an elegant dining room serving typical French cuisine prepared with flourish. Some of the seating comes from old cinemas. **Les Dames Tartines** serves excellent French and Belgian cuisine (horse, rabbit, and snails) that has restaurant critics and diners reaching for superlatives. **Au Brabançon**'s pink dining room wall is covered with paintings of horses. But Black Beauty wouldn't last long here, since the menu is heavy with horse steaks, blood sausage, and other traditional Belgian cooking, just like your grandma used to make (if your grandma happened to be Belgian). Like Au Brabançon (said to be the inspiration of the Belgo chain), *La Bonne Humeur is easy to miss: the nondescript window looks like just any other café. But inside, the place serves some of the city's best *moules et frites* in a diner setting. *L'École Buissonnière, meanwhile, offers serious value-for-money continental grub. The school cafeteria interior's nothing to write home about, but the mix of businessmen, students, and locals make it a fun dining experience. If freshly prepared pasta is more your thing, *Senza Nome is the place. The candy-pink walls border on tacky, but who cares? Chances are you'll keep your eyes on your *plat du jour* in any case.

cafés, bars & clubs

Being mostly residential, St-Josse and Scharbeek are where the corner café thrive; you can get a hot shot of java along with serious second-hand fumes on pretty much every street. **L'Art du Café** is a more upscale affair, taking its coffee very seriously; freshly ground beans make up the java, and the interior, if a tad twee, is a relief from Starbuck's. Those after hard liquor are out of luck. But knocking back a few beers or shots of *jenever* is possible at *De Ultieme Hallucinatie ↲, a local landmark and a period gem. In an Art Nouveau house dating back to 1850, it also serves excellent, if a tad expensive, French and Belgian cuisine. Suits and Eurocrats dine up front in the posh dining room, while other pun-

ters have drinks and snacky food in the winter garden out back.

Other areas beat St-Josse in sheer number of clubs, but a dynamic duo of discos keeps punters coming back week after week. Put on your best Gucci knock-off for *Mirano Continental, where Brussels' beautiful people flock for a

Saturday night boogie. Radio-friendly house and R'n'B provide the soundtrack here. *Chez Johnny is Essex boy *à la Belge*; half-nostalgic (1970s French pop), half-ironic (resort-from-hell decor: hammocks hanging from the ceiling, rubber chickens hanging around, lifebuoys), with most punters missing the joke decor.

🎵 directory

À la Petite Vache 🍴*B4*
69 chaussée de Louvain
02.217.39.69

L'Art du Café 🍴*C4*
98 chaussée de Louvain
02.280.47.12

À Table 🍴*B2*
290 rue Royale
02.223.48.68
ⓜ–ⓜⓜ

Au Brabançon 🍴*B3*
75 rue de la Commune
02.217.71.91
ⓜⓜ–ⓜⓜ

La Bonne Humeur 🍴*C3*
244 chaussée de Louvain
02.230.71.69 ⓜⓜ

Chez Johnny 🍴*B4*
24 chaussée de Louvain
02.227.39.99

Les Dames Tartines 🍴*B2*
58 chaussée de Haecht
02.218.45.49

DeGrif 🍴*B4*
11–25 chaussée de Louvain
02.219.64.59

Le Dépôt 🍴*B3*
103 rue de Liedekerke

De Ultieme Hallucinatie 🍴*B2*
316 rue Royale
02.217.06.14

Le Deuxième Souffle 🍴*C4*
15 rue Braemt
02.219.17.70

Dod 🍴*B4*
44 chaussée de Louvain
02.218.24.68

L'École Buissonnière 🍴*B3*
13 rue Traversière
02.217.01.65 ⓜ–ⓜⓜ

Manon 🍴*B4*
9A chaussée de Louvain
02.217.45.00

MC Négoces 🍴*A2*
130 rue de Brabant
02.219.22.46

Merci-Cash 🍴*A2*
53 rue de Brabant
02.223.49.03

Mirano Continental 🍴*B4*
38 chaussée de Louvain
02.227.39.70

Senza Nome 🍴*B1*
22 rue Royale Ste-Marie
02.223.16.17 ⓜⓜ

Yoca 🍴*B4*
16 chaussée de Louvain
02.217.16.17

st-josse & schaerbeek

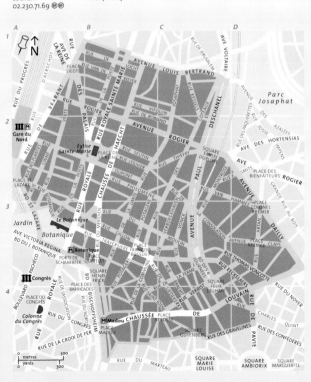

around belgium

Belgium's only been around for 170 years, so it's no surprise that its regions are so diverse. Plump for the instant charms of Flanders; or for lovers of the great outdoors, heaven in the hills and valleys of Wallonia.

getting your bearings

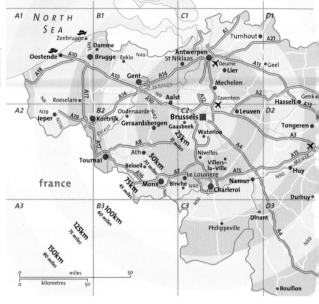

🔖 directory

Aalst (Alost) 🔖 B1
🏛 290BF (26 mins)

A medieval trading point, with an elegant balconied belfry, Aalst became a major industrial centre in the 19th century, with slums to match. No slums today, but a boisterous carnival on Shrove Tuesday.

Antwerpen 🔖 C1
[→50–53]

Bastogne 🔖 D3
🏛 1160BF (2 hrs, 50 mins)

A Sherman tank in the main square recalls American defence of the town during the Battle of the Bulge (1944). The Colline du Mardasson memorial and Bastogne Historical Centre offer sombre insights on the conflict.

Beloeil 🔖 B2
🚗 E19 to Mons, then N526

Home to the wealthy de Ligne family for 700 years, the Château de Beloeil is a lavish, if soulless, castle stuffed with antiques, tapestries and furniture. The gardens, landscaped in the 18th century, are spectacular.

Binche 🔖 C2
🏛 520BF (1 hr, 9 mins)

The only Belgian town with complete medieval walls, Binche hosts one of Europe's

biggest carnivals on Shrove Tuesday [→119]. The Musée International du Carnaval et du Masque explains all.

Bouillon 🔖 D3
🚗 A4, then N89 until N828

This picture-postcard town, crowned by a medieval fortress, was home to Godefroid de Bouillon, the first crusader to conquer Jerusalem. The Musée Ducal has Islamic plunder and the press used to print works by Voltaire and Diderot.

Brugge 🔖 A1
[→56]

Charleroi 🔖 C2
🏛 520BF (43 mins)

A much-derided industrial town, reinventing itself as an eco-centre by turning its slagheaps into nature reserves. Magritte grew up here; see his work at the Musée des Beaux-Arts. The suburban Musée de la Photographie is world class.

Damme 🔖 B1
🚗 A10 to Brugge, then north

Once Brugge's main port, Damme is an elegant backwater with a tree-lined canal and a medieval centre. Now overrun with bookshops, it's perfect for boat or cycling trips.

Dinant 🔖 C3
🏛 700BF (1 hr, 34 mins)

The birthplace of Adolphe Sax, inventor of the saxophone, is a low-key, pretty town on the banks of the Meuse. Take a cable car to the top of the 19th-century citadel for grand views.

Durbuy 🔖 D2
🚗 N4, then N63, then N929

Although keen to milk the tourist dollar, the self-styled 'smallest town in the world' possesses considerable charm: cobbled streets, half-timbered houses and a castle, all set in sprawling greenery.

Gaasbeek 🔖 C2
🚗 N8 (follow sign for Gaasbeek)

Gaasbeek Castle is a Renaissance pile in the picturesque Pajottenland, with wooded grounds and a large tapestry collection. Art-lovers can follow a Brueghel trail, starting at the church in St-Anna-Pede.

Geraardsbergen (Grammont) 🔖 B2
🏛 400BF (1 hr, 6 mins)

Welcome to weirdsville. From the stone elephant padding the steep hill to the bizarrely ornate church, from the elegant Stadhuis to the Manneken Pis museum, this is an odd, but addictive, place.

on tap

Les Artisans Brasseurs place de la Station, Namur
Brewpub with a fine selection of beers, some with impossible names. ☎ 081.23.16.94 ◐ 10am–7pm Mon–Sat.

Nationaal Jenevermuseum 19 Witte Nonnenstraat, Hasselt
Restored 19th-century *jenever* (gin) distillery and museum.
☎ 011.24.11.44 [BF] 80BF ◐ 10am–5pm Tue–Sun (to 6pm Sat–Sun).

Musée des Bières Belges rue de la Gare 19, Lustin
A bona fide living museum housed in a classic pub house.
☎ 081.41.11.02 [BF] 60BF ◐ 11am–8pm daily.

E1

etherlands

N

E2

germany

Liège • Verviers

Spa • Francorchamps

Stavelot

E3

La Roche-
en-Ardenne •

• Bastogne

luxembourg

Gent (Gand) ⌂B1
[→54–55]

Hasselt ⌂D1
▮▮▮ 700BF (1 hr, 30 mins)

Fashionistas love the shopping and the Stedelijk Mode-museum, devoted to trendy togs from the 19th century on. The Nationaal Jenevermuseum explores the history and production of *jenever* (gin).

Huy ⌂D2
▮▮▮ 700BF (1 hr, 38 mins)

A beguiling, twisty little place, adored by Victor Hugo. The Collégiale-Notre-Dame has a resplendent rose window. Atop a hulking riverside cliff, the citadel, a Gestapo prison in WWII, is now a museum.

Ieper (Ypres) ⌂A2
▮▮▮ 960BF (1 hr, 37 mins)

'Wipers', as it was known by the thousands of Brits who died here in WWI trenches, was rebuilt after the Germans razed it. The In Flanders Fields Museum is powerful, the area's dotted with cemeteries, memorials, and battle sites.

Kortrijk (Courtrai) ⌂B2
▮▮▮ 700BF (1 hr, 3 mins)

An unashamedly well-heeled Flemish town near the French border, with up-market shops

and laid-back terraces on the main square. The white-washed Begijnhof is one of the loveliest in the country.

Leuven (Louvain) ⌂C2
[→57]

Lier (Lierre) ⌂C1
▮▮▮ 380BF (42 mins)

A sleepy, romantic town southeast of Antwerpen, with fab canal walks, a bizarre astronomical clock, and the Stedelijk Museum Wuyts, home to works by Brueghel and Rubens.

Liège (Luík) ⌂D2
▮▮▮ 810BF (1 hr, 34 mins)

Grim at first glance, this fading industrial city has hidden charms, notably in the Outremeuse area, with its bars, restaurants, and jazz cafés. The Musée d'Art Moderne has work by Picasso, Gauguin, and Ensor.

Mechelen (Malines) ⌂C1
▮▮▮ 240BF (26 mins)

Mechelen has been gracefully declining since the 16th century, when it was more important than Brussels. Concerts ring out from the late-Gothic cathedral tower, delighting visitors but driving locals dotty.

Mons (Bergen) ⌂B2
▮▮▮ 520BF (41 mins)

Its bar-heavy Grand' Place is a drinker's dream, and there's an outstanding late-Gothic church. The 19th-century Grand-Hornu complex, built as housing for workers, now holds contemporary art exhibitions.

Namur (Namen) ⌂C2
▮▮▮ 490BF (59 mins)

An eccentric town given extra edge by the student population. Baroque churches and 18th-century mansions have an Italianate feel, while the Citadel was once considered the least stormable in Europe. Painter/pornographer Félicien Rops was born here; see his drawings in the Rops Museum.

Oostende (Ostende) ⌂A1
▮▮▮ 920BF (1 hr, 9 mins)

People usually go through, not to, Oostende, but this atmospheric beach town is worth a stop. The fine arts museum has great works by local boy Ensor, whose house is open to the public. If art ain't your bag, get some just-caught seafood and hit the beach.

La Roche-en-Ardenne ⌂D3
🚌 A3 to Liège, then G25

Steep, wooded hills, riverside location, and ruined castle. High season can be tourist hell, but outdoor types trek the wild stretches of the River Ourthe.

Spa ⌂E2
▮▮▮ 1070BF (2 hrs, 17 mins)

Monaco may have the myth, but Spa-Francorchamps is the drivers' favourite circuit. The F1 circus hits town in late August. Otherwise, the world's first health resort is a gracefully crumbling affair, with a casino and a summer theatre festival providing a little life.

Stavelot ⌂E2
🚌 A3, then G25, then N66

This rambling hilltop town, with a ruined abbey, is great for post-prandial promenades. Come carnival time, white-robed figures with pointy noses batter passers-by with pigs' bladders.

Tongeren (Tongres) ⌂D2
▮▮▮ 890BF (1 hr, 51 mins)

Belgium's oldest town. The Onze Lieve Vrouwbasiliek is a Gothic masterpiece visible for miles around. Follow the Roman walls to the Gallo-Romeins Museum, with an array of objects from antiquity.

Tournai (Doornik) ⌂B2
▮▮▮ 700BF (1 hr, 33 mins)

Tournai has a colossal five-towered cathedral, Roman-esque bridges and houses, and rowdy riverside bars. The airy, Horta-designed Musée des Beaux-Arts has two fab Manets and Renaissance gems aplenty.

Villers-la-Ville ⌂C2
▮▮▮ 330BF (1 hr, 1 min)

The haunting remains of a Cistercian abbey, partially reclaimed by the surrounding woodland, is sometimes used for open-air concerts and theatre performances.

Waterloo ⌂C2
▮▮▮ 200BF (22 mins)

My, my... at Waterloo, Napoleon did surrender – but the Bona-parte memorabilia in the souvenir shops might make you think he won. Avoid the modern town unless you want to see Wellington's HQ or the less-than-enthralling visitors' centre. The fields around the Butte de Lion are the place to remember 1815. Catch the annual re-enactment [→118].

getting your bearings

All prices are return; journey times may vary

the fashion mecca

Antwerpen (Antwerp) is at the forefront of everything it turns its hand to: the world's largest uncut-diamond market, the second-biggest port in Western Europe, a business hub, a fashion mecca, and a magnet for culture. It's progressive, cosmopolitan, and crammed with bars, clubs, shops, and eateries, yet has a weirdly conservative undertow. In Belgium's most radical city, support for the far-right Vlaams Blok reaches 25%. For a town of 500,000 souls, it's a complicated place.

antwerpen

exploring antwerpen

III 200BF (45 mins)

Antwerpen may be a city of the future, but don't neglect its past. The charming, cobbled Vlaeykensgang dates back to the Middle Ages, but it's the glory days of the Renaissance that provide Antwerpen's most spectacular sights. Head for the historic centre using the tower of the Gothic **Onze Lieve Vrouwekathedraal** as a guide. The Hôtel de Ville and guildhouses of the Grote Markt are much as they were in Rubens' day, though what he would have made of the square's Irish pubs is hard to say. Ponder the statue of a Roman soldier hurling a hand he'd chopped off the city's hated toll-levying giant into the air – hence the name *Hantwerpen* ('hand-throwing'). Spoilsports will tell you a less gory tale about how the name comes from *Aan de werpen* ('on the wharf').

The waterfront west of the Grote Markt is disappointing at first glance – the view across the river is of grey apartment blocks and there's no obvious place to stroll. Instead turn your attention to the 12th-century **Het Steen**, a former prison that now houses a maritime museum, or to the **Ethnografisch Museum's** impressive array of pottery, jewellery, masks, and musical instruments from around the world.

Those of a bookish bent will love the **Museum Plantin-Moretus**. Located west of the cobbled Vrijdagmarkt, in the former marble-floored printing house and mansion of Renaissance publisher Christopher Plantin, it features a stunning collection of presses, rare books, and sketches by Rubens. Plantin's greatest achievement was the Polyglot Bible, written in four languages, although font fanatics might know him as the originator of the Plantin and Garamond sets, both still in use today.

Art-lovers should stroll south along the Schelde to 't Zuid, a hip hang-out with restaurants, bars, and cultural venues arranged around a filled-in former dock between the Waalse and Vlaamse Kaais. At the northern edge of this once grim area, **MUHKA** (Museum voor Hedendaagse Kunst van Antwerpen), hosts international contemporary art shows. The best-known commercial art gallery is **Gallery Ronny van de Velde**, a four-floored house that shows retrospectives of modern masters like Marcel Duchamp, plus the latest in contemporary art. The southwestern corner of the square is home to the **Museum voor Fotografie**, an old warehouse devoted to photography and film-making. Besides quality contemporary shows, it has a superb permanent collection featuring work by the likes of Cartier-Bresson and Man Ray. Further inland, the **Koninklijk Museum voor Schone Kunsten** (Fine Arts Museum) is the neighbourhood's oldest temple to the arts. Located within an overblown, neoclassical building, the collection includes lesser-known, but worth-seeing, works by Van Eyck, Van der Weyden, James Ensor, and René Magritte.

Heading towards the northern docklands, you'll hit the city's red-light district, where tales of illegal immigration and exploitation lie behind the neon-lit shopfronts displaying prostitutes from all corners of the globe. The Falconplein is home to Antwerpen's Little Russia, where traders from the former Soviet Union sell anything from vodka to radio sets. It's a reminder of the city's growing links with Russia, from bona fide diamond traders to dodgy businessmen exporting stolen cars.

To sample Antwerpen's brash, commercial character, head east from the centre along the tacky Meir, a pedestrianized shopping street, towards the station. Check out the **Rubenshuis**, a red-brick 17th-century mansion where Rubens lived and worked. You can see some of his minor works inside before taking a break in the formal, but cozy, garden out back. West of the house you'll find the **Mayer van den Bergh Museum**, a private collection with one of Breughel's most famous paintings, *Dulle Griet*. You'll reach the stunningly flamboyant, neo-Baroque **Centraal Station**, completed in 1905 as a celebration of industrial progress. Its splendour contrasts with the somewhat seedy streets around the Diamond District, which are dotted with tacky, shack-like jewellers' shops. Traditionally run by Hassidic Jews, a significant portion of this secretive business is also handled by traders from India and, most recently, Russia. The vast, 150-year old **Antwerpen Zoo**, home to some 4000 animals, is worth a visit if you've a soft spot for 19th-century exoticism, best illustrated by the elephant house that resembles an Egyptian temple.

shopping

In the late 1980s, a group of six former students from Antwerpen's Royal Academy of Fine Arts (now known as the Antwerp Six) conquered the fashion world, and since then there's been no stopping the pilgrimage of style victims and shopaholics to the city. Hot areas take in De Wilde Zee, a network of pedestrianized streets, very trendy Kammenstraat, and St-Antoniusstraat, home to two Antwerp Six members – Walter van Beirendonck and Dirk van Saene. Clothes are displayed here like gallery installations in a converted garage. It is a perfect backdrop for labels like Bad Baby Boys, Wild and Lethal Trash, and the newer Aesthetic Terrorists. **Modepaleis** is the realm of Dries Van Noten. Even if you're not after a super-feminine dress or a shirt from his menswear collection, the shop, a beauty from 1881 warrants a visit on architectural merits alone. **Ann Demeulemeester**, meanwhile, focuses on the intimate relationship between clothes and the individual. Her cool corner shop – opposite the Fine Arts Museum – sells the perfect clothes for women taking a stand in a man's world – she was one of the first designers to create city-style pinstripe suits for women. The Antwerpen store is the only one in the world to stock both her men's and women's ranges.

New wave Antwerpen designers – including Raf Simons, Jurgi Persoons, Véronique Branquinho, Martin Margiela, and AF Vandervorst to name a few, can be found at **Louis**. For footwear to complement such cutting-edge designer fare try **Coccodrillo**.

If you were surprised you could fit into a smaller size, head straight for bakery **Goossens** and queue up with the rest of Antwerpen for the finest rye raisin bread and sweet delicacies you've ever tasted. With renewed energy, hit the Kammenstraat, which has a medley of shops for lovers of 50s, 60s, and 70s gear. At **Fish & Chips** ✓ you can buy into the lifestyle of the raver, skater, and clubber. Walk up the stairs of this one-time warehouse, grab a snack, and get your hair done up in a beehive at **Housewives on Fire**. If their soundtrack makes you music-mad, jump

a couple of houses and dive into **Metrophone** or **Lowlands & Stereophonic Records** to get the latest elektro, drum 'n' bass, hip-hop, techno, hard-core, acid jazz, or tempo. You can even get that classic wild dragon tattoo. For a cultural refill, **Copyright** has what seems like every book on art and architecture in a cool black-and-white setting. For vintage fashion from the 1960s and 1970s go for **Naughty I** or for clubland fashions **Fetisj**. And it's women-only at nearby **De Erotische Verbeelding** where erotic underwear and sexual aids can be bought by those who know what turns them on.

If all this makes you feel like Alice in Wonderland, wait until you reach Kloosterstraat, paradise of curiosities and the bizarre. Lovers of antiques might find their missing treasure here. The façade of **Tony Boogaert Antiques** is as weird as its interior.

Take in the smell of old books at **Antiquariaat Erik Toonen** or hunt for old mirrors and desks at **Oude Spiegels & Bureau's**. If you're more 40s to 70s, **Fiftie-Fiftie** has plastic furniture on sale.

To keep the under 10's in high fashion, head for **De Groene Wolk**. And for decking out their bedrooms or for natty accessories like jewellery and scarves go to **De Prinses op de Erwt** ('the princess on the pea').

Then make a beeline for the **Horta Complex** in Hopland, an upmarket shopping centre that includes Emporio Armani, DKNY Jeans, and Essentiel, an Antwerpen women's label for twenty-somethings. Spitting distance from the centre is avant-garde **Lieve van Gorp**'s boutique. She's the one who favours the black leather goth look. From there on it's full steam ahead along Schutterhofstraat for a blend of top lifestyle stores and other exclusive fashion labels.

restaurants

Antwerpen's restaurant scene is strong on orthodox Belgian fare and newer, trendier places too. Head to 't Zuid, and indulge. **Farine's Food & Future** seats everybody together at one big table and spoils them for choice with an array of world cuisines. If you don't fancy sharing, try **Grand Café Leroy**, which lives up to its name in terms of both food (mostly fusion) and decor. Tuck into a Soul Fingers ratatouille or a Boogie Wonder Lamb at **Funky Soul Potato**, or make tracks to **Chez Fred** for down-to-earth Mediterranean dishes at decent prices. Brasserie fare is available at **De Kaai**, in a mirrored warehouse that doubles up as a late-night dancing joint. A combination of Italian, French, and local food rules at **Cargo**; or ditch those francophone tastes and focus on Italian flavours at **Danieli il Divino**. The seafood is to die for, as are the Art Deco interior and the garden. For the best desserts ever, hit **Popoff**, in the shade of the cathedral. Try their home-made hot chocolate and cheesecake. Combine a dive into cyberspace with a non-virtual snack at **Lollapalooza**. **Hungry Henrietta** ✔ serves an eclectic menu to students and professors alike. **Kei Kei** is a stylish oriental canteen. From *ebi tempura* to *chawan moshi*, baked noodles and rice; you name it, they serve it – and at very reasonable prices. Set in an old grocery shop, **Lenny's** dishes out the best salads in town.

If you're into organic stuff, **Fair Food** has it all. Honest, healthy, and affordable. Smack in the middle of the Jewish quarter, kosher fish, meat, and vegetables are the Hoffman brothers' specialities. **Hoffy's** will take great pains to explain to you the ins and outs of their cuisine.

And whatever you do, don't forget to get fantastic takeaway lobster bisque from the **Van Bladel** stall in the middle of De Wilde Zee area where there's also an impressive line-up of traiteurs and juice bars.

bars, cafés & clubs

God said, let there be fun and he created Antwerpen. At **Zillion**, videowalls, fog-machines, and moving robots entertain to deep house, techno, soul, and funk. What used to be an old church and then cinema has turned into a funky hall hung with chandeliers. Smack in the middle of the red light district, techno and happy, garage and mellow is what's happening at **Café d'Anvers**. Latin lovers hit **La Bodeguita**, a down-to-earth café that serves up salsa. If you're not so confident on the dance floor, try **Café Locale**. For Latino in fab settings, head for the **Bar Room ►**. **Lebozo** is the snob spot at the edge of the docks. Enjoy the music on the plush red velvet. And on Saturdays, join the hordes of gay men who come from all over to dance to kitsch disco tunes and score at **Red & Blue**.

Kulminator is the best beer bar in the city, with about 600 brews on offer. Fine modern architecture by Bob Van Reeth makes you seem like you're floating on the Scheldt in **Zuiderterras**. Don't miss a fine example of one of Antwerpen's trad old cafés, especially as **De Vagant** has 400 different kinds of *jenever* (gin). Grand and theatrical, with as much neo-classicism as you can handle in the foyer of an old theatre, **De Foyer** has legendary brunches, for which you must book weeks in advance. For old-fashioned, knees-up-style entertainment, **Café Beveren** has an authentic 1933 organ belting out old tunes. Live music, food, café, and cinema – you get it all at **Kladaradatsch! Cartoons**. Get there early or you won't get in. Philosophize day and night at **L'Entrepôt du Congo** – note the ironic inclusion of a portrait of King Baudouin, the only thing hanging on the walls. In the early hours, join the fashion crew, writers, designers, and actors at **Bar Tabac**. If red velvet and cocktails are your thing, the Bar Room has a great lounge to while away the hours and **Café Hopper**, across the street, is the best jazz venue in town. Set in an old factory, converted by architect Bob Van Reeth, **Foyer Zuiderpershuis** provides food for stomach and soul – check out their cultural agenda for world music concerts, expositions, and dance. End the day with a prayer in the 16th-century **Het Elfde Gebod** ('The Eleventh Commandment') – it's chocka with religious statues. May the saints be with you.

directory

Ann Demeulemeester
A0
Leopold de Waelstraat
03.216.01.33

Antiquariaat Erik Toonen
48 Kloosterstraat
03.237.94.66

Antwerp Zoo
26 Koningin Astridpl
03.202.45.40

Bar Room
30 Leopold De Waelplaats
03.257.57.40

Bar Tabac
43 Waalse Kaai
03.238.19.37

Café d'Anvers
15 Verversrui
03.226.38.70

Café Beveren
2 Vlasmarkt
03.231.22.25

Café Hopper
2 Leopold De Waelstr
03.248.49.33

Café Locale
25 Waalse Kaai
03.238.50.04

Cargo
24b Leopold De Waelplaats
03.260.60.10

Centraal Station
Koningin Astridplein

Chez Fred
83 Kloosterstraat
03.257.14.71

Coccodrillo
9 Schuttershofstraat
03.233.20.93

Copyright
22 Haarstraat
03.232.94.16

Danieli il Divino
12 Beukenlaan
03.825.37.38

De Erotische Verbeelding
10–12 IJzerenwaag
03.226.89.50

De Kaai
94 Rijnkaai, Hangar 26
03.233.25.07

Ethnografisch Museum
19 Suikerrui
03.232.08.82

L'Entrepôt du Congo
42 Vlaamse Kaai
03.238.99.32

Fair Food
60 Graaf van Egmontstraat
03.238.92.96

Farine's Food & Future
40 Vlaamse Kaai
03.238.37.76

Fetisj
55 Kammenstraat
03.289.33.68

Fiftie-Fiftie
156 Kloosterstraat
03.237.43.72

Fish & Chips
36–38 Kammenstraat
03.227.08.24

De Foyer
18 Komedieplaats
03.233.55.17

Foyer Zuiderpershuis
Waalse Kaai
03.248.70.77

Funky Soul Potato
76 Volkstraat
03.257.07.44

Gallery Ronny van de Velde
3 IJzerenpoortkaai
03.216.30.47

Goossens
31 Korte Gasthuisstraat
03.226.07.91

Grand Café Leroy
49 Kasteelpleinstraat
03.226.11.99

De Groene Wolk
20 Korte Gasthuisstraat
03.234.18.47

Het Elfde Gebod
10 Torfbrug
03.289.34.65

Het Steen
1 Steenplein
03.232.08.50

Hoffy's
52 Lange Kievitstraat
03.234.35.35

Horta Complex
Hopland

Hungry Henrietta
19 Lombardenvest
03.232.29.28

Kei Kei
34–36 Minderbroedersrui
03.213.22.26

Kladaradatsch! Cartoons
4–6 Kaasstraat
03.232.96.32

Koninklijk Museum voor Schone Kunsten
Leopold De Waelplaats
03.238.78.09

Kulminator
32 Vleminckveld
03.232.45.38

La Bodeguita
21 Ernest Van Dijckkaai
03.226 01 12

Lebozo/Le beau zoo
50 Godefriduskaai Willemdok
03.238.41.45

Lenny's
47 Wolstraat
03.233.90.57

Lieve Van Gorp
1 Hopland
03.231.19.17

Lollapalooza
28 Pelgrimstraat
03.227.41.42

Louis
2 Lombardenstraat
03.232.98.72

Lowlands & Stereophonic Records
70 Kammenstraat
03.232.98.70

Mayer van den Bergh Museum
19 Lange Gasthuisstr
03.232.42.37

Metrophone
47 Kammenstraat
03.231.18.65

Modepaleis
16 Nationalestraat
03.233.94.37

MUHKA
Leuvenstraat
03.238.59.60

Museum Plantin-Moretus
22 Vrijdagmarkt
03.221.14.51

Museum voor Fotografie
47 Waalse Kaai
03.242.93.10

Naughty I
65–67 Kammenstraat
03.213.35.90

Onze Lieve Vrouwekathedraal
Handschoenmarkt
03.213.99.40

Oude Spiegels & Bureau's
68–79 Kloosterstraat
03.238.73.62

Popoff
18 Oude Korenmarkt
03.232.00.38

De Prinses op de Erwt
65 Volkstraat
03.216.41.18

Red & Blue
9 Schipperskapelstr
03.232.47.12

Rubenshuis
9–11 Wapper
03.201.15.55

Tony Boogaert Antiques
81 Kloosterstraat
03.237.89.55

De Vagant
25 Reyndersstraat
03.233.15.38

Visdelicatessen van Bladel
25 Schrijnwerkerstraat
03.233.23.09

Walter
12 St-Antoniusstraat
03.213.26.44

Zillion
4 Jan van Gentstraat
03.248.15.16

Zuiderterras
37 Ernest van Dijckkaai
03.234.12.75

gent real

No less charming than Brugge, tourist-free Gent (Gand) has canals and cobbles aplenty, yet it's anything but a museum town. Sedition has been the style in this forward-thinking city since 1540, when Charles V quashed a revolt by forcing burghers to parade with nooses round their necks. There are great bars and mucho culture, and the proud locals love a party, especially during July's Gentse Feesten [→118–119].

sightseeing

III 245BF (50 mins)

Gent's rich mix of medieval and Gothic architecture reflects a heady past, when the wool and cloth trades made it as prosperous as Paris and Bologna. The most striking legacy is the three-spired skyline of the austere, Romanesque **St-Niklaaskerk**, the Gothic **St-Baafskathedraal**, and the 14th-century **Belfort (Belfry)**, crowned with a gilded dragon that symbolizes Gent's jealously guarded freedom. The cathedral also houses the city's greatest treasure, Jan van Eyck's astonishing *Adoration of the Mystic Lamb*. The view is best seen from the **St-Michielsbrug** bridge across the River Leie (very romantic at night).

When you tire of the view, head north on either side of the canal (Graslei and Korenlei), admire the Renaissance houses that line it, and stroll to the **Gravensteen** (a dark, sober fortress with a horribly graphic torture chamber). Then to the Patershol, a gentrified former slum district with a cluster of hip but cozy restaurants and desirable dwellings for young urbanites. On the waterfront, the **Museum voor Sierkunst** is a well-assembled tribute to

the applied arts, with a strong collection of Belgian Art Nouveau and Modernist pieces, as well as international-quality shows.

If you're into industrial heritage, the **Museum voor Industriële Archeologie en Textiel** gives the lowdown on Gent's 19th-century revival (kick-started by the theft of a spinning jenny from Manchester), and has splendid city views. Get back to Gent's roots at the **Bijlokemuseum**, a medieval abbey with a collection exploring

local history from the 7th century to the French Revolution. The **Museum voor Schone Kunsten**, in Citadelpark, has a haunting Bosch, *The Bearing of the Cross*, but its fine-arts collection has been overshadowed by its ultra-contemporary cousin, the **Stedelijk Museum voor Actuele Kunst** (aka SMAK). The brainchild of Belgian curating legend Jan Hoet, it's housed in an old casino and showcases Hoet's cutting-edge personal collection, which includes works by Francis Bacon and Andy Warhol.

shopping

If you're a dedicated follower of Belgian fashion, head to **Obius** for men's shoes and clothes by the likes of Dirk Bikkembergs and Ann Demeulemeester. For something a little less obvious, try Ria Dewilde's **Sjapoo**. Dewilde designs her own hats and, if you're after an interesting dress or the perfect accessory, you've come to the right spot. Avant-garde fashion for both sexes can be yours at Ann Huybens' **Double Face**. **Au Bon Marché** carries handbags, trinkets, slippers, and jewellery. If interiors are your weak spot, **Curiosa** has superb handmade lamps and other design

goodies, while the **Fallen Angel Gallery** is *the* shop for retro freaks – old tin cans, kitsch postcards, and model cars. If food is more your thing, **Mosterdwinkel Tierenteyn** offers fine vinegars, rare herbs, and spicy mustards in a wonderfully preserved interior.

eating

Patisserie **Alsacienne Bloch** may not look like much, but this Jewish bakery tempts Belgians from all over; its croissants and coffee are the business. Or start the day in style at the **Brood-Huys**, which serves excellent, hearty breakfasts, brunches, and salads. Design freaks should make a beeline for **Pakhuis**, a flamboyant warehouse conversion by Antonio Pinto (of Quincaillerie fame), where the cavernous green roof and scores of whirring fans give an Apocalypse Now feel; the comfy leather chairs and classy brasserie fare, however, hold no horrors at all. It's closed on Sundays. **Fast Food/Global Design** is trendy and homey, with an open fire in winter; in summer you can wine and dine on the canal. The excellent French cuisine is the main pull at **Het Blauwe Huis**. But if you're talking Italian, **Il Mezzogiorno** is waiting, with bright-coloured walls and extravagant antipasti. For more down-to-earth Italian fare, try the spaghetti at **De Grote Avond**, a typical old café with a great outdoor terrace.

Sticklers for tradition will love **Waterzooï**, one of the oldest restaurants in Gent. Order the namesake dish, Gent's special addition to cuisine, a delicious, creamy and filling soup-cum-stew with chicken or fish. Somewhat more exotic, at least for Belgian palates, the flock-free **Raj** is all cushions, red velvet and mysterious candlelight, and the food is luscious and authentic Indian (closed Mondays).

55

gentgent

drinking & clubbing

Culture vultures congregate at the Art Nouveau **Vooruit** building, erected as a workers' cultural centre and now the city's main avant-garde arts venue; the café's decor is sparse and proletarian, although the switched-on punters are anything but. Poetic souls should head for **Trefpunt**, a more intimate hub for the culturally inclined, or take a trip down memory lane (well, a medieval alley) to **'t Dreupelkot**, which serves mind-clearing jenevers in chilled glasses. Neighbouring **'t Galgenhuisje** (the Gallows House), the smallest and most crowded bar in the city, is set in 14th-century cellars opposite the square where public executions once took place.

Kitsch rules at the **Pink Flamingo's Lounge**, with its 100 statues of the Virgin Mary and a collection of old records by corny local singer Eddy Wally. Less mannered but no less eccentric, **De Tap en de Tepel** is a rambling joint with a blazing fire and a marvellously secluded garden, serving excellent wines and platters of pungent cheese. Incurable romantics will feel right at home at **Rococo**, an informal candlelit bar with a piano in the corner. Beer monsters may prefer **Het Waterhuis aan de Bierkant**, with a splendid canalside terrace and more than 100 beers on offer; the 'menu' provides notionally humourous explanations of each brew in four languages (the jokes are different in each language, though not necessarily more amusing). If you're still standing, world music and swinging ambience are assured at **Damberd**, which has been a café since the 15th century.

directory

Alsacienne BlochAlsacienne Bloch
60–62 Veldstr ☎ 09.225.70.85

Au Bon Marché
Hoornstraat ☎ 09.269.02.60

Belfort (Belfry)
Emile Braunpl ☎ 09.233.39.54

Bijlokemuseum
Godshuizenlaan ☎ 20.225.11.06

Het Blauwe Huis
17 Drabstraat ☎ 09.233.10.09

Brood-Huys
12 Jakobijnenstr
☎ 09.225.77.65

Curiosa
19 Onderbergen
☎ 09.233.02.41

Damberd
19 Korenmarkt
☎ 09.225.84.33

De Grote Avond
40 Huydevetterskaai
☎ 09.224.31.21

De Tap en de Tepel
7 Gewad ☎ 09.223.90.00

Double Face
2 Trommelstraat
☎ 09.371.56.37

Fallen Angel Gallery
29–31 Jan Breydelstraat
☎ 09.233.39.04

Fast Food/Global Design
36 Jan Breydelstraat
☎ 09.225.29.41

Gravensteen
St-Veerleplein ☎ 09.225.93.06

Il Mezzogiorno
17 Baudelokaai ☎ 09.224.33.29

Mosterdwinkel Tierenteyn
3 Groentemarkt
☎ 09.225.83.36

Museum voor Industriële Archeologie en Textiel
9 Minnemeers ☎ 09.223.59.69

Museum voor Schone Kunsten
5 Jan Breydelstraat
☎ 09.267.99.99

Museum voor Sierkunst
5 Jan Breydelstraat
☎ 09.225.66.76

Obius
12 Meersenierstraat
☎ 09.233.82.69

Pakhuis
4 Schuurkenstr ☎ 09.223.55.55

Pink Flamingo's Lounge
55 Onderstraat ☎ 09.233.04.56

Raj
43a Kraanlei ☎ 09.225.18 .95

Rococo
57 Corduwaniersstraat
☎ 09.224.30.35

Sjapoo
29 Sluizeken ☎ 09.225.75.35

St-Baafskathedraal
St-Baafsplein ☎ 09.269.20.65

Stedelijk Museum voor Actuele Kunst (SMAK)
Citadelpark ☎ 09.221.17.03

St-Niklaaskerk
Korenmarkt ☎ no phone

't Dreupelkot
12 Groentemarkt
☎ 09.224.24.55

't Galgenhuisje
5 Groentemarkt
☎ 09.233.42.51

Trefpunt
18 Sint-Jacobs ☎ 09.233.58.48

Vooruit
23 St-Pietersnieuwstraat
☎ 09.223.82.01

Het Waterhuis aan de Bierkant
9 Groentemarkt
☎ 09.225.06.80

Waterzooï
2 St-Veerlepl ☎ 09.225.05.63

history repeating

Known as the Venice of the north, Brugge (Bruges) certainly lives up to its reputation. Cynics point out that much of the 'medieval' stuff was built in the 19th century, and in summer it's a citywide game of sardines, but who cares? Brugge is somewhere you'll never forget.

brugge

sightseeing

Romantics pause at the **Minnewater** (the 'lake of love' of a famous legend) before heading for the **Onze-Lieve-Vrouwekerk** (Church of Our Lady). Here you can marvel at an early Michelangelo sculpture, a white marble *Madonna and Child*. Just around the corner, the **Gruuthuse**, built by a noble family in the 1400s, has fantastic Gothic halls. Next door, the **Hans Memling Museum**, a 13th-century former hospital, is home to six outstanding paintings by the Flemish Primitive. For more world-class art, the **Groeningemuseum** houses works by the likes of Van Eyck, Brueghel, Bosch, and Magritte. Then hit the city's most famous square, the Burg, home to the 12th-century **Heilig-Bloedbasiliek**. The *pièce de résistance* of this church is a phial said to contain the blood of Christ. Feeling energetic? Then climb the 366 steps of the **Belfort (Belfry)** for awesome views of the city; to see it with your feet up, catch a boat from one of the jetties along the Dijver.

shopping

Brugge's shops are, on the whole, limited to tack and tat: lace is everywhere, and the smell of praline wafts down every street. Hit Wollestraat for Belgian goods, Steenstraat for mainstream ware, and Hoogstraat for less-touristy stuff.

restaurants

Brugge brims with restaurants – most of them vying for tourists' money. Of a different mould, **Breydel-De Konick** is where chefs from Michelin-starred restaurants go on their days off. Sit at one of **In den Wittekop**'s two tables to try the house specialities: *waterzooï* (chicken or fish stew with white wine), *bouil-labaisse*, or Flemish stews (beef stewed in beers). Or have lamb or seafood in the cozy **Cafedraal**. This eatery's green terrace is an ideal spot for lunching al fresco. For a health fix, **De Lotus** is *the* place. But you only have the choice of one organic dish at lunch.

III 390BF (75 mins)

directory

Bauhaus
133–137 Langestraat
☎ 050.34.10.93

Belfort (Belfry)
17 Markt ☎ 050.44.87.67

Breydel-De Konick
xx xxxxxxxx ☎ 050.??.??.??

't Brugs Beertje
5 Kemelstraat ☎ 050.33.96.16

Cafedraal
38 Zilverstraat
☎ 05.034.08.45

Café Vlissinghe
2a Bleekerstr ☎ 050.34.37.37

't Ei
13 Eiermarkt ☎ 050.33.20.85

Groeningemuseum
12 Dijver ☎ 050.44.87.50

Gruuthuse
17 Dijver ☎ 050.44.87.62

Hans Memling Museum
38 Mariastraat
☎ 050.44.87.70

Heilig-Bloedbasiliek
13 Burg ☎ 050.31.65.29

In den Wittekop
14 St-Jakobsstr
☎ 05.033.20.59

Lokkedize
33 Korte Vulderstraat
☎ 050.33.44.50

De Lotus
5 Wapenmakersstraat
☎ 050.033.10.78

Minnewater
Minnewater Park

Onze-Lieve-Vrouwekerk
Dijver

West Flanders Tourist Info
12 Burg ☎ 050.44.86.86
w www.brugge.be

bars & cafés

For a fine real beer experience and a good range of brews, try **'t Brugs Beertje**. Or soak up the history at **Café Vlissinghe**, the oldest bar in town (from 1552). **Lokkedize** is a great local joint with fab *jenevers* (gins), while salsa and tapas await at trendy **'t Ei**. International crowds at **Bauhaus** lounge on leopard-skin seats behind wooden carved tables.

sweet leuven

Home to the world's oldest Catholic university (1425), this historic Flemish town comes alive during term-time, when its cafés fill with students and its cobbled streets rattle with chatter and bicycles.

leuven

sightseeing

Despite being bombed by the Germans in both world wars, and the scene of violent linguistic riots during the 60s, Leuven is steeped in dignity and tradition. At its heart is the ornate **Stadhuis**, a Gothic town hall sporting lace-like stonework. Opposite is the less flamboyant **St-Pieterskerk**, whose treasures include an extravagant baroque pulpit and a rich collection of medieval art. South of the main square lies the cobbled **Oude Markt**, with quaint gabled houses and cafés. Head south on Naamsestraat to find the 14th-century **Cloth Hall (Lakenhallen)**, the city walls, and the **Groot Begijnhof**, one of the largest in the country, now used as university accommodation. East of the Grote Markt is the **University Library (Universitaire Bibliotheek)**, rebuilt in Flemish Renaissance style after the original was destroyed in a 1914 bombardment. Round off the day with a waterside walk or bike ride around the university area.

shopping

Try Mechelsestraat and Parijsstraat for a few worthy stop-offs. If you're after furry handbags and stylish Italian coffee machines plunge into **Pakjeshuis'** eclectic world. **Profiel** is a vibrantly decorated boutique selling

clothes by all the Flemish fashion gurus, while the tiny but stylish **Sumô** stocks footwear by Prada, Bikkembergs, and Pavelko. If you've been bitten by the Bande Dessinée bug, **Het Besloten Land** has stacks of comics in Dutch, English, and French.

eating

Leuven's cheap 'n' trendy eateries offer anything from mod Med to comforting tavern fare. Named after an African tribe, **Kapsiki** has a New York Soho feel thanks to its radiant silver walls. The chef is as much at ease with classic French cooking as he is with world food. If you've got more cash to blow (on an organic steak, maybe), head to **De Blauwe Zon**. Or, to forget Belgium's wintry chills, warm up with some Mediterranean food at **Ombre et Soleil** – best to sit by the open fire upstairs. Off the beaten track, but oh-so-trendy, **Ananas & Ramanas** is an intimate joint for salad or pasta.

bars & cafés

Designed by the Belgian architect of the same name, the **Literair Café Henry van de Velde** is the place for coffee. Run by the same family since 1896, sumptuous **Café Gambrinus** has fancy woodwork, cozy booths, and a terrace with great views of the Stadhuis. For an arty trip, **D'Adario**

is a refuge for soul-searching philosophers, with live jazz on Saturday. Also known for its jazz and blues concerts is café **De Blauwe Kater**.

III 145BF (30 mins)

directory

Ananas & Ramanas
10 Vaartstraat ☎ 016.22.01.73

Het Besloten Land
16 Parijsstraat ☎ 016.22.58.40

Café Gambrinus
13 Grote Markt ☎ 016.20.12.38

Cloth Hall (Lakenhallen)
22 Naamsestr ☎ 016.32.46.60

D'Adario
21–33 Ravenstr ☎ 016.29.01.23

De Blauwe Kater
1 Hallengang ☎ 016.20.80.90

De Blauwe Zon
25 Tiensestraat ☎ 016.22.68.80

Groot Begijnhof
Schapenstraat ☎ no phone

Kapsiki
34–36 Parijsstr ☎ 016.20.45.87

Literair Café Henry van de Velde
4 Rijschoolstr ☎ 016.50.16.72

Ombre et Soleil
20 Muntstraat ☎ 016.22.51.87

Pakjeshuis
30 Mechelsestr ☎ 016.29.09.11

Profiel
37 Mechelsestr ☎ 016.23.72.62

Stadhuis
Grote Markt ☎ 016.15.25.39

St-Pieterskerk
Grote Markt ☎ 016.29.51.33

Sumô
7 Mechelsestraat
☎ 016.22.14.85

University Library (Universitaire Bibliotheek)
21 Ladeuzepl ☎ 016.32.46.15

brussels' top sights

A1 **B1** **C1**

Ⅲ Gare du Nord
Église Royale • Ste-Marie
De Ultieme • Hallucinatie
M Yser
RUE DU PROGRÈS
RUE ROYALE
CHAUSSÉE DE HAECHT
M Rogier
AVENUE VICTORIA REGINA
Le Botanique
M Botanique
Église St-Jean-Baptiste
FNAC
BD DU JARDIN BOTANIQUE
Congrès Ⅲ
Ste-Catherine M
L'Autre Musée
Place des Martyrs
Centre Belge de la Bande Dessinée Ⅲ
M Madou
RUE DE FLANDRE
A2 De Brouckère M
B2S
Bourse M
Colonne du Congrès
RUE DU CONGRÈS
ste-catherine
Église Ste-Catherine •
•La Monnaie M
Artesia Center for the Arts
central
13 Rue Royale
Jeanneke Pis
Halles St-Géry
Église St-Nicolas •
La Bourse
Théâtre de Toone
Cathédrale St-Michel & St-Gudule
M Arts–Loi
Hôtel de Ville GRAND PLACE
Gare Centrale M
RUE ROYALE
RUE VAN ARTEVELDE
Anneessens M
M Parc
Parc de Bruxelles
RUE DE LA LOI
Chapelle de la Madeleine
Palais des Beaux-Arts
A3 PLACE ROUPPE **B3**
•Manneken Pis
Magasins Old England/ Musée des Instruments Musique
Recyclart
Église Protestante
Église Protestante
PLACE ROYALE
M Lemonnier
Chapelle
Musée d'Art Moderne
Notre Dame de la Chapelle
Musée d'Art Ancien
Église St-Jacques-sur-Coudenberg
Palais Royal
Église des Brigittines
Église Notre-Dame du Sablon
le sablon
PLACE DU TRÔNE
M Trône
les marolles
Synagogue • Communauté Israélite de Bruxelles
Porte de Namur
Gare du Quartier Léopold Ⅲ
PLACE POELAERT
M Louise
CHAUSSÉE D'IXELLES
Gare du Midi Ⅲ
Palais de Justice
Église • St-Boniface
AVENUE DE TERVUREN
A4 **B4** **C4**
Porte de Hal
Porte de Hal
Hôtel des Monnaies
Musée d'Ixelles •
CHAUSSÉE DE WATERLOO
ixelles (east)
Parvis de St-Gilles M
Fondation pour l'Architecture •
st-gilles
Église Orthodoxe Russe •
A5 M Horta **B5** **C5**
St-Gilles Hôtel de Ville •
Musée Horta •
Rue de la Vallée •
Parc de Forest
ixelles (west)
Place Albert M
Hôtel Hannon/ Espace Photographique Contretype
Rue de Belle Vue •
AVE DUCPÉTIAUX
Parc Tenbosch
Musée Constantin • Meunier

0 metres 500
0 yards 500

🎧 directory

getting your bearings

tourist passport

A one-day Tourist Passport
provides a tram and bus pass,
discounts on train tickets, and
reductions on the admission
prices of sights and museums
across Brussels, saving up
to 2000BF per person.

TIB, Hôtel de Ville,
1 Grand' Place, Central
☎02.513.89.40
BF 300BF

tours

ARAU

Organizes Art Nouveau and
Art Deco architecture tours.
55 boulevard Adolphe Max,
Central ☎ 02.219.33.45
Ⓜ Rogier BF varies
◑ 9am–5pm daily (tours in
French: daily; tours in English:
Sat mornings only).

La Fonderie

15 city tours, most of which
are concerned with industrial
history.
27a rue Ransfort, Molenbeek
☎ 02.410.99.50
Ⓜ Comte de Flandre
BF varies ◑ times vary
(call for details).

Arcadia

Explores art history and
architecture on walking
tours around Brussels.
38 rue du Métal, St-Gilles
☎ 02.534.38.19
Ⓜ Parvis St-Gilles
BF 250BF–750BF ◑ times
vary (call for details).

Pro Velo

Cycling tours with 18
different themes, like forest
and fauna.
15 rue de Londres, Ixelles
(East) ☎ 02.502.73.55
Ⓜ Trône BF 500BF (bike
hire and guide)
◑ Apr–Oct: times vary.

De Boeck's Sightseeing Tours

City-wide bus tours.
8 rue de la Colline, Central
☎ 02.513.77.44
Ⓜ De Brouckère BF 800BF
◑ 8am–5.30pm daily (to 2pm
Sat–Sun).

Chatterbus

Walking and public-transport
tours, plus once- or twice-
weekly themed excursions.
Start at: Galeries St-Hubert,
Central ☎ 02.673.18.35
Ⓜ Centrale BF 300BF
◑ times vary.

TIB

Dozens of walking and
car day tours of the 19 communes of Brussels. The focus
is largely on art and architecture. They also publish
a comic-strip map.
TIB, Hôtel de Ville,
1 Grand' Place, Central
☎ 02.513.89.40
Ⓜ De Brouckère BF varies
◑ times vary.

city of culture

Forget Brussels' dreary Eurocrat image: scratch the city's surface to find a bewitching blend of Baroque splendour, fin-de-siècle flamboyance and monumental pomposity.

↓ brussels landmarks

Arc de Triomphe (Triomfboog) | parc du Cinquantenaire, Quartier Européen

The BBC's backdrop of choice for EU stories, the arch was inspired by Paris's Arc de Triomphe and Berlin's Brandenberg Gate. Léopold II built it to celebrate 50 years of Belgian independence in 1880, eventually having to use his plundered Congo fortune to complete the arch in 1905.

Atomium | boulevard du Centenaire, Heysel

This model of an iron atom, magnified 165 billion times (standing at 102m), was built for the 1958 *Exposition Universelle* (World Fair) and has an appropriately dated, Flash Gordon feel. Despite local affection for the distinctive grey balls, nobody seems willing to capitalize on its touristic potential: bar the view, there's little worth seeing inside.

Basilique du Sacré Coeur (Heilig Hert Basiliek) | 1 parvis de la Basilique, Koekelberg

This chunky Art Deco basilica, another big-is-beautiful Léopold II project, is the fifth-largest church in the world and took 66 years to complete (1970). Some call it monstrous, others appreciate its surreal grandeur. A bizarrely tacky red-neon crucifix glows on top of its green copper dome at night[→71].

Le Botanique | 236 rue Royale, St-Josse

This airy early 19th-century glasshouse (one of the city's lovelier landmarks) is now the Centre Culturel de la Communauté Française, with a cinema, theatre, and exhibition halls [→75]. The French-style gardens [→76] feature statues by Meunier, but are known as a night-time haunt for drug dealers; better to join the arty crowd in the centre's café.

La Bourse (Beurs) | 2 rue Henri Maus, Central

The flamboyant neoclassical stock exchange, which boasts sculptures by Rodin, stands in splendid isolation on the shoddy boulevard Anspach. It's still active and its steps, flanked by two imposing lions, are a favourite haunt for activists and demonstrators.

Cathédrale St-Michel-&-St-Gudule (St-Michiels & St-Goedele Kathedraal) | 15 rue du Bois Sauvage, Centrale

Out on a limb between the upper and lower towns – and surrounded by soulless modern buildings – this masterpiece of Brabant Gothic architecture dates back to 1226. Curiously, for such a dreamily medieval pile, it's only been a cathedral since 1962 [→70].

sights, museums & galleries

Colonne du Congrès (Congreszuil) | place du Congrès, Central

Completed in 1859 to celebrate the founding of Belgium's constitutional monarchy, this poignant monument is the focus for memorial services on Armistice Day (11 Nov). An eternal flame burns at the base of the 47m-high column in memory of the Unknown Soldiers of the two world wars.

Eglise Ste-Marie (Kon. Ste-Mariakerk) | place de la Reine, St-Josse & Schaerbeek

An eclectic, eccentric 19th-century church at the northern end of rue Royale; the architect was inspired by London's St Paul's Cathedral and Istanbul's Haghia Sofya, which explains the bizarre neo-Byzantine influence. Regularly threatened with demolition, it was saved by local action groups and restored in 1996 [→70].

Grand' Place (Grote Markt) | Central

Yes, it's touristy, but Brussels' centrepiece has too much magic to be ruined by the hordes who traipse its cobbles. Louis XIV's artillery razed the square in 1695, aiming for but missing the Hôtel de Ville [→68]. Brussels' burghers rebuilt the rest in Flemish Renaissance Baroque style, in three years. Visit at night, when gentle lighting illuminates the gilt edges of the guildhouses.

Manneken Pis & Jeanneke Pis | 1 rue de l'Étuve, Central & rue du Chêne, Central

Brussels' no. 1 postcard image is the disappointingly small (30cm) statue of a boy peeing; even worse, he's only a copy of the 1619 original which was stolen and smashed in 1817. A female equivalent, the Jeanneke Pis, crouches round the corner; the result of an entrepreneurial restaurant owner trying to woo tourists his way [→xx].

La Monnaie (De Munt) | place de la Monnaie, Central

The city's elegant neoclassical opera house (1817) was built on the site of a 17th-century theatre. It saw revolution in 1830 when, fired by a nationalistic Auber opera, theatre-goers poured onto the square and raised the Brabant flag, the first step in Belgium's fight for independence.

Palais de Justice (Poelaert) | 1 place Poelart, Le Sablon

The construction of this mock-classical law court (the highest in the land) required mass local evictions. A typically overstated Léopold II project, it was conceived as the largest building on the continent. Candles burn outside to remember Julie and Mélissa, alleged victims of Belgium's notorious paedophile, Marc Dutroux.

Palais Royal (Koninklijk Paleis) | place du Palais, Le Sablon

This is where tourists who don't read Hello! discover that Belgium has a royal family. Its members prefer to hang out at their Laeken pad, away from the public eye, although they deign to appear at the balcony of this Léopold II-era mock-Louis XVI affair on special occasions, like the Belgian National Day [→118].

Place des Martyrs (Martelaarsplein) | Central

Built in 1775, this neoclassical square, which honours the 450 citizens killed in the 1830 uprising, is a sad symbol of the divide that has dogged Belgium since the 1960s. Those in favour of a united Flemish and Franco-phone country were horrified when the Flemish Regional Government planted its headquarters, awash with their flags, here.

Place Royale (Koningsplein) | Le Sablon

An opulent 18th-century square built over the Habsburg emperors' 15th-century palace. At its centre is a statue of Godefroid de Bouillon, a crusader king who captured Jerusalem; behind is the Eglise St-Jacques-Sur-Couden-berg [→70]; and in front is Calder's *Whirling Ear* sculpture brought out for Brussels' stint as European City of Culture in 2000.

Porte de Hal (Hallepoort) | boulevard du Midi, Les Marolles

This lonesome tower, sole survivor of the city's second medieval wall, provides a mournful contrast to the office blocks on boulevard du Midi. It served as a prison from the 16th to the 18th centuries, but is now home to the Musée du Folklore. It's one of few medieval rem-nants not ruined by modern developments.

Tour et Taxis (Thurn et Taxis) | 5–7 rue Picard, Molenbeek

This colossal, derelict 19th-century customs depot is the focus of an acrimonious battle between heritage enthusiasts and developers who want to turn it into an entertainment complex. Meanwhile, it's a suitably grand venue for the Couleur Café festival [→113], and an impressive place for an illicit stroll.

Tunnels | around central Brussels

Both the bane and the joy of motorists, the tunnels that bypass central Brussels were built for the 1958 *Exposition Universelle*. They ease traffic, but when there's an acci-dent, drivers get stuck in polluted under-ground jams. Newcomers often struggle to navigate the underground whirl.

↓ government buildings

Parlement Européen (Europees Parlement) | rue Archimède, Quartier Européen

Built for 600+ MEPs, many of whom complain about the rabbit-warren corridors and pokey rooms, this glass-and-steel edifice earned its nickname of *Les Caprices des Dieux* for two reasons: one, locals thought it pretentious, hence the 'whim of the gods'; two, it resem-bles the French cheese of the same name.

Résidence Palace | rue de la Loi, Quartier Européen

This yellowbrick Art Deco complex, in the European quarter, was conceived as a luxury residential complex for the bourgeois set of the 1920s, with an on-site restaurant, theatre, hairdresser, and a gorgeous mock-Moorish indoor swimming pool. It now houses the country's fearsome immigration office.

St-Gilles Hôtel de Ville (Stadhuis St-Gillis) |
place Maurice van Meenen, St-Gilles

The *St-Gillois* are proud of their ornate,
Renaissance-style 19th-century town hall, the
most impressive in Brussels bar the one on the
Grand' Place [→68]. It's a sign of the bygone
wealth of this neighbourhood [→29–32], now
one of the poorer parts of the city, with a
large immigrant population.

Brussels' rolling roads have created an up-and-down cityscape. High ground buildings in the Upper Town provide
the best views, with further-out points of interest giving
a greater overall perspective.

↓ viewpoints

sights, museums & galleries

hotel heights

Hilton Brussels

The Hilton towers over
Brussels' most exclusive
shopping district and
overlooks Egmont Palace.
Head to the 27th floor for
the best outlook.

boulevard de Waterloo, Ixelles
(West) ☎ 02.504.11.11 Ⓜ Porte
de Namur ⟦BF⟧ free

Sheraton

The rooftop pool and open-
air terrace provide an
amazing stance from which
to look south over Brussels'
inner ring. Catch this vista for
Sunday brunch, with access
to the pool and organized
kids' activities. [→123]

3 place Rogier, Central
☎ 02.224.34.56 Ⓜ Rogier
⟦BF⟧ free

cultural vistas

Arc de Triomphe

Climb to the top of the Arc
de Triomphe through the
Musée Royal de l'Armée et
d'Histoire Militaire [→65] for
fantastic views over the
Quartier Européen.

Parc du Cinquantenaire,
Quartier Européen
☎ 02.737.78.11 Ⓜ Mérode
⟦BF⟧ free

Atomium

The top pod of this 102m-
high landmark (model of an
iron atom, magnified 165
billion times) provides a
fantastic view over the whole
of Brussels' cityscape. [→60]

boulevard du Centenaire,
Heysel ☎ 02.474.89.77
Ⓜ Heysel ⟦BF⟧ 200BF

Basilique du Sacré-Coeur

Climb right to the top of
the dome in this landmark
basilica for a fantastic
panorama of Brussels city
centre from further afield.

1 parvis de la Basilique,
Koekelberg ☎ 02.425.88.22
Ⓜ Simonis, then 🚌 87
⟦BF⟧ free

Manhattan Center

Take the lift to the top of this
humongous office block
complex which houses many
multinational companies,
three floors of shops and a
multi-storey car park. The
view's all about distance, not
detail, as this place towers
way above its neighbours.

21–34 avenue du Boulevard,
St-Josse & Schaerbeek
☎ 02.23.36.36 Ⓜ Rogier
⟦BF⟧ free

Mont des Arts

Just a little way down the hill
from place Royale is this little
piece of serenity. Sit on the
fountain's wall and gaze
down onto the *jardin* and
across the lower town.

rue Montagne de la Cour,
Le Sablon Ⓜ Centrale
⟦BF⟧ free

Magasin Old England

This one-time department
store has shut up shop for
good and now houses the
Musée des Instruments de
Musique. The top-floor restaurant provides magnificent
views over downtown Brussels.

2 rue Montagne de la Cour,
Le Sablon ☎ 02.545.01.30
Ⓜ Centrale ⟦BF⟧ free

Place Poelaert

Stand in awe at the Palais
du Justice [→61] then turn
around and gawp at the
view this square has over the
Lower Town. On a clear day
you can see right across
the city to the Atomium and
the Basilique du Sacré-Coeur
to the north.

Place Poelaert, Le Sablon
Ⓜ Toison d'Or ⟦BF⟧ free

Le Roy d'Espagne

This former bakers'
guildhouse-turned-bar, with
the best address in town, is
spread over a series of floors,
each slightly different from
the next. Its architecture is
amazing, but the real draw
is the view over the Gothic
Grand' Place [→68],
particularly impressive at
night. So grab a window seat
in one of the upper rooms
and drool.

1 Grand' Place, Central
☎ 02.513.08.07 Ⓜ De
Brouckère ⟦BF⟧ cost of a drink

↓ the big six

Centre Belge de la Bande Dessinée (Belgisch Centrum van het Beeldverhaal) ▶

Epitomising Belgians' fascination with all things *bande dessinée* (comic strip), this centre shows just how seriously they take the eighth art. The museum (which shows some 300 of its 6000 original plates at any one time) is housed in one of the city's Art Nouveau gems, a converted department store designed by the grand master himself, Victor Horta, in 1903. Get yourself re-acquainted with Belgium's two most famous comic exports, the Smurfs and Tintin. The former were, rather disappointingly, born out of a silly conversation about salt between their creater, Peyo, and fellow illustrator Franquin. Tintin, meanwhile, has been the centre of controversy since Hergé's death, due to the illustrator's debatable political views (the quiffed reporter first appeared in 1930 in a strip called *Tintin in the Land of the Soviets*, which made no effort to hide its Bolshevik-bashing intentions; and during WWII Hergé carried on illustrating for the Nazi-controlled *Le Soir*). Although a lot of the museum is a pull for all ages, some is purely for those in long trousers. On the top floor are images to make your grandma blush – bloody babies being pulled from the womb, erotic encounters in bathtubs, and a graphic guide to mastur-bation. Younger eyes can see how cartoons are made, wander round a life-size animation set, then peek in the world's largest comic library.

👁 Showroom of Imagination.
↻ 1| If comics aren't your bag, but Art Nouveau is, look around the lobby (or grab a bevvy in the café) without paying the entrance fee. 2| The museum shop has a great collection of Belgian comic books, some in English, as well as Tintin paraphernalia.

20 rue des Sables, Central
☎ 02.219.19.80 🅼 De Brouckère; Rigier; Botanique 🆖🅱🅵 250BF 🚇 none
🌓 10am–6pm Tue–Sun. ♿🖙 By reserva-tion (1600BF) 🐾 🏛

Musée D'Art Ancien (Museum voor Oude Kunst)

The façade's colossal pillars and the cavernous entry hall proclaim this a serious space, a temple from which to worship the god of fine art. And why not, when you've got one of Europe's best collections of Flemish masters at your disposal?

The museum is split into two main sections, with a sculpture hall (Rodin, Meunier, George Minne) in the basement: the blue route takes in a daunting 35 rooms devoted to 15th- and 16th-century artists, while the brown route covers the 17th and 18th centuries. The blue is the more impressive, with an awesome array of Flemish Primitives. The obvious draw is the Brueghel room, with the magnificent *Fall of Icarus* and the haunting *Massacre of the Innocents*. Alongside Bouts, Memling, Matsys, Pourbus, and Bosch, look out for a strong German collection dominated by Lucas Cranach. If you're over-whelmed by altarpieces and biblical scenes, the brown route offers secular relief, but if you're left cold by banqueting tables and portraits of Dutchmen you've never heard of, you'll be through in a jiffy. Stop, though, in the first of several Rubens rooms, with its intriguing small-format works as well as the signature swirling religious dramas.

👁 The Brueghels; Cranach's *Adam and Eve*; Bouts' *Judgement of the Emperor Otto*; Gerard David's *Madonna with the Porridge Spoon*; Van der Weyden's *Lamentation*; Rubens' *Four Negro Heads & Martyrdom of St Ursula*; Rembrandt's *La Morte*; Jordaens' *The King Drinks*.

♻ 1| The shop has good stock and prices are reasonable. 2| Pleasant sculpture garden just outside.
♻ You can only buy a combined ticket for the Musées d'Art Ancien et Moderne.

3 rue de la Régence, Le Sablon ☎ 02.508. 32.11 **w** www.fine-arts-museum.be Ⓜ Parc 🎫 150BF (combined with Musée d'Art Moderne) 🚆 all ◑ 10am–5pm Tue–Sun. ♿☞ By reservation (3500BF–4000BF) ♂ 🍴

Musée D'Art Moderne (Museum voor Moderne Kunst) ⌐

A slightly misleading name, given that much of the collection dates from the early 19th century, but think of it as a sample of Belgian art since the country's creation and you won't be disappointed. Like its sister museum, the Musée d'Art Ancien, it is divided in two: the yellow route on the upper floors for the 19th century, and the green route, housed in a subterranean complex, for the 20th.

Upstairs, the tourists go for David's overstyled *Death of Marat*, but the real highlights are the Belgian Impressionists and Pointillists (Monet, Bonnard, Seurat, Signac), Meunier's sculptures and industrial paintings, and the macabre, mask-filled works of James Ensor, usefully shown alongside his accomplished early landscapes. A rough-hewn wooden Zadkine sculpture, *Diana*, ushers you onto the green track, which takes in the world's biggest Magritte collection (on level -6). There are also works by Dalí, Miró, and the even weirder Surrealism of Paul Delvaux, plus an enlightening selection of less famous but equally talented Belgians, notably the intense, proto-noir works of Léon Spilliaert, and Constant Permeke's hulking, gloomy figures. On the international front, the collection opts for quality, not quantity, with top dogs represented by one or two prime-period efforts rather than a slew of artists' studios. Many museums could do with a similar policy.

👁 Marat, if you must; Meunier's *Old Mine Horse*; Emile Claus' Luminist works; Ensor's *Skeletons Fighting Over a Kipper*; Spilliaert's *The Beach*; Permeke's *Potato Eaters*; Delvaux's *Crucifixion*; Bacon's *Pope With Owls*; Magritte's *Empire of Lights*; Broodthaers' *Red Pot of Mussels*.
❶ There are 12 levels, so pace yourself.

3 rue de la Régence, Le Sablon ☎ 02.508. 32.11 **w** www.fine-arts-museum.be Ⓜ Parc 🎫 150BF (combined with Musée D'Art Ancien) 🚆 all ◑ 10am–5pm Tue–Sun. ♿☞ By reservation (3500BF–4000BF) ♂ 🍴

Musée Royal de l'Armée & d'Histoire Militaire (Koninklijk Museum van het Leger & de Krijgskunde)

You don't have to be a war buff to appreciate this museum. If time's of the essence, head straight to the fourth floor where there's an exhibition of fairly well-preserved military helmets, swords and badges of honour from the Napoleonic era. The 19th-century Belgian section covers the 1830 Revolution (which resulted in Belgium's independence) and features wall displays of swords and guns. Neaby, the *Section Air et Espace* (in a hall built to house the *Exposition Universelle de 1910*) holds over 130 flying machines to keep any plane buff in paradise for hours. Or step outside into the courtyard and take the display of WWII tanks head on.

One of the most interesting areas is the Resistance and Deportation display, which charts Nazi occupation in Belgium during WWII – see how and why Léopold III abdicated, and how some Flemish nationalists cooperated with the Germans, lured by false promises of independence. Shop windows from the era (with a 'potatoes sold out' sign outside) and an otherwise cozy kitchen (which has a radio tuned into the news of that era) give a feel for everyday life in wartime. Follow eyewitness accounts of victims of the Nazi occupation on video screens and headphones. Part of the charm of the museum is its haphazardness and lack of explanation for what's on display – it's not unusual to find a statue or an old map hidden in a dark corner.

♻ 1| The Titeca Collection of weapons and uniforms occupies a room above the Arc de Triomphe – you can step out onto the roof for amazing views over the Quartier Européen. 2| Free admission.

3 Parc du Cinquantenaire, Quartier Européen ☎ 02.737.78.11 **w** www.klm-mra. be Ⓜ Mérode 🎫 free ◑ 9am–12pm, 1–4.45pm Tue–Sun. ☞ By reservation ♂ 🍴

sights, museums & galleries

Musée Royal d'Art & d'Histoire (Koninklijke Musea voor Kunst & Geschiedenis)

From images of kings cavorting with half-human, half-beast creatures, to punk wedding dresses with safety-pins, the exhibits in this museum leap from one epoch to another with furious abandon. It houses about a thousand artefacts, the sacred competing with the profane for space. There's no shortage of visual stimulation, yet the lack of obvious logic to the layout, its poor signposting and the fact that much of its cataloguing is exclusively in Flemish may baffle. Trying to catch everything is neither practical nor advisable. Some gems worth hunting for include the limestone relief of Queen Tiy from 1375 BC Egypt, the colossal stone figure of a man from Easter Island, and the immaculately preserved biblical tapestries from 16th-century Belgium. But the most intriguing thing about this museum is that its curators seem to have a Monty Python-like sense of humour. Across from tombs bearing heavy images of death, for example, they have an oddball collection of heart-shaped objects in a room dedicated to the late cardiologist, Dr Boyadjian. They also have a section showing how the costumes of baptism, communion and matrimony have never been based on good taste or sense.

♿ There's an exhibition space for the blind.
❶ The Treasure Room (with medieval jewellery) has limited opening hours, so head there first if it's open.

3 parc du Cinquantenaire, Quartier Européen ☎ 02.741.72.11 w www.kmkg-mrah.be Ⓜ Merode 🚋 150BF ◐ 9.30am–5pm Tue–Sun (from 10am Sat–Sun). ♿ ☞ By reservation ♨ 🛍

Musée Royal de l'Afrique Centrale (Koninklijk Museum voor Midden-Afrika)

At its foundation in 1897, this exhibition space was called the Musée du Congo. It was originally built to celebrate, and even brag about, Belgium's imperial expansion into the Congo. Its stance at the time was very much 'see how the savages of Africa live', with Congolese performers regularly brought over for major celebrations. Almost from the moment Léopold II took his place on the throne, he revealed his ambition to create a Belgian empire. By 1884, he had taken personal control of the Congo and, over the next two decades, he made an immense fortune from ivory and rubber, most of it off the work of slaves. Léopold's rule was so harsh that even other imperialistic countries, like Britain, expressed concern about conditions; Conrad based *Heart of Darkness* on the notorious brutality of the Belgian Congo.

This museum holds the remnants of decades of colonial rule (the Congo was granted independence in 1960). The museum still bears the hallmarks of its past as an imperial showcase (there's no mention of the millions of Congolese who died under Léopold's rule), but the boastfulness has been replaced by an almost apologetic stance. The museum has a comprehensive collection of insects, masks, and sculpture. But there are other gems worth seeking out: a 22.5m *pirogue* (canoe) that can hold 100 men and was built from the trunk of a single tree; a pickled coelacanth (a living fossil fish believed to have been extinct for 70 million years until its discovery off Africa in 1938); and a wonderful technicolour display of ceremonial African dress.

♿ Tervuren Park [→77], around the museum, offers a peaceful escape.
♨ For information about exhibits in English, buy the guidebook (100 BF).
❶ Temporary exhibitions are usually far more exciting than the permanent ones.

13 chaussée de Louvain, Tervuren ☎ 02.769.52.11 w www.africamuseum.be 🚌 29 🚋 200BF 🚇 none ◐ 10am–5pm Tue–Fri; 10am–6pm Sat–Sun. ♿ 🎧 🛍

↓ famous houses

Musée Constantin Meunier (Constantin Meunier Museum)

Tucked away on a residential street, this modest 19th-century town house was the home and studio of an unjustly neglected sculptor, Constantin Meunier (1831–1905), described by the British art critic Brian Sewell as 'a Belgian who deserves to be famous'. Originally a painter of religious scenes, Meunier changed tack completely following a trip to Belgium's industrial heartland, the Borinage, where he was shocked by the conditions endured by miners and steel-workers. The resulting sculptures recall Rodin in their muscular power, while the blend of pain, endurance, and dignity on the faces of his working-class heroes sets a benchmark for social realism throughout Europe, an impassioned reaction against stuffy academies and their narrow conception of fine art. In his group pieces, the energy and dynamo of new technologies shines through, but the intolerable strains they imposed upon the human workers were Meunier's real concern. This coherent collection, displayed on the ground floor and in the studio at the back, includes sketches and paintings as well as imposing bronze sculptures of working men.

👁 *The Reaper; Pain; Le Retour des Mineurs*, one of his best-known paintings.

59 rue de l'Abbaye, Ixelles (West) ☎ 02.648.44.99 🚋 93, 94 🎫 free 🚌 none 🕐 10am–12pm & 1–5pm Mon–Fri, plus every 2nd Sat. ☞

Musée David et Alice van Buuren (Museum David en Alice van Buuren)

The wealthy Dutch banker and art collector David van Buuren built this delightful 1930s Art Deco

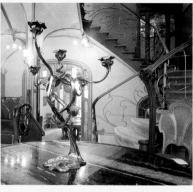

villa on an elegant suburban street in Uccle. Don't be alarmed when the curators ask you to schlep about in ragged overshoes: it's a small price to pay for padding on gorgeous Art Deco carpets and the almost voyeuristic sensation of sneaking round someone's home. Mind you, it's hardly your average home: the lounge is adorned with paintings by Belgian artists Rik Wouters and James Ensor, sketches by van Gogh, and a version of *The Fall of Icarus* thought to be one of three on the theme by Pieter Brueghel the Elder, though some experts claim it was painted after his death. Stylish furnishings include Lalique vases and, in the upstairs office, a magnificent desk with a lush *shagreen* (sharkskin) surface. In fine weather you can explore the garden, which features a labyrinth designed by celebrated Belgian landscapist René Péchère.

41 avenue Léo Errera, Uccle ☎ 02.343.48.51 🚋 23, 90 🎫 300BF (house & gardens), 250BF (gardens only) 🚌 none 🕐 2–6pm Mon; 1–6pm Sat. ♿ ☞ 🎁

Maison d'Erasme (Erasmushuis)

Renaissance philosopher Desiderius Erasmus may only have spent a grand total of five months here, but he might as well have spent his whole life in this

impressive gabled house. Someone must have gone to a lot of trouble to get a piece of his coffin, a cast of his skull and numerous portraits all depicting the man in his signature beret-like hat. They all look similar to each other, except for the unflattering watercolour featuring a pale-looking Erasmus shortly before his death. But even those who are not Erasmus groupies will appreciate the old stuff here, and it's easy to get a feel for what life was like back then. Fortunately, the museum provides thick guidebooks describing all the objects on display, but one would be well-advised to read up on the humanist philosopher beforehand so as not to feel intimidated by this shrine to academia.

31 rue du Chapitre, Anderlecht ☎ 02.521.13.83 🌐 www.ciger.be/erasmus Ⓜ St-Guidon 🎫 50BF (combined ticket with Musée du Béguinage) 🚌 none 🕐 10am–12pm; 2–5pm Mon; Wed–Thu; Sat–Sun. ♿ limited ☞ By reservation 🎁

Musée Horta (Hortamuseum) ↓

Few can resist the full-on enjoyment of this house and studio which Victor Horta, the pioneer of Art Nouveau architecture, built for himself between 1898 and 1901. The façade is far from the movement's most flamboyant,

sights, museums & galleries

but there's a glorious glow to the interior, thanks to the warm ochre and amber colours of the furnishings. This is Horta at his purest and most inventive, without the vulgar flourishes some of his clients demanded: no expense has been spared, from the exquisite wood panelling and wrought iron, to the swirling door handles and coat hooks. The centrepiece is the stairwell, topped by a glass canopy from which light streams through the house, while the small, peaceful upstairs balcony offers a fine view of the surrounding private gardens. Horta lived here until 1919, by which time the horrors of war and a new austerity had cast a shadow over the excesses of Art Nouveau.

♻ The shop has great books about Art Nouveau.
❶ There's a limit of 45 people in the house at any one time; and it's less crowded on weekdays.

26 rue Américaine, Ixelles (West) ☎ 02.543.04.90 ⍟ 81, 82 ⊞ 150BF (200BF Sat–Sun) 🚫 none ◑ 2–5.30pm Tue–Sun. ☞ By reservation 🛈

Musée René Magritte (René Magrittemuseum)

True Surrealist art fans should bypass the city's main art museums – crammed with lots of other stuff – and head straight for the house where Belgium's most famous Surrealist lived for 24 years. The home is rather modest – René Magritte was not a collector of others' art – but it is quite extraordinary to see the fireplace and the black bowler hat immortalized in Magritte's work on the coat rack in the hallway. There is just a small smattering of his work on display, but a rather impressive assortment of personal effects, like his wife's piano notes and Magritte's own camera collection. The room where a dozen or so Belgian Surrealists used to gather at a time is surprisingly tiny. Beginning with the moment you ring the doorbell, visiting this place, where the artist did about half his work, is a very intimate and rewarding experience.

❶ Sat–Sun can be crowded

135 rue Esseghem, Evre ☎ 02.428.26.26 ⍟ 18 ⊞ 240BF 🚫 none ◑ 10am–6pm Wed–Sun. ☞ 🛈

Musée Wiertz (Wiertzmuseum) ✓

A monument to ludicrous delusions of grandeur, the former home and studio of artist Joseph Wiertz (1806–65) offers welcome light relief from the office-block monotony of the Quartier Européen. It's stuffed with overwrought, oversized canvases by a painter whose ego exceeded his talent: a

competent neoclassical artist, he saw himself as the equal of Rubens and Michelangelo. Inspired by classical and biblical themes, his paintings alternate between the macabre and the mildly pornographic, with the moral consistency of a modern slasher flick: lithe nudes rub shoulders with gruesome depictions of hell, hunger and the horrors of contemporary medicine. Think *Enfant Brûlé* (Burnt Child) and *Inhumanation Précipitée* (Premature Burial) and you'll get the idea. They went down a storm with his contemporaries, but his continued fame is principally due to a canny deal with the state: build me a studio, and I'll leave you my work when I die. Perhaps prophetically, Wiertz believed that Brussels would one day eclipse 'provincial Paris'; good foresight as the museum is next door to the Parlement Européen.

62 rue Vautier, Quartier Européen ☎ 02.648.17.18 ⍟ 21, 34, 80 ⊞ free 🚫 none ◑ 10am–12pm & 1–5pm Tue–Fri & every other weekend. ☞ By reservation

---

grand' place

The heart of Brussels in every sense, the Grand' Place is a magnet for tourists, a site for all manner of entertainment (from jazz orchestras to volleyball), and a symbol of the commercial clout Brussels has enjoyed since the 14th century. The influential guilds, who rebuilt the square (1695–1698) after the French bombardment, have long since disappeared, but first-timers can have endless fun guessing which house each house represents. A relief of Apollo shooting an arrow is a giveaway (No. 5, the archers' guild), as is the ship-shaped gable of Le Cornet (No. 6, boatmen), but the dancing figure of Fame on the dome of Nos. 1 and 2, now Le Roy d'Espagne bar [→105], offers few clues as to the identity of the former owners, the bakers' guild. The Confederation of Brewers now occupies the Brewers' House (No. 10), home to the unthrilling Musée de la Brasserie. Several of the buildings have celebrity pasts: Victor Hugo spent part of his 1852 exile from France in No. 26, while across the road (No. 8), Marx and Engels penned the Communist Manifesto (1848). The building, Le Cygne, now houses a swanky restaurant.

♻ The night-time floodlights are very romantic.
♺ 1| The night-time son et lumière is very unromantic. 2| Some bars are on the pricey and touristy side.
❶ Events on the Grand' Place: the Jazz Marathon [→119]; Ommegang [→118]; open-air opera in summer; the flower carpet [→118]; Christmas market [→119]; and ice-rink in Dec–Jan [→119].

↓ one-offs

Hôtel de Ville (Stadhuis)

The newly cleaned and blindingly spruce town hall, dominated by a slimline 96m tower, is among the city's most beautiful sights, and arguably the finest Gothic structure in Europe. Started in 1402, the spire was completed 50 years later by Jan van Ruysbroeck, and was one of the few buildings on the Grand' Place [→68] to survive the French bombardment of 1695. Its charming asymmetry is the result of regulations that forbade building over the nearby rue Tête d'Or. A more interesting local rule is that civil marriage ceremonies for the commune's citizens take place in the town hall – a great reason to live in downtown Brussels. Join a tour and you can view the function rooms, adorned with 18th- and 19th-century tapestries, 19th-century depictions of bygone Brussels, and full-length portraits of Mary of Burgundy, Charles V and other rulers.

❶ The inner Baroque courtyard, with its fountains, is a cool spot for escaping the Grand' Place scrum; and it hosts concerts in summer.

Grand' Place, Central
☎ 02.279.43.65 Ⓜ De Brouckère ⒝ 100BF 🚇 none ◑ *Guided tours only: 11.30am & 3.15pm Tue (year round); 3.15pm Wed (year round); 12.15pm Sun (Apr–Sep only).* ☞

Manneken Pis & Jeanneke Pis

What can you make of a city that promotes a 30cm widdling youth as one of its greatest assets? If you can bear to be seen there, it's worth checking out Brussels' favourite 'little man', if only to see the bemused faces of onlookers and hear the cries of 'but he's so small'. The legends that surround him are less of a let-down. Is he a homage to a quick-thinking medieval lad who put out a firebomb by pissing on it? Or the boy Godrey, future 12th-century Duke of Brabant, who manfully peed on the enemy when taken to battle? Or perhaps he was the creation of a thankful farmer who lost his son during carnival and found him calmly doing a wee? What we do know is that the Manneken Pis was created in 1619, that there have, incredibly, been several attempts to steal him (one successful, in 1817, meaning this is a copy), and that he has been showered with outfits, now exceeding 600. Examples of his fancy dress, including Mickey Mouse and Elvis suits, are in the Maison du Roi. The Jeanneke Pis, off the tacky rue des Bouchers, was created in 1985 by a restaurateur who hoped the statue of a grimacing, peeing girl with pigtails would attract more trade. For locals, she's a shameless travesty, but the tourists look set to make her a fixture.

Manneken Pis: corner of rue du Chêne & rue de l'Etuve, Central; Jeanneke Pis: Impasse de la Fidélité, Central Ⓜ Bourse ⒝ free 🚇 none ◑ *24 hours daily.*

Musée Bruxellois de la Gueuze (Brussels Museum van de Geuze)

Founded in 1900 by Paul Cantillon, who left the family brewery in Flanders following a fight with his brother, this is the only surviving Brussels brewery dedicated to the production of *gueuze*, a distinctively sour beer unique to the region, and of the famous fruit beers *kriek* and *framboise*. Family-run, and using age-old techniques that rely on natural, spontaneous fermentation, the museum is equally dedicated to educating a public that is used to the ersatz *krieks* produced by Belle-Vue and others: taste the real thing and you'll never forget it. After a wonderfully impassioned introduction, you're free to wander the building and marvel at its magnificent machinery, including a vast copper vat, before heading back to the foyer for a tasting session. The still-working brewery grinds into life in winter, when cooler weather ensures hygienic fermentation; the brewing season kicks off and ends with open days (late Nov and early Mar). If you'd rather savour your *gueuze* in peace, drop in on working days through the rest of the year.

❶ Best time to visit is Oct–Apr when the beer is being produced.

56 rue Ghuede, Anderlecht
☎ 02.520.28.91 Ⓜ Gare du Midi ⒝ 100BF 🚇 none ◑ *9am–5pm Mon–Sat (from 10am Sat).* ☞ *By reservation* ☞ 🛈

Musée des Instruments de Musique (Muziek-instrumentenmuseum)

If you don't know your Gambian harp lute from your Tunisian rebab, you're in for a treat. Housed since 2000 in the Art Nouveau Magasin Old England [→73], this is a stunning collection of historical instruments from around the world. Interactive headsets, which respond to infrared signals from some of the displays, allow you to hear what

the instruments sound like. The recordings are sometimes a touch out of sync, but the irritant factor is outweighed by the pleasure of watching people jiggling their heads to get the music. An extravagant collection of keyboard instruments includes an 18th-century pyramid piano, one of the earliest upright pianos, and a 17th-century Italian harpsichord coated with bouncing cherubs. Touring the World Instruments collection, where you can pour over ancient African lyres and fantastically long Tibetan trumpets, is like speed-travelling through thousands of years of musical history. The café on the sixth floor has superb views of central Brussels [→63], beautifully framed by crescent-shaped wrought-iron windows.

♫ 1| Stylish café with terrace, mod-Med and Belgian cuisine. 2| Excellent shop with specialist music books.
♬ Beautiful but impractical lift, which gets stuck when people forget to close the double doors, which they invariably do.

2 rue Montagne de la Cour, Le Sablon ☎ 02.545.01.30
w www.mim.fgov.be
Ⓜ Centrale ⊞ 150BF
🖭 V ◑ 9.30am–5.30pm Tue–Fri; 10am–5pm Sat–Sun.
♪ ♫ ⌂ 🛈

Théâtre de Toone (Theater Toone VII) →

There can't be many places in the world where you can watch papier-mâché puppets lampoon politicians by performing Macbeth in an incomprehensible dialect. Brussels' tradition of subversive puppetry goes back to the days of Spanish rule, when theatres were closed to stifle local protest and a less obvious form of satire developed. The Théâtre Royal de Toone, founded by Antoine Toone in the

Marolles in 1835, moved to this secluded medieval alley in 1966. Shows take place in an intimate atmosphere on a tiny stage. The dialect, Vloms, a weird mix of French, Dutch and Spanish, is taken very seriously by current master puppeteer José Geal (Toone VII) and a small group of enthusiasts dedicated to preserving a language that nobody speaks. In the unlikely event that you understand the lingo, you'll be in for a feast of Rabelaisian mischief. Otherwise, hold out for performances in English.

♫ Atmospheric bar, great for tasting local beers.
♬ The museum is only open during performance intervals.

6 petite rue des Bouchers, Central ☎ 02.513.54.86
Ⓜ Bourse ⊞ performances from 400BF 🖭 none
◑ varies. ☞ ⌂ 🛈

↓ religious buildings

Basilique Nationale du Sacré-Coeur (Heilig Hat Basiliek)

This early 20th-century twin-towered building is the duckling among Brussels' churches. Still, it has its charms, like the bold colourful windows – especially in the side chapels – which brighten up the drab interior. One wonders what the place looked like before the huge restoration project. The folk here also run their own tourist office and a Christian comic-book store [→60].

👁 Climb up the dome for a spectacular view.

1 parvis de la Basilique, Koekelberg ☎ 02.425.88.22
Ⓜ Simonis ⊞ 100BF
🖭 none ◑ 9am–6pm daily.
♪ ☞ ♫ 🛈

Cathédrale St-Michel & St-Gudule (St-Michiels & St-Goedele Kathedraal)

If you only have time for one church in Brussels,

this is the one. A one-stop shop, it has everything a Gothic cathedral (started in 1226) should have – impressive towers, a grand collection of golden chalices and other holy artefacts, paintings by famous artists, and a souvenir store to boot. No wonder Belgian royalty, Prince Philippe and Princess Mathilde, chose to get married here.

parvis St-Gudule, Central
☎ 02.217.83.45 Ⓜ Centrale
⊞ free 🖭 none ◑ 8am–7pm daily. ♪ ☞ 🛈

Chapelle de la Madeleine (Magdalenakapel)

This quaint little brick church, part of a convent in the Middle Ages, is oozing cuteness. It is decorated with a modern flair: the unusual stained-glass designs could be something out of a Cubist painting, and the ceramic depictions

of the stations of the cross are most unusual.

rue de la Madeleine, Central
☎ 02.511.28.45 Ⓜ Centrale
⊞ free 🖭 none
◑ 7am–7.30pm Mon–Sat; 7am–12pm & 5–8pm Sun.
♪ ☞ ♫ 🛈

Eglise des Brigittines (Brigittinenkapel)

You'll be drawn to this building by its elaborate gabled façade, with intricate light-stone carvings set against darker brick. Unfortunately, there's not much else to see except the remainder of an old 17th-century convent. Today, the building, which has undergone numerous facelifts over the years, serves as a theatre [→116] and exhibition hall.

1 petite rue des Brigittines, Les Marolles
☎ 02.506.43.00
Ⓜ Anneessens ⊞ free
🖭 none ◑ 8am–7.30pm daily.

Eglise Notre Dame du Sablon (Kerk van Onze-Lieve van de Zavel) ↓

The place du Grand Sablon's Gothic showpiece is surprisingly not as dark and musty as other religious buildings of the same period. In fact, it is a rather uplifting place, from the glistening pipes on the huge organ topped by a trumpet-playing cherub, to the brilliant stained-glass windows. At night these windows, if viewed from the outside, give the square a magical ambiance. This is one of few consumer-friendly churches, replete with a nun-run gift shop.

3 rue de la Régence, Le Sablon ☎ 02.511.57.41 Ⓜ Louise 🆓 free 🚫 none ◑ 9am–5pm daily (from 10am Sat; from 1pm Sun). ♿

Eglise Protestante (Protestante Kerk)

This petite church, across the courtyard from the Palais des Beaux-Arts [→74], is as glisteningly white on the inside as it is on the outside. Chandeliers and marble give it an unsurpassed elegance, with black and gold railings adding just the right amount of colour. The acoustics are also amazing, so definitely sneak a peak and whisper a few words.

Chapelle Royale, 2 place du Musée, Le Sablon ☎ 02.513.23.25 Ⓜ Centrale 🆓 free 🚫 none ◑ 10.30–11.30am Sunday & by request. ♿ ☞ By reservation

Eglise St-Boniface (St-Bonifaaskerk)

Named after a local saint who hailed from a noble Brussels family, this unassuming church has some worthwhile gems, despite the somewhat shabby exterior. The elaborately carved wooden confessionals and stations of the cross might entice anyone to become Catholic. A good

place for peace and quiet, far, far removed from the hustle and bustle outside.

rue St-Boniface, Ixelles (East) Ⓜ Porte de Namur 🆓 free ◑ varies.

Eglise Ste-Catherine (St-Katelijnekerk)

This 19th-century church, with a parking lot for a front yard and a row of gourmet fish restaurants at its rear, is worth a trip if only to see the temporary exhibitions housed there from time to time. The building, which was almost converted into the stock market, is in sore need of a paint job. The Black Virgin statue was fished out of the River Senne by Catholics in 1744 after the Protestants had dumped it there, so they're pretty proud of it.

place Ste-Catherine ☎ 02.513.34.81 Ⓜ Ste-Catherine 🆓 free 🚫 none ◑ 8.30am–6pm daily. ♿ ☞ 🎧 🐾

Eglise Royale Ste-Marie (Kon. Ste-Mariaskerk) ↖

From an architectural point of view, this is undoubtedly the most unusual religious building in Brussels. An odd mix somewhere between a mosque, a church and a temple, this cream-coloured beauty, with side chapels and towers jutting every which way, has a very exotic feel to it. The large blue dome, speckled with green and

orange stars, has photo opportunity written all over it.

rue Royale, St-Josse & Scharbeek Ⓜ Botanique 🆓 free ◑ varies.

Eglise St-Jacques-sur-Coudenberg (Kerk van St-Jacob op de Koudenburg)

Only the very dull are able to resist the temptation to enter this building after viewing one of the city's most amazing façades. The blindingly white church, with its ornate gold-plated frieze, seems to be a cross between a Greek-Roman temple and an American colonial courthouse. The interior, painted in a cheerful pale yellow, is not as impressive as one would expect, though it is pleasantly refreshing.

1 impasse Borgendael, Le Sablon ☎ 02.511.78.36 Ⓜ Parc 🆓 free 🚫 none ◑ 10am–6ppm Tue–Sun (from 3pm Sun). ♿ ☞

Eglise St-Nicolas (St-Niklaaskerk)

This unpretentious Catholic church, one of the oldest in the city, is dedicated to the patron saint of merchants, though he is more commonly known as Santa Claus. Though clearly not the most beautiful, this cluttered church, with its sea of votive candles, is one of the city's most endearing. It's in amazingly good shape, having undergone one restoration after another since a battle between Catholics and Protestants in the late 16th century.

👁 The unique diorama depicting Christ's birth in Brussels, with the amusing by-line 'times and places have been slightly displaced for our purposes'.

1 rue au Beurre, Central ☎ 02.513.80.22 Ⓜ Bourse 🎫 free 🍴 none ⏱ 8am–6.30pm Mon–Sun. ♿

Musée du Béguinage (Begijnhofmuseum)

It's difficult to imagine what the women – all single or widowed – who once lived here did for fun. As members of the *béguines* (a Christian sisterhood that, despite not taking vows, lived an austere life with strong religious values), their lives were devoted to prayer, care of the sick and elderly, and making

arts and crafts in the *bollewinkel* (sweat shop). This tiny museum is just as exciting, though it makes a sincere (but feeble) attempt to show the area's history.

🔑 One ticket gets you in both here and the Maison d'Erasme [→67], round the corner.

8 rue du Chapelain, Anderlecht ☎ 02.521.13.83 Ⓜ St-Guidon 🎫 50BF (combined with Musée d'Erasme) 🍴 none ⏱ 10am–12pm & 2–5pm Mon, Wed–Thu. ♿ ☞ 🎧 🎁

Notre-Dame de la Chapelle (Onze-Lieve-vrouw-ter-Kapelle)

Like most Brussels churches, this 13th-century one has had its fair share of damage and patch-ups – a fire in 1405 and the 1695 French Bombardment saw to that. But you would hardly know it when inside this peaceful escape, simple yet elegant with light-72stone walls and transparent windows. The travelling exhibitions on modern art sometimes seem out of place next to the old religious paintings, and pale in comparison to the detailed sculptures of the four Apostles.

4 rue des Ursulines, Central ☎ 02.512.07.37 Ⓜ Anneessens 🎫 free 🍴 none ⏱ 9am–5pm Mon–Fri; 1.30–5pm Sat–Sun (to 3.30pm Sun). ♿ 🚻 🎧 🎁 🍴

Synagogue Communauté Israélite de Bruxelles (Synagoge van de Israëlitische Gemeenschap van Brussel)

Brussels' main synagogue, built in Romano-Byzantine style, will not disappoint. The exterior is dramatic, with a gabled façade topped by a giant star of David. Go through the large wooden door and enter an enchanted world. Climb the stairs to get a full glimpse of the ornate interior (lit by lights on golden lampposts), metal chandeliers, and a dome decorated with religious symbols in bright shades of gold, red and turquoise.

2 rue Joseph Dupont, Le Sablon ☎ 02.512.43.34 Ⓜ Louise 🎫 free 🍴 none ⏱ 9.30am Sun & by request. ♿ ☞

↓ art nouveau

Brussels, capital of Art Nouveau? You'd hardly have known it a few years ago, when the clamour for office space left heritage trailing a very distant second (a situation not helped by the authorities' lack of haste in listing buildings of architectural value). Many classic structures were torn down in the name of commerce, the most mourned being La Maison du Peuple, a workers' cultural centre designed by the movement's grand master, Victor Horta, and toppled amid howls of protest in 1965. Since the 1980s, the city has

treated its legacy with a little more respect, promoting itself as the cradle of Art Nouveau, with some of the finest examples in the world.

The advocates of 'New Art' favoured flamboyant glass- and ironwork, swirling, organic shapes, delicate *sgraffiti* (a decorative effect achieved by scratching into layers of plaster to reveal different colours in the layers behind) and an abundance of natural light. They believed every detail of a house, down to the doorknobs, should be in keeping with the style. Horta even went

to the extent of telling women what clothes would suit his furnishings. Despite the movement's socialist leanings, the style was embraced by Brussels' wealthy middle classes as a symbol of Belgium's break with a past marked by foreign styles and occupation, and as an irresistible opportunity to show off.

Even the most mundane neighbourhoods can boast a few examples of the *fin-de-siècle* fad, but there are several must-sees. Start in the Quartier Européen, with the resplendent square

Marie-Louise and square Ambiorix, crowned by Horta's superb **Hôtel Van Eetvelde**, built for Baron Edmond, Léopold II's administrator in the Congo (and later Secretary of State). Take an **Arau** guided tour (complete with cheeky commentary about the rights and endless wrongs of town planning) if you want to drool over the interior: mosaic floors, green onyx walls, crystal doors and an octagonal stairwell topped with a Tiffany-glass cupola. Gustave Strauven's extraordinarily frilly **Maison du St-Cyr** shows the movement at its most elaborate (and ultimately ridiculous). *Sgraffiti* can be seen at **Maison de Paul Cauchie**, the house of this architect, a fan of Rennie Mackintosh. Once earmarked for demolition, it was listed in 1975 and its Symbolist-influenced friezes have since been painstakingly restored. Heading towards the centre of town, **13 rue Royale** is a fine example of the sober architecture of Paul Hankar, who favoured red-brick structures over flamboyant metalwork. Take a breather in the bar of **De Ultieme Hallucinatie** [→104], which has a mosaic floor and a tendril-like green-metal conservatory.

Wander down to place Royale and admire Paul Saintenoy's **Magasin Old England** ✓, a glorious iron-and-glass department store that is now home to the Musée des Instruments de Musique [→70]. The **Centre Belge de la Bande Dessinée** [→64] is housed in a former warehouse, built by Horta for draper Charles Waucquez in 1893. Abandoned in the 1960s, when squatters moved in and used the shop fittings for firewood, it became a museum in 1989. The centrepiece is

the airy hallway and double-glass ceiling, but if cartoons aren't your thing, have a swiftie in the brasserie, where the chink of glass and cutlery resounds around the high ceilings.

In southern Brussels, the **Musée Horta** [→67] is the main draw as, perhaps, the purest illustration of Horta's harmonious style, followed closely by the streets around the Étangs d'Ixelles, examples of more affordable Art Nouveau residences built for the middle classes. Don't miss Ernest Blérot's town houses on **rue Belle Vue** (Nos. 42, 44, 46) and a mass of dwellings by the Delune brothers, Aimable, Ernest and Léon, along **rue de la Vallée**. The former **Hôtel Hannon** was built in 1903 by Jules Brunfaut for his amateur photographer friend, Edouard Hannon. The curvaceous exterior is more delightful than the inside, where the *trompe-l'oeil* ceiling verges on bad taste. Appropriately, it's now home to the Contretype photography gallery [→75].

art nouveau tours

Arau
☎ 02.219.33.45
Arcadia
☎ 02.534.38.19
Pro Vélo (bicycle tours)
☎ 02.502.73.55

directory

Centre Belge de Bande Dessinée (Belgisch Centrum van het Beeldverhaal)
20 rue des Sables, Central
☎ 02.219.19.80 Ⓜ De Brouckère; Rogier; Botanique
💶 250BF 🚭 none ◐ 10am–6pm Tue–Sun. ♿ ☜ 🏛

Hôtel Hannon
1 ave de la Jonction, St-Gilles ☎ 02.538.42.20
Ⓜ Mérode

Hôtel van Eetvelde
4 avenue Palmerston, Quartier Européen
Ⓜ Schuman

Magasin Old England
2 rue Montagne de la Cour, Le Sablon ☎ 02.545.01.30
Ⓜ Centrale

Maison de Paul Cauchie
5 rue des Francs, Etterbeek
☎ 02.673.15.06 Ⓜ Mérode

Maison du St-Cyr
11 square Ambiorix, Quartier Européen
Ⓜ Schuman

Musée Horta
26 rue Américaine, Ixelles (West) ☎ 02.543.04.90
🚌 81, 82 💶 150BF (200BF Sat–Sun) 🚭 none
◐ 2–5.30pm Tue– Sun.
☞ By reservation 🏛

rue de la Vallée
Ixelles (East) 🚌 93, 94

42, 44 & 46 rue de Belle Vue
Ixelles (East) 🚌 93, 94

13 rue Royale
Central Ⓜ Parc

De Ultieme Hallucinatie
316 rue Royale Ste-Marie, St-Josse & Scharbeek
☎ 02.217.06.14 🚌 92, 93, 94
💶 free 🚭 MC/V ◐ 11–2am Mon–Sat (from 4pm Sat). ♿ ☜

↓ exhibition spaces

Artesia Center for the Arts

Brussels' European Capital of Culture 2000 nerve centre, this renovated department store displays a permanent exhibition of 35 contemporary international artists, including Alicia Framis and Stephen Wilks, the fruits of Artesia bank's expendable cash.

50 rue de l'Ecuyer, Central
Ⓜ De Brouckère

L' Autre Musée

Without its own collection, this place is literally 'the other museum', as it fills in the blanks of the city's public art scene. It includes sculptures, installations and paintings of lesser-known European contemporaries.

41 rue St-Michel, Central
☎ 02.226.12.11 Ⓜ De Brouckère ⓘ free ◐ 2–6.30pm Tue–Sat.

Le Botanique

Ornamental greenhouses offer perfect lighting and calm for these disparate displays. One space shows off-the-wall photography, such as family snaps collected from Communist Hungary. The upper, larger gallery attracts contemporary touring displays.

236 rue Royale, St-Josse & Scharbeek ☎ 02.226.12.11 Ⓜ Botanique ⓘ 180BF ◐ 11am–6pm Tue– Sun. ♿ ☞ By reservation ℗ 🛈

Centre d'Art Contemporain

The French-speaking Community's gallery is devoted purely to contemporary art. Whatever's bubbling under the surface in the Francophone Belgian art scene will be exhibited or referenced here. Unheard-of artists often get shown.

63 ave des Nerviens, Quartier Européen ☎ 02.735.05.31 Ⓜ Schuman ⓘ free ◐ 9am–1pm & 2–7pm Mon–Fri; 1–6pm Sat.

FNAC

Linger while CD-hungry companions browse in the record shop [→15]. The smallish room behind the shop's cash desks displays photography, with a preponderance for modern black and white.

City 2, 16 rue Cendres, Central ☎ 02.275.11.11 Ⓜ Rogier ⓘ free ◐ 10am–7pm Mon–Sat (to 8pm Fri). ♿

Fondation pour l'Architecture

This impressive building rotates its art and architecture exhibits every few months. Sound, sculpture, installations and models make up hybrids featuring themes as varied as urban movement or use of plastics.

55 rue de l'Ermitage, Ixelles (East) ☎ 02.644.91.52 🚃 71 ⓘ 250BF ◐ 10.30am–6.30pm Tue–Sun. ♿ 🛈

Halles St-Géry (St-Gorikshallen)

By day, this ex-meat market houses exhibitions. Belgian art, given a wide definition, links shows of diverse subjects. At night, it's a bar and concert hall.

1 place St-Géry, Ste-Catherine ☎ 02.502.44.24 Ⓜ Bourse ⓘ 100BF ◐ 10.30am–6pm Tue–Fri; 2–5pm Sat–Sun. 🔲

Hôtel de Ville (Stadhuis)

This superb gallery makes the Grand' Place more than just a pretty face. It attracts quality international artists such as the Chilean, Matta, as well as some late 19th- and early 20th-century work.

Grand' Place, Central ☎ 02. 279.64.71 Ⓜ De Brouckère ⓘ 100BF ◐ Guided tours only: 11.30am & 3.15pm Tue (year round); 3.15pm Wed (year round); 12.15pm Sun (Apr–Sep only). ♿ ☞

Musée d'Ixelles (Museum van Elsene)

This one-time slaughterhouse is now used to display mainly 20th-century European art – it's big on retrospectives and lesser-known movements. A permanent collection keeps original Toulouse-Lautrec posters away from the more central throngs.

71 rue van Volsem, Ixelles (East) ☎ 02.515.64.21 🚃 71 ⓘ varies ◐ 1–6pm Tue–Fri; 10am–5pm Sat–Sun. ♿ ☞

Palais des Beaux-Arts (Palais voor Schone Kunsten)

Diverse exhibitions from embroidery to video installations can be found in the Palais des Beaux-Arts, a purpose-built Art Nouveau exhibition space, theatre, and cinema. [→113–115]

10 rue Royale, Le Sablon ☎ 02.507.84.66 w www.net point.be/abc/psk Ⓜ Parc ⓘ 250BF–350BF ◐ 10am–6pm Tue–Sun (to 8pm Fri). ♿ ☞ By reservation ℗ 🛈

Recyclart

Minding the gaps around Chapelle train station is this urban space that rotates installations and sculptures, often as backdrops for musical events. The group (Recyclart is their name, not the space's) aims to breath new life into the run-down surrounds.

25 rue des Ursulines, Les Marolles ☎ 02.502.57.34 w www.go.to/recyclart Ⓜ Lemonnier ⓘ varies ◐ varies. ♿ ℗

what's on

Find out what's on through Art Expo *and the* Arts, Antiques and Auctions *magazine, available at all newsagents, or online at www.gotim.be/artexpo. Less specialized is the English-language* The Bulletin *or the listings in Wednesday's edition of* Le Soir [→111].

↓ commercial galleries

Voyeurs are welcome in Brussels' galleries but it's worth a call first as galleries tend to take long holidays. The run-down area by the canals is art central – whether for cheap space or the hope that a docklands recovery is around the corner, two buildings now jam in over a dozen galleries. **Kanaal** and **Kanaal II** rent both poky and spacious areas to galleries. Windows is one of the best known, but the others, such as La Lettre Volée and the second branch of Artiscope, add to the fresh ambiance. Round a couple of corners is the minimalist gallery of **Meert Rihoux**, whose conceptual works show a preference for the 1970s and America. Nearby, **CCNOA** promotes non-objective art, one of the most radical 20th/21st-century art movements.

The established galleries are by no means less innovative; indeed, **Aeroplastics** would win the contest for hosting the most bizarre exhibitions. This space still buzzes with installations from the recesses of strange, usually sick, and debatably genius minds. Less far-out – but just as contemporary – is **Damasquine**, owned and run by the same people. The original **Artiscope** gallery tends to show its better-quality work here: mixed media from names like Warhol and Shapiro have adorned the walls. On rue Madeleine, a series of shop displays artistic wares. The most established of these is **J Bastien Art**, where sculpture and paintings fill a small space. Nothing too cutting-edge, but usually good-quality and interesting. **Xavier Hufkens** is in a different league, showcasing the likes of Louise Bourgeois. Less exclusive, but also trading on a reputation for quality, is the

Sabine Wachters Fine Art Gallery, which is as good for installations and photography as it is for paintings. Another classic is the **Pascal Polar** gallery, whose paintings and photography are French and Belgian. Painting is the niche of **Rodolphe Janssen**, where glass ceilings provide fantastic natural light. **Espace Photographique Contretype**, meanwhile, specializes in photography. Good, varied exhibitions vye for attention with the gallery building itself – the Art Nouveau Hotel Hannon [→73]. Also into photos, with some paintings too, is **Dorothée de Pauw**'s gallery. The contemporary works are judiciously selected. More varied is **Atelier 340**; less central than other galleries, this building is run by a Polish collector well known for giving space and opportunities to up-and-coming artists. Having bought stock through the years, permanent and motley collections are on view in this non-profit-making house. Another for-love collection is in the tiny **Salon d'Art et de Coiffure**. As the name suggests, hairdressing is the bread-winning venture, coupled with the gallery, which has mainly Belgian paintings, drawings and photography. New, and still establishing reputations, are the **Orion Art Gallery** (whose European sculpture and painting exhibits rotate every four months), and the **Taché-Lévy Gallery**, which had a real coup showing Tracey Emin's works. For Egyptian antiquities and avant-Russian work stop in at **Art Kiosk**.

Art Kiosk
9 ave Jean Volders, St-Gilles ☎ 02.534.66.11 🄼 Porte de Hal; Parvis St-Gilles

Atelier 340
340 drève de Rivieren, Jette ☎ 02.424.24.12 **III** Jette

CCNOA
2 rue Notre Dame du Sommeil, Ste-Catherine ☎ 02.502.69.12 🚋18

Espace Photographique Contretype
1 ave de la Jonction, St-Gilles ☎ 02.538.42.20 🄼 Albert

Damasquine
62 rue de L'Aurore, Ixelles (East) ☎ 02.646.31.53 🚋93, 94

Dorothée de Pauw
70 rue de Hennin, Ixelles (East) ☎ 02.649.43.80 🚋93, 94

J Bastien Art
61 rue de la Madeleine, Central ☎ 02.513.25.63 🄼 Centrale

Kanaal/Kanaal II
20 blvd Barthélemy, Ste-Catherine ☎ 02.735.52.12 🚋18

Meert Rihoux
13 rue du Canal, Ste-Catherine ☎ 02.219.14.22 🄼 Ste Catherine

Orion Art Gallery
19 rue aux Laines, Les Marolles ☎ 02.512.63.55 🄼 Hôtel des Monnaies

Pascal Polar
108 chaussée de Charleroi, St-Gilles ☎ 02.37.81.61 🚋91, 92

Rodolphe Janssen
35 rue de Livourne, Ixelles (West) ☎ 02.538.08.18 🚋93, 94

Sabine Wachters Fine Arts
26 ave de Stalingrad, Les Marolles ☎ 02.502.39.93 🄼 Lemonnier

Salon d'Art et de Coiffure
81 rue de l'Hôtel des Monnaies, St-Gilles ☎ 02.537.65.40 🚋Hôtel des Monnaies

Taché-Lévy Gallery
74 rue Tenbosch, Ixelles (West) ☎ 02.344.23.68 🚋93, 94

Xavier Hufkens
6–8 rue St-Georges, Ixelles (West) ☎ 02.646. 63.30 🚋93, 94

Aeroplastics
32 rue Blanche, Ixelles (West) ☎ 02.537.22.02 🚋93, 94

Artiscope
35 boulevard St-Michel, Etterbeek ☎ 02.735.52.12 🄼 Montgomery

With almost 14% of Brussels' metropolitan area being parkland, it's the second greenest city in the world. The capital's parks, woods, and gardens are varied: some wild, some sculpted and many, the most alluring, tucked away.

↓ the green scene

parks & gardens

Bois de la Cambre (Ter Kamerenbos) ↙

The manicured northern edge of the Forêt de Soignes is one of Brussels' most pleasant surprises, with hilly wooded sections, an artificial lake and acres of sweeping lawns. There's no better place to rollerblade, especially on weekends when the roads are closed to traffic. The Pélouse des Anglais, a picnicker's paradise, hosts free open-air jazz and classical concerts in summer. It's named after British troops who allegedly played cricket here before the Battle of Waterloo.

↪ Théâtre de la Poche; outdoor Sunday summer concerts [→118–119]; water towers.
↪ Drivers treat the roads through the park as a Formula One track.

Entrance: ave Louise (Ixelles (West) ☎ 02.775.75.75
🚌 23, 90, 93 🚊 38 🎫 free
◑ 24 hours daily. ◐ canoeing, rollerblading, pony trekking, horse riding, cycling ♂♀

Château de la Hulpe (Kasteel van Ter Hulpe)

This sprawling estate south of Brussels was landscaped by the sun-

worshipping Marquis de Béthune in 1842; he put in a Loire-style château, a gamut of exotic trees, and a gigantic stone obelisk. Its proximity to the lake, into which an incredibly steep flight of stone steps disappears, has led many to speculate that the whole thing is a hymn to fertility; a cozy hilltop summer house, with splendid views, may tempt you to get natural.

↪ Café in 19th-century farmhouse.

Entrances: chaussée de Bruxelles (La Hulpe)
☎ 02.653.64.04 🚊 La Hulpe 🎫 free ◑ summer: 8am–9pm daily; winter: 9am–6pm daily. ◐ cycling, horse riding ♂♀

Forêt de Soignes (Zoniënwoud)

An explosion of amber in autumn, Europe's largest beech forest stretches 43km/sq south and east into Flemish Brabant, an unbroken expanse of greenery that the locals call Brussels' 'green lungs'. Snaking paths take you through elegant, slender trunks, their uniformity the result of the 18th-century Austrian occupation, when fast-growing beeches were planted as an antidote to pillaging. Some *Bruxellois*

want the forest restored to its original oak character, but the joggers, riders, walkers, cyclists and lovers who flock here at weekends don't seem to mind. Take a break from the beeches at the Rouge-Cloître, a delightful site developed around a 14th-century abbey; the south wing is now a restaurant that offers hungry walkers a barbecue in good weather. The forest is also home to wild boar, deer, pheasants, and sparrow hawks.

↪ 1| In summer, trams from the Musée du Transport run through the wood. 2| Jean Massart Experimental Garden, with 5600 species.

Entrance: chaussée de la Hulpe (Boondael)
☎ 02.775.75.75 🚇 Hermann-Debroux 🎫 free ◑ 24 hours daily. ◐ cycling, horse riding, golfing, fishing ♂♀ 🍴

Jardin d'Egmont (Egmonttuinen)

An oasis of calm, this secluded secret garden

alternative retreats

Take a stroll through **Parc Léopold (Leopoldpark)** and you might bump into MEPs taking a break from the European Parliament [→62] which overshadows this landscaped park with its little lake and natural history museum. For a surprisingly natural feel, wander along the artificial ponds and sloped lawns of the English-style **Parc Woluwe (Park van Woluwe)**. Heading south, hilly **Parc Duden (Dudenpark)** has a pleasingly untamed atmosphere. Local hideaway **Parc Tenbosch (Park van Tenbosch)** has a boules pitch and a neat children's playground. Surrounded by some of the city's most desirable Art Nouveau and Art Deco houses, the willow-swept **Étangs d'Ixelles (Vijvers van Elsene)** municipal ponds are a must for architecture enthusiasts. One of the city's best rural retreats lies west of Anderlecht in the sloping vales of the **Vallée de la Pède**.

Étangs d'Ixelles
Entrances: ave des Eperons; ave du Général de Gaulle

Parc de Woluwe
Entrance: ave de Tervuren

Parc Duden
Entrances: ave du Parc, ave des Villas & Mont Kemmel

Parc Léopold
Entrance: chaussée de Wavre

Parc Tenbosch
Entrances: chaussée de Vleurgat; place Tenbosch

is a welcome antidote to this bustling area. There's a fine view of the Palais d'Egmont, named after the 16th-century count whose opposition to Spanish rule cost him his head, and now home to the Foreign Affairs Ministry. And ponder the merits of EU membership, for this is where Britain pledged to join in 1972.

☼ The Peter Pan statue is a hit with kids.

Entrance: blvd de Waterloo (Le Sablon) ☎ 02.775.75.75 🚌 92, 93, 94 🆓 free ◑ 24 hours daily.

Parc de Bruxelles (Warandepark)

Once the game reserve of medieval Dukes of Brabant, this central park was redesigned in ultra-neat French classical style in the 19th century. Formal, and a touch arid, it comes to life during holidays and festivals, especially the Belgian National Day [→118–119]. Alongside the unthrilling statuary is a memorial to paedophile victims Julie and Mélissa, whose deaths in 1996 provoked a national crisis.

Entrances: rue Royale, rue Ducale & place des Palais (Central) ☎ 02.775.75.75 🚇 Parc, Arts-Loi, Luxembourg 🆓 free ◑ 6am–9pm daily.

Parc de Laeken (Park van Laken)

Léopold II's exotic pretensions are perfectly illustrated by this rolling park, where he commissioned a Chinese pavilion and a six-storey Japanese tower, with parts shipped over from the Far East – pop in if you're a fan of Samurai armour or Chinese porcelain. If, and only if, you can stand the queues, the colossal royal greenhouses, filled with exotic flora, open for a fortnight Apr–May [→118–119].

Entrances: ave du Parc (Laeken) ☎ 02.775.75.75 🚌 19, 23, 81 🆓 free ◑ 8am–8.30pm daily.

the canals

If you want a waterfront, there's no point in trying to track down the trickles of the River Senne, which was buried in 1866 after cholera outbreaks in the city. Instead, head west to the city's canals, in the communes of Molenbeek and Anderlecht – once so industrial they were known as Brussels' 'Manchester'. The northern part of the canal, opened in 1561 to connect the city to Antwerpen and the North Sea, is one of the oldest in Europe. In its heyday, the port stretched up to place Ste-Catherine, which sported a splendid iron-and-glass fish market; its demolition in 1955 symbolized the canals' decline. The waterside neighbourhoods are hardly beautiful, but there's a new buzz thanks to the increasingly prosperous port and artist-friendly rents. La Raffinerie, an old sugar refinery (rue Manchester), is being converted into a dance venue, Quai Mariemont is home to jazz and hip-hop venue Fool Moon, and boulevard Barthélemy has been colonized by the Kanaal art complex [→75]. Take a boat tour by the industrial-heritage group La Fonderie (☎ 02.410.99.50) to get the true story of Brussels' canals. It leaves from the Quai des Péniches, opposite the smart new promenade at Bassin Béco at 2pm every Sunday (check in advance).

Parc du Cinquantenaire (Jubelpark)

Overshadowed by the Arc de Triomphe [→60] and its museums [→65–66], this severe symmetrical garden is another monument to Léopold II's ego. Look out though, for the Mosque and the Pavilion of Human Passions, a neoclassical temple built by a young Victor Horta. Inside is an erotic relief that outraged public decency on its opening in 1889 and has been off-limits ever since. On summer weekends, the Esplanade is transformed into a faux-50s drive-in cinema [→118–119].

Entrance: ave JF Kennedy (Quartier Européen) ☎ 02.775.75.75 🚇 Mérode; Schuman 🆓 free ◑ 24 hours daily.

Parc Tournay-Solvay (Park van Tournay-Solvay)

It's worth a detour to leafy Boitsfort to stroll through this little-known gem, an eclectic mix of wilderness and land-scaped sophistication. The peaceful park is also home to the European Sculpture Foundation, with a perilously

balanced permanent piece near the entrance and temporary outdoor shows by top artists from across the EU. Eco-tourists should check out activities organized by the park's Ecology Initiation Centre Tournesol.

☼ The rose garden.

Entrance: chaussée de la Hulpe (Watermael-Boitsfort) ☎ 02.775.75.75 (Ecology Centre ☎ 02.675. 37.30) 🚌 94 🆓 free ◑ summer: 8am–8.30pm daily; winter: 8am–5.30pm daily.

Parc de Wolvendael (Wolvendaalpark)

One of the beauties of this wooded park is its steep hill, transformed in snowy weather into a chaotic whirl of sledges and toboggans. Another, despite the excruciatingly slow service, is the open-air summer café, an extension of the Louis XV restaurant, housed in a splendid 17th-century pavilion. This relaxed locals' hangout is great for observing Belgian family life, especially in the children's playground.

☼ Dieweg Cemetery, the city's oldest.

Entrances: ave Paul Stroobant, ave Wolvendael (Uccle) ☎ 02.348.65.47 🚌 92 🆓 free ◑ 8am–4pm daily.

parks & gardens

Brussels is just made for kids: with masses of parkland, fantastic interactive museums, and some of the best theme parks in Europe nearby.

↓ kicks for kids

family fun

Bruparck Village

A purpose-built pleasure park that includes Océade (a swimming complex with slides, pools, saunas, and Turkish baths), Kinepolis (a 29-screen multiplex cinema), and Mini-Europe (notable buildings from EU countries, like the Acropolis, at a scale of 1:25). It's tacky, commercial, but a great place for the kids.

1 avenue du Football, Heysel ☎ Mini-Europe: 02.478.05.50; Océade: 02.478.43.20; Kinepolis: 02.474.26.04 Ⓜ Heysel 🚇 Combined tickets for 3 attractions: 750BF ◑ Mini-Europe: Mar–Jan: 9.30am–6pm daily (Jul–Aug: to 8pm). Océade: Apr–Aug: 10am–6pm Tue–Thu; 10am–10pm Fri–Sun; Sep–Mar: 10am–6pm Tue–Fri; 10am–10pm Sat–Sun. 🚻 all ages ♿ ☞ 🏠

Nautisports

Nautisports has four pools, from one of fairly large proportions if you want to notch up laps to a baby bath with mini slides. It's set on the edge of Chateau d' Enghien's land, with its Chinese pavilion, ornamental gardens, and duck ponds.

36 chaussée de Soignies, Enghien ☎ 02.397.01.80 Ⅲ Enghien 🚇 180BF adults; 120BF children; free under 12 yrs ◑ 9am–12.30pm Mon–Fri; 1.30–9pm Sat; 9am–7pm Sun. 🚻 all ages ♿ 🏠

Planckendael Zoo

This breeding ground for Antwerp Zoo has acres of parkland, including a stork colony, ape house, beaver dam, and rhino enclosure. There's an adventure playground, African-style mud-hut village, and farmyard.

582 Leuvensesteenweg, Muizen, Mechelen ☎ 015.41.49.21 Ⅲ Mechelen, then 🚌 284, 285 🚇 460BF adults; 295BF 3–11 yrs; free under 3 yrs ◑ 9am–6pm daily. 🚻 all ages ♿ ♿ 🏠

Walibi & Aqualibi

Theme park Walibi has 50 attractions, from a Vampire rollercoaster that travels at 81km/hr and with a 30m-plunge, to traditional carousels. Take it easier at Aqualibi next door, which boasts a 29°C heated tropical wave pool, rapids and a 140m-long Boa slide.

9 rue Joseph Dachamps, Wavre ☎ 010.42.17.17 Ⅲ Bierges 🚇 Walibi & Aqualibi: 995BF adults; 445BF 1–1.4m tall; free

under 1m. ◑ Apr–Jun: 10am–6pm daily; Jul–Aug: 10am–9.30pm daily; Sep–Oct: 10am–6pm Sat & Sun. 🚻 all ages ♿ ♿ 🏠

kids' culture

Beersel Castle (Kasteel van Beersel)

This 14th-century ruined fortress comes complete with a moat, towers, dungeons, and torture chambers. Children are encouraged to play and explore. There's a picnic area and a small playground for younger kids.

65 Lotstraat, Beersel ☎ 02.331.00.24 Ⅲ Beersel 🚇 100BF adults; 50BF kids ◑ Mar–Nov: 10am–12pm, 2–6pm Tue–Sun; Nov–Dec & Feb: weekends only. 🚻 all ages ♿

Musée de l'Enfant ↓ (Kindermuseum)

This kids' museum is filled with all sorts of goodies: giant interactive puzzles, a theatre and dressing-up area,

kids' shops

Brussels' most up-market toy store is *Serneels*, where rich mums and dads shop for wooden puzzles, handmade dolls and soft toys by the likes of Steiff. Serious dolls' house collectors should head for *La Courte Echelle* for miniature hand-crafted furniture. Don't miss out on a trip to one of rue du Lombard's joke and costume shops: *Picard* has been here since the turn of the century. Belgian children's wear is celebrated for its chicness rather than

its practicality. The city's smartest parents go to *Basile et Boniface* to buy top-of-the-range Belgian and French clothes and baby equipment at prices to match. *Jardin des Fleurs* is the place for doting relatives of the under 18-months, specializing in Italian knitwear and shawls. Check out trendy stores *Kat & Muis* or *Claude Hontoir* for cutting-edge designer labels.

Basile et Boniface
77 rue Washington, Ixelles (West) ☎ 02.534.81.18

Claude Hontoir
14 place Brugmann, Ixelles (West) ☎ 02.346.59.47

La Courte Echelle
12 rue des Eperonniers, Central ☎ 02.512.47.59

Jardin des Fleurs
60 rue Darwin, Ixelles (West) ☎ 02.344.18.89

Kat & Muis
32 rue Antoine Dansaert, Ste-Catherine ☎ 02.514.32.34

Picard
71 rue du Lombard, Central ☎ 02.513.07.90

Serneels
69 avenue Louise, Ixelles (West) ☎ 02.512.97.60

painting and cooking workshops, a nature section, as well as indoor and outdoor play areas.

15 rue du Bourgmestre, Ixelles (East) ☎ 02.640.01.07 🚋 23, 90 💷 220BF ◑ 2.30–5pm Wed, Sat, Sun, school holidays (closed Aug). ☃ 4–12 yrs ♿ 🖶

Institut Royal des Sciences Naturelles (Kon. Belgisch Instituut voor Natuurweten- schappen)

If you can't tell your diplodocus from your Tyrannosaurus Rex, the Natural Sciences Museum will set you straight with its impressive dinosaur displays. Check out the Neanderthal and the stuffed animal sections. Mollusc fans will find one of the world's largest collections.

29 rue Vautier, Quartier Européen ☎ 02.627.42.11 Ⓜ Maelbeek 💷 150BF adults; 100BF 6–16 yrs; free under 6 yrs ◑ 9.30am–4.45pm Tue–Fri (10am–6pm Sat–Sun). ☞ By reservation ☃ 5 yrs & up ♿ ♿ 🖶

Musée du Jouet (Speelgoedmuseum)

This toy museum is chocka with antique toys and interactive games. Don't miss the free demo of vintage clock-work toys and the string-puppet show.

24 rue de l'Association, Central ☎ 02.219.61.68 Ⓜ Madou; Botanique 💷 100BF adults; 60BF 6–16 yrs; free under 6 yrs ◑ 10am–12.30pm & 2–6pm daily. ☃ 4 yrs & up ♿ 🖶

Scientastic Museum

Discover the fun in physics and puzzle over illusions at this small interactive science museum. For would-be Einsteins, there are 80 experiments to try, either individually or as a guided group (English spoken).

Bourse Metro, blvd Anspach, Central ☎ 02.732.13.36 Ⓜ Bourse 💷 160BF adults; free children under 4 yrs ◑ school holidays: 2–5.30pm Sat–Sun; term: by appoint-ment. ☃ 4 yrs & up ♿ 🖶

showtime

Brussels has a rich variety of entertainment aimed at kids, much of which is seasonal: travelling circuses from late autumn to January; English Christmas pantos by expat theatre groups; carnival parades around Shrove Tuesday/Mardi Gras; and puppet shows. The two best puppet shows for the young are **Théâtre du Peruchet**, and **Théâtre du Ratinet** (both closed during July and August). The former's wooden marionettes act out fairy tales and fables; the latter presents trad children's tales in an old farm building. Also recommended is **Peruchet's Interactive- Puppet Museum**.

Théâtre du Peruchet
50 avenue de la Forêt, Ixelles (East) ☎ 02.673.87.30 🚋 94

Théâtre du Ratinet
44 avenue de Fré, Uccle ☎ 02.375.15.63 🚋 91, 92

Peruchet's Interactive- Puppet Museum
23 rue Ravenstein, Le Sablon ☎ 02.673.87.30 Ⓜ Gare Centrale

kids' eats

Provided kids watch their p's and q's, they are extended a warm welcome in most restaurants. One of the best deals for kids is at the Belgian frites et moules institution **Chez Léon**. If parents buy a 495BF meal of mussels, chips and a beer, children under 12 get a free set menu that isn't limited to shellfish. Fifties-style milk bar **Le Balmoral**, a laid-back, American diner, has a great children's menu of club sandwiches, burgers, and pasta dishes, which can be washed down with milkshakes. It's a popular brunchtime haunt.

Le Balmoral
21 place Brugmann, Ixelles (West) ☎ 02.347.08.82 🚋 91, 92 ◑ 9am–8.30pm Tue–Sun (to 7.30pm Sun).

Chez Léon
18 rue des Bouchers, Central ☎ 02.513.08.48 Ⓜ Bourse; De Brouckère ◑ 12–11pm Mon–Sun.

playtime

Brussels has a wealth of green spots where adults can unwind and kids can let off steam. A best-kept secret is the **Parc de la Sauvagère**, on the Sauvagère Nature Réserve, which keeps young kids happy with a playground, mini wildlife zoo, duck pond, and woods. **Parc Régional Tenbosch** [→76] is ano-ther find: it's got a pond with terrapins, a sandpit, a well-kept tots' play-ground, and a basketball court. Kids zip about at **Parc de Wolvendael** [→77], with its two play-grounds, pony rides and a grassy slope for ball games. Check out the **Bois de la Cambre** [→76] lakeside area on Sundays, when the road is closed to traffic and it becomes Belgium's answer to Central Park.

On the edge of the Forêt de Soignes is **L'Abbaye de Rouge Cloître** – spot the carp in the lakes and run riot in the playground.

L'Abbaye Rouge Cloître
Forêt de Soigne ☎ 02.775. 75.75 Ⓜ Hermann-Debroux 💷 free ◑ 24 hours daily. ♿ ♿ 🖶

Bois de la Cambre
Entrances: ave Louise, ave Franklin, Uccle ☎ 02.775.75.75 🚋 23, 90, 93, 94 💷 free ◑ 24 hours daily.

Parc Régional Tenbosch
Entrances: rue Américaine, Mélèzes, chaussée de Vleur-gat ☎ 02.775.75.75 🚋 93, 94 💷 free ◑ summer: 8am–9pm; winter: 8am–6pm. ♿

Parc de la Sauvagère
ave de la Chênaie, Uccle 🚋 43 💷 free ◑ 9am–dusk daily. ♿

Parc de Wolvendael
ave Paul Stroobant, Uccle ☎ 02.348.65.47 🚋 92 💷 free ◑ 7.30am–6 or 7pm daily ♿

children

Let yourself go with any or many of these fun-filled activities.

↓ play the game

Ballooning

Enjoy gliding, sightseeing, navigation tricks and balloon hide-and-seek as the pilot steers across forests and through quiet valleys.

Aerovlare, Office: 82 ave van Crombrugghe, Woluwe St-Pierre ☎ 02.762.45.73
🚌 39 💷 5950BF per person ⏰ May–Sep: by appt.

Bowling

The Bowl Factory calls itself the 'most beautiful alley in the world', while Bowling Crosley has 20 lanes in the tradition of pin-smashing.

Bowl Factory, 29 chaussée de Nivelles, Waterloo ☎ 02.387.54.31 🚌 365 💷 95BF–145BF ⏰ 12pm–midnight daily (to 2am Fri–Sat).
Bowling Crosley, 43 quai au Foin, Ste-Catherine ☎ 02.217.28.01 Ⓜ Ste-Catherine 💷 120BF ⏰ 12pm–midnight daily.

Breakfast Cinema

Join the breakfast club at Petit Déjeuners du Cinéma, where new releases and a few oldies are shown on Sundays.

UGC Toison d'Or, 8 ave de la Toison d'Or, Ixelles (West) ☎ 02.223.20.20 Ⓜ Louise; Porte de Namur 💷 280BF ⏰ 9.30am Sun.

Climbing Walls

New Roc and Stadium Centre are suitable for all skill levels with heights of up to 16m. Walls are regularly re-designed by professional climbers.

New Roc, 136 chaussée de Watermael, Auderghem ☎ 02.675.17.60 Ⓜ Demey 💷 300BF ⏰ 12pm–midnight daily.
Stadium Centre, 1 ave Sippelberg, Koekelberg ☎ 02.414.40.41 Ⓜ Ossegheim 💷 300BF ⏰ 9am–midnight daily.

Dance

Tango, flamenco, even Hungarian dance lessons are on offer at La Tentation. Those with two left feet can practise castanets, bagpipes, and accordion, or enjoy the art gallery and concerts.

La Tentation, 28 rue de Laeken, Ste-Catherine ☎ 02.537.45.47 Ⓜ De Brouckère 💷 200BF–450BF ⏰ 11am–11pm Mon–Sat.

Go-Karting

City Kart offers plenty of practice to perfect your racing skills on a 1000m track. For more lengthy rides, Brussels Kart has the biggest indoor track.

City Kart, 5a squ E des Grées du Lou, Forest ☎ 02.332.36.96 🚌 15, 50, 98 💷 350BF–500BF per 15 mins ⏰ 12pm–midnight (from 9.30am Sat–Sun).
Brussels Kart, 11 Gossetlaan, Groot-Bijgaarden ☎ 02.467.28.00 🚌 19 💷 350BF–500BF per 15 mins ⏰ 12pm–midnight daily (from 9.30am Sat–Sun).

Horseback Riding

In Bois de la Cambre [→76], the Royal Étrier Belge provides horseback treks, lessons, and workouts. The best option is to take a riding tour of the majestic Forêt de Soignes.

Royal Étrier Belge, 19 champ du Vert Chasseur, Uccle ☎ 02.374.28.60 🚌 41, 375 💷 750BF per hour ⏰ 9am–sunset Tue–Sun.

Paintball

Games with rules are organized to lend some form of order to an otherwise mad firing of paint. ⓘ Wear old clothes!

Paintball Sport ASBL, 13 rue Zwartebeek, Uccle ☎ 02.376.36.67 🚌 55 💷 950BF–1200BF ⏰ 10am–8pm daily (daylight permitting).

Rollerblading & Skateboarding ⓘ

Brussels' cobblestones don't make for good blading and boarding. So head to Bois de la Cambre (with its free rink) [→76] or pay to play at Rollerpark.

Rollerpark, 300 quai de Biestbroeck, Anderlecht ☎ 02.522.59.15 🚌 Veeweyde 💷 180BF–200BF ⏰ 10am–10pm daily.

Skating

Olympic-sized and semi-covered Poseidon has a rink a stone's throw from the pool, sauna, and hammam of this sports centre.

Patinoire Poseidon, 4 ave des Vaillants, Woluwe-St-Lambert ☎ 02.762.16.33 Ⓜ Tomberg 💷 12BF–160BF ⏰ Sep–Apr: 12–10pm daily (from 10am Wed–Sun).

fever pitch

Ask football fans about Brussels pre-millennium and they'd talk of match-rigging and hooliganism at Heysel. And, since Euro 2000, the images are of fighting fans of numerous Euro countries. But while the city is hardly a mecca for lovers of the game, its smaller clubs offer a glimpse into the amateur roots of football. **Anderlecht** are the Belgian Man United, all corporate hospitality and fans from out of town. While they can't afford to fork out for a Figo or even a Foé, the Mauves boast a smattering of international stars and can mix it in the Euro competitions. To sample Brussels' football heritage, though, head for Parc Duden and the fabulous Art Deco Stade Joseph Marien, home to fallen heroes **Union St-Gilloise**. Their pre-war heyday is gone, but the few hundred fans who still flock to the ground come Saturday treat every game like a champions' celebration.

Anderlecht
Stade Constant Van der Stockt, 2 avenue Théo Verbeeck, Anderlecht ☎ 02.522.15.39

Union St-Gilloise
Stade Joseph Marien, 223 chaussée de Bruxelles, Forest ☎ 02.344.16.56

Although the term 'spa' comes from the Belgian town of the same name, the *Bruxellois* don't go in for high pampering. But there are some gems...

↓ feelgood factor

hair care

Santi's

Frédéric Blondel's flamboyant salon reflects St-Gilles' faded Art Nouveau splendour. The loyal crowd is all ages, genders, and sexual orientations. Cuts: 1300BF for women, 750BF for men.

22 ave Paul Dejaer, St-Gilles ☎ 02.534.64.22 Ⓜ Horta

Herminio

Herminio's multilingual staff specialize in precision cutting (from 1700BF) and subtle colour techniques (1300BF–3000BF) in this sleek, chic salon.

119 rue Stévin, Quartier Européen ☎02.230.48.88 Ⓜ Maelbeek

Guillaume Sénéchal

Clubby comfort for guys only at this branch of Parisian barber Defossé. The range of care includes a facial massage and shave combo (700BF). Cuts from 1000BF.

85 ave Louise, Ixelles (West) ☎ 02.534.33.36 Ⓜ Louise

health clubs

Champney's

This luxurious centre offers a gym, dance studio, gorgeous pool, and sauna as well as Swedish massage, reflexology, Shiatsu, and Reiki. Choose between two one-day packages: entry with two treatments (1500BF +1000BF per option) or with three treatments, and lunch (8500BF).

Conrad Hotel, 71 ave Louise, Ixelles (West) ☎ 02.542.46.66 Ⓜ Louise ♨

manicures

Ruby's Nail Art
17 rue Lesbroussart
☎ 02.644.22.487

Beauté & Esthétique
94 avenue Louise
☎ 02.511.28.01

Azur
42 galerie du Centre
☎ 02.223.03.86

Sauna & Beauty Farm Thermae Grimbergen

A full day of luxury includes services such as rebirthing and chroma-therapy (3200BF–5950BF). For the 490BF entry fee you get jacuzzis and a Japanese sauna. Treatments cost 250BF–2800BF.

74 Wolvertemsesteenweg, Grimbergen ☎ 02.270.81.93 🚌 231 ♨

Thermen Dilbeek

Get-togethers in the buff are *de rigueur* here. The entrance fee (690BF) gives access to Turkish baths, saunas, herb baths, and heated indoor and outdoor pools. Pay for extras like a massage with essential oils (1450BF).

290 Kattebroekstraat, Dilbeek ☎ 02.466.00.88 🚌 to St-Antoon, then 🚌 ♨ 🚻

body art

Ritual Piercing & Tattoo

This kinky boutique provides a huge selection of excellent-quality jewellery, and they'll pierce almost any part of your body (500BF–2000BF). Henna tattoos are done on request (500BF).

3 passage St-Honoré, Central ☎ 02.223.49.58 Ⓜ Bourse

Hannya Tattoo

Thumb through the hundreds of designs available, or bring your own. For 3000BF per hour free-hand specialist PsychoPat creates tribal and Polynesian tattoos.

9 passage St-Honoré, Central ☎ 02.219.22.76 Ⓜ Bourse

beauty

Make-up Forever

This (expensive) staple for pro make-up artists and beauty addicts offers heaps of extraordinary selections. Many treatments (facials, waxing, make-overs, etc) are by appointment only.

62 rue du Midi, Central ☎ 02.512.10.80 🚌 34, 48, 95, 96

Espace Beauté

Serious pampering is the deal here, with treats like full-body seaweed wraps (1750BF) or Finnish sauna (500BF). Indulge in their menu of eight combinations from two hours (2900BF) to a half day (4900BF).

11 chaussée du Charleroi, St-Gilles ☎ 02.537.42.63 Ⓜ Louise

fitness

Centre Energetique Humaine

Individual or collective classes (500BF) such as contemporary dance and Qi Gong soothe your soul in this bright, calm studio. They also do shiatsu and massotherapy.

6 rue du Prévôt, Ixelles (West) ☎ 02.513.85.01 🚌 54, 71

Piscine Victor Boin ⚱

The pool in this *fin-de-siècle* gem is surrounded by tiers of elegant *cabines* (changing rooms). The Turkish baths look as they did in 1905, with mosaic tiles and marble benches. It alternates between ladies' and gents' days (790BF–990BF). Entry to the pool alone is 70BF.

38 rue de la Perche, St-Gilles ☎ 02.539.06.15 Ⓜ Horta ♨ 🚻

Yogashram-Centre de Bien Être

This 18th-century town house is a peaceful downtown sanctuary. Hatha, Egyptian yoga, breathing, and anti-stress classes (private and group, 350BF) are provided by 80-year-old Christiane Brandt and her team.

27 rue des Minimes, Le Sablon ☎ 02.512.64.92 🚌 93, 94

body & soul

getting your bearings

brussels' top shopping zones

♫ directory

Avenue Louise ♫C4–C5: With a mix of international chains and one-off boutiques, avenue Louise is a shopper's paradise.

Boulevard de Waterloo & Avenue de la Toison D'Or ♫C3: The Guccis, Versaces, and Hermès of this world have chosen the late 18th-century former mansions on boulevard de Waterloo for their flagships. Modernized avenue de la Toison D'Or is dominated by the designer label mecca Francis Ferent.

Chaussée de Charleroi ♫B4: An earthy thoroughfare with a diverse blend of up-market jewellers and galleries, made-to-measure dressmakers, and old-fashioned outfitters. Also home to German art supplies and stationery shop Schleiper.

Chaussée d'Ixelles ♫C3–C4: Vibrant artery of mainstream chain stores, fast-food outlets, and electrical stores. Includes cash-for-goods store Cash Converters and Dutch department store Hema. The busy Porte de Namur end backs onto the central African quarter, the Matongé, with its colourful fabric shops and foodstores.

Chaussée de Waterloo ♫B4–C5: It's kilometres long and the type of shops changes as you pass through the different communes. The buzzier northern end, in St-Gilles, is good for Spanish and Turkish delis and halal butchers. The bourgeois Uccle end is known for antiques, clothes stores, and florists.

Grand' Place area ♫B2: Touristy lace and chocolate shops dominate the square, but there are a few surprises in the surrounding labyrinth of streets. Rue du Midi and rue du Marché au Charbon are firmly trendy, with hatmaker Elvis Pompilio setting the tone.

Place du Châtelain, Tenbosch & Rue du Bailli ♫C4–C5: The Wednesday afternoon market on place du Châtelain draws foodies from all over Brussels. The lively rue du Bailli is good for trendy clothes shops. There's also a hub of one-off boutiques around Tenbosch park's main gates on rue des Mélèzes and rue Washington.

Place du Grand Sablon & Rue de Rollebeek ♫B3: There's a chocolate war on the main

st-josse & schaerbeek

quartier européen

ixelles (east)

| Ste-Catherine [→6–12] |
| Central [→13–19] |
| Le Sablon [→20–24] |
| Les Marolles [→25–28] |
| St-Gilles [→29–32] |
| Ixelles (West) [→33–37] |
| Ixelles (East) [→38–41] |
| Quartier Européen [→42–44] |
| St-Josse & Schaerbeek [→45–47] |

getting your bearings

markets

Grand' Place *B2*: Small daily flower market isn't the city's best, but it adds local colour to the square.

Midi market *A3*: A melting pot of ethnic food stalls, fruit, vegetables, plants, and cheap clothes (Sunday mornings).

Parvis St-Gilles *B4*: Morning market for no-frills fruit, veg, and meat (closed Mondays).

Place Flagey *D4*: Great for cut flowers, farm produce, and Italian delis (every morning except Mondays).

Place du Jeu de Balle *B3*: Daily flea market good for vintage clothes, picture frames, and miscellaneous junk.

Place du Grand Sablon *B3*: Weekend market, excellent for silver trinkets, jewellery, and antique chairs; but no bargains here.

galeries

Galeries de L'Agora *B2*: One-off shops selling leatherwear and watches. Weekend stalls sell tacky jewellery as well as leather bags and jackets.

Galeries Bortier *B2*: Shares the same architect as Galeries Royales St-Hubert. It's quiet, charming, and lined with antiquarian book and map shops.

Galeries Louise *C3*: This is where avenue Louise's window shoppers pile in at the first sign of rain or cold weather. It's lined with international chain stores.

Galeries Royales St-Hubert *B2*: The jewel in the crown of Brussels' *galeries*. Beautifully restored mid-19th-century arcade with up-market one-off clothes and jewellery shops, Neuhaus' flagship store, and a branch of Delvaux, the up-market Belgian designer shop.

Galeries de la Toison D'Or *C3*: Mall shopping is a national pastime, and this modern warren of mid-range boutiques is one of the most popular in town.

shopping complexes

Wiltcher *B4–C4*: Swanky home to toy store Serneels and the up-market health and beauty spot Champneys.

City 2 *B1–C1*: Modern redeveloped centre dominated by the media store FNAC.

Anspach Center *B2*: Vast modern centre good for electrical and computer stores.

square: Wittamer's, Pierre Marcolini and Godiva vie for the attention of the well-heeled who flock here for the weekend antiques market, select fashion stores, and art galleries. The pedestrianized rue de Rollebeek is lined with boutiques.

Place Georges Brugmann *B5*: A weekend hangout for the chattering classes. Shops include pricey kids' boutiques, an international newspaper store, women's fashion, antiques, and the city's top florist Catleya. Shops are open on Sundays.

Rue Antoine Dansaert & Place St-Géry *B2*: The trend-setting part of the city, with cutting-edge fashion from the best of Belgium's

designers. Shops include the Antwerp Six at Stijl, hat shop Christophe Coppens, womenswear store Azniv Afsa,r and jewellers Christa Reniers.

Rue Blaes & Rue Haute *B3*: Junk shops, chichi furniture and lifestyle stores, Art Deco specialists and wood restorers – this is a home decorator's heaven. The daily flea market on nearby place du Jeu de Balle draws in the crowds.

Rue Neuve & Boulevard Anspach *B1–B2*: Rue Neuve is a tacky walkway lined with mainstream chain stores and department store Inno. Nearby boulevard Anspach is a quirkier affair, with a mixed bag of fashion, second-hand vinyl and comic-strip shops.

Brussels' very best shops by category...

↓ stand-out stores

accessory designers

Annick Tapernoux | Ste-Catherine [→8]

Christa Reniers | Ste-Catherine [→8]

Christophe Coppens | Ste-Catherine [→8]

Elvis Pompilio | Central [→14]

Les Précieuses | Ste-Catherine [→8]

Théo Dépôt | Ste-Catherine [→8]

antiques/brocantes

Bleue comme... une orange | Ixelles (West) [→35]

Espace 161 | Les Marolles [→26]

Faisons un Rêve | Ixelles (West) [→35]

Fin de Siècle et Plus | Les Marolles [→26]

Ma Maison de Papier | Le Sablon [→21]

Marché place du Grand Sablon | Le Sablon [→21]

Marjolaine | Central [→14]

Scènes de Ménage | Ixelles (West) [→35]

Senses Art Nouveau | Le Sablon [→21]

Table d'Hôtes | St-Gilles [→30]

Yannick David | Le Sablon [→21]

belgian designerwear

Annémie Verbeke | Ste-Catherine [→7]

Azniv Afsar | Ste-Catherine [→7]

Kaat Tilley | Central [→14]

Martine Doly | Ixelles (West) [→33]

Stijl | Ste-Catherine [→6]

Studio Pitschon | Ste-Catherine [→7]

Van V | Ste-Catherine [→7]

books & magazines

Anticyclone des Açores | Central [→14]

FNAC | Central [→15]

Librairie Candide | Ixelles (West) [→35]

Librairie de Rome | Ixelles (West) [→35]

Nijinsky | Ixelles (West) [→35]

Pêle Mêle | Les Marolles [→26]

Peinture Fraîche | Ixelles (West) [→35]

Sterling | Central [→14]

Waterstone's | Central [→14]

CDs, records & tapes

Musicmania | Central [→15]

Virgin Megastore | Central [→15]

childrenswear, books & toys
[→78]

chocolates

Godiva | Le Sablon [→22]

Léonidas | Central [→14]

Manon | St-Josse [→45]

Mary's | Central [→14]

Neuhaus | Central [→13]

Pierre Marcolini | Le Sablon [→22]

Wittamer | Le Sablon [→22]

comic strips

Le Deuxième Souffle | St-Josse [→46]

Tintin | Central [→15]

Ziggourat | St-Gilles [→30]

euro fever

The English Shop | Quartier Européen [→ 42]

Kenlis | Quartier Européen [→42]

food

african asian foods

MC Négoces | St-Josse [→45]

Merci-Cash | St-Josse [→45]

Himi | Ixelles (East) [→39]

Tagawa Superstore | Ixelles (East) [→39]

cheese/drink

À la Petite Vache | St-Josse [→45]

Degroof | Ixelles (West) [→37]

confectionery

Maison Dandoy | Central [→14]

gourmet

L'Atelier de la Truffe Noire | Ixelles (West) [→34]

L'Atelier Gourmand | Ixelles (West) [→34]

Le Déjeuner sur l'Herbe | Ixelles (West) [→34]

La Ferme Landaise | Ste-Catherine [→8]

Mary's | Ixelles (East) [→39]

Matthys van Gaever | Ste-Catherine [→8]

healthfoods

Biodrome | Central [→14]
Den Teepot | Ste-Catherine [→8]
Dolma | Ixelles (East) [→39]
La Tsampa | Ixelles (West) [→34]

patisserie

St-Aulaye | Ixelles (West) [→34]

international designerwear

Camelot | Ixelles (West) [→34]
Le Chien du Chien | Ste-Catherine [→8]
Harmony | Ixelles (West) [→34]
Kenzo | Le Sablon [→21]
Ming Tsy | Ixelles (West) [→34]
Smadja Femme | Ixelles (West) [→34]
Tast | Central [→13]
Via della Spiga | Ste-Catherine [→7]

kitchenware & cutlery

Au Grand Rasoir | Central [→15]
La Coutellerie | St-Gilles [→30]
Dille en Kamille | St-Gilles [→30]
Fahrenheit | Ixelles (West) [→35]
Lauffer | Central [→15]
Noire d'Ivoire | Central [→15]

lifestyle stores

Antithèse | Ixelles (West) [→35]
Cinabre | Ixelles (West) [→35]
Compagnie de l'Orient et de la Chine | Ixelles (West) [→35]
Da Zia | Ixelles (West) [→34]
Graphie Sud | Ixelles (West) [→35]
MagicLand | Ixelles (West) [→35]
Natan | Ste-Catherine [→7]
New De Wolf | Les Marolles [→26]
Noire d'Ivoire | Central [→15]
L'Objet du Désir | Le Sablon [→22]
Rambagh Asian Homestyle | Les Marolles [→26]
La Vaisselle à Kilo | Le Sablon [→22]

lingerie

Les Charmes d'Hélène | Les Marolles [→26]
Stijl Underwear | Ste-Catherine [→7]
Undressed | Ixelles (West) [→34]

menswear

Balthazar | Central [→14]
Kwasi | Ste-Catherine [→7]
Degand | Ixelles (West) [→34]
Michiels | Les Marolles [→26]
Natan | Ste-Catherine & Le Sablon [→7 & 21]
Smadja Homme | Ixelles (West) [→34]
Stijl | Ste-Catherine [→6]
Via della Spiga | Ste-Catherine [→7]

secondhand & vintage

Les Enfants d'Édouard | Ixelles (West) [→35]
Idiz Bogam | Ste-Catherine [→7]
Look 50 | Ixelles (East) [→38]
Modes | Les Marolles [→26]
Nicolas Woit | Ste-Catherine [→7]
Palace | Les Marolles [→26]
Les Petits Riens | Ixelles (West) [→35]

shoes

Hatshoe | Ste-Catherine [→8]
Shoe'svictim.com | Central [→14]
Le Silla | Ste-Catherine [→8]

souvenirs

Het Plaizier | Central [→14]
Mont-de-Piété | Les Marolles [→26]

womenswear

Amandine | Ixelles (West) [→34]
Cachemire | Ixelles (West) [→34]
Gérald Watelet | Ixelles (West) [→34]
Isabelle Baines | Le Sablon [→20]
Natan | Ste-Catherine & Le Sablon [→7 & 21]
Nina Meert | Ixelles (East) [→39]
Rue Blanche | Ste-Catherine [→7]

top shops

Brussels may not have the cachet or choice of London or New York, but it's sure got the style. First-timers imagine row upon row of chocolate and comic shops; while the more experienced know that Belgian designer gear and accessories, trendy vintage togs, and fine antiques are the real draw. And though much of it is centred in the inner ring, each of Brussels' 19 communes retains neighbourhood shopping at its best, with specialities the name of the game.

brussels' top shops

belgian designers

Antwerpen was put firmly on the fashion map in 1986 when six former students from Antwerpen's Royal Academy of Fine Arts got together and showed their work during London Fashion Week. They called themselves the 'Antwerp Six', and the name stuck. There's been no letdown since then. The Six are still major players, and have now been joined by a new wave of designers garnering international success.

Louis [→51], in Antwerpen, owned by Geert Bruloot, was one of the first shops to stock collections by the Six, and remains Antwerp's champion of new Belgian talent. But most of them have their own stores now: **Ann Demeulemeester**'s [→51] is a year old; **Walter** [→51] is owned by Walter van Beirendonck and Dirk van Saene; **Lena Lena** is Marina Yee's; **Verso** [→51] sells Dirk

Bikkembergs; and most famous of all is Dries van Noten with his **Modepaleis** [→51]. More recent fashion stars are Martin Margiela (chief stylist at Hermès) and Brussels-born Olivier Theyskens (who replaced Alexander McQueen at Givenchy). Both these designers approached Louis first, and still sell there.

Don't despair, though. If Antwerpen doesn't figure in your travel plans there's a Brussels equivalent: Sonia Noël. She's been in the fashion biz for yonks, and was one of the first people to have faith in the Dansaert area of Ste-Catherine, 16 years ago, by opening her ultra-trendy clothes store **Stijl** [→6] there. Noël has also done much to boost Brussels' general fashion profile. She was one of the original pioneers of Parcours de Stylistes – an annual celebration of fashion that consumes the city centre for a weekend.

Stijl stocks most of the Antwerp Six and second-wave designers: Margiela, Jurgi Persoons, Olivier Theyskens, and AF Vandervoorst. Collections by the so-called third-wave avant-garde set are also here. Brussels-born Xavier Delcour made a beeline for Stijl, as did (Italian-born, but Antwerpen Academy graduate) Angelo Figus. About the only leading lights in Belgian fashion missing are **Lieve Van Gorp** [→51] (she has an Antwerp shop), Yee (who has a branch of Lena Lena on Dansaert), and van Beirendonck.

For clothes by avant-garde designers that haven't quite made the international circuit yet, stay in the Dansaert area. Those home-grown designers currently taking Brussels by storm include: **Annémie Verbeke** [→7], **Azniv Afsar** [→7], Belgo-Brazilian duo **Marien Perez** [→7] and **Van V.** [→7]. Watch this space.

vintage

Die-hard trend followers are the first to make a beeline to vintage fashion boutiques. If you know there's an 1980s or 1920s revival why not buy original one-offs secondhand? Brussels ain't Paris or London when it comes to quantity, but it sure wins out on price. Current up-market favourite has to be Jacqueline Ezman's women's and men's shop **Idiz Bogam** [→7]. She buys at auction and scours the flea markets of Paris and New York for stylish classics. Gladstone bags, flapper-style foxes and minks, slinky maxi-dresses, distressed leather jackets and crimplene shirts are Ezman's staples. It's also good for period footwear too – mostly unworn. This is as expensive as it gets in Brussels, but most items are still a bargain. Nearby, **Nicolas Woit** [→7] remakes women's classics from bygone eras using vintage fabrics and trimmings that he finds at auction. His Dansaert store is especially good for glam eveningwear, while **Gabriele** [→7] around the corner is best for 1940s croc handbags and pill-box hats. Men are catered for, too, with felt trilbies in winter and panamas during summer. Meanwhile, fashions closer to the millennium can be had at Bernard Gavilan's store **L'Homme Chrétien** [→14]. His speciality is clothes for boys and girls from the 1950s to 1970s. Rails of vintage jeans and jackets are there for the rummage alongside dressier evening numbers from the 1970s. Canny shoppers can find their own bargains: the **place de Jeu de Balle flea market** [→25] in Les Marolles is fab hunting ground for such things. Not far from the market square is **Modes** [→26], which is unbeatable for odd buttons – jet, plastic and Bakelite – men's braces from the 1940s, grandad shirts, and hats for men and women from the 1920s.

top shops

accessory designers.

Hotfoot it down to rue Antoine Dansaert and you won't be disappointed on the accessories front. The city's best designers are here alongside the hardcore of the avant-garde fashion set. Jeweller **Christa Reniers** [→8] is a fave with style queens. Silver flower cluster rings and pendants are among her top signatures, but diversity is the key to her success. Happily her prices won't break the bank – earrings and rings without semi-precious rocks start at 1500BF. Rival **Annick Tapernoux** [→8] is a stone's throw away. Her penchant is beaten silver *objets d'art* and austere jewellery. And she made the spoons at superchef Alain Ducasse's eaterie Spoon, Food & Wine in Paris. A softer approach is taken by fashion designer Pili Collado at **Les Précieuses** [→8]. This is a sideline to her day job so the opening hours a re erratic. Collado makes gorgeous costume jewellery for the modern twinset brigade – glass-bead chokers, bracelets, and earrings threaded onto silver wire. Jamin Puech's collectable beaded bags are also on sale here. But nothing comes cheap – expect to pay 3500BF for a necklace. Belgian hat designers are renowned. Twenty-something **Christophe Coppens** [→8] was less talked about than mad hatter **Elvis Pompilio** [→14] until he opened a first shop. He's been garnering attention ever since, and his handmade hats have graced many a Paris fashion show.

Gillis [→14], bang opposite Pompilio, is *the* hat shop for men and women with classic tastes. It's been here since the 1940s and the milliners still use authentic wooden casts from bygone days.

antiques

The city's architecture is testimony to Brussels' rich heritage in Art Deco and Art Nouveau, so fans of period pieces in these styles are in for a treat. The best specialist shops for this type of furniture are **Fin des Siècle** [→26] and **Essence de Siècles. Faisons un Rêve** [→35] is better for Bakelite (a Belgian invention) jewellery, ceramics, and more portable Art Deco *objets* such as candlesticks and mirrors. And **Table d'Hôtes** [→30] is a reliable bet for Val St-Lambert crystal vases and ashtrays, dinner services, and scent bottles. For more possibilities, mosey around the Marolles [→25–26] where there are many smaller shops specializing in pieces from the same era.

Hunting grounds for older, finer antiques are scattered liberally around the city. Indisputably the richest pickings are to be had in the Sablon [→20–22]. The downside is that this is where prices run sky high, although it has been known for early birds to get a bargain at the weekend market [→21] – credentials run high here, and the chances of being ripped off are slim. Those on a mission should check out the city's auction houses (salles de ventes in French or veilinghuizen in Flemish). Most prestigious is the **Salle de Ventes au Palais des Beaux-Arts**, closely followed by **Hôtel des Ventes Horta** and **Hôtel des Ventes St-Georges**. **Hôtel des Ventes Vanderkindere** is on a smaller scale, but well worth a look. These addresses used to target dealers only, but now they have evening viewings and auctions to try to attract private buyers. All the above sell a diverse line-up of antiques.

Hôtel des Ventes Horta
70–74 avenue de Rodebeek, St-Gilles ☎ 02.741.60.60

Hôtel des Ventes St-Georges
199 ave Louise, Ixelles (West) ☎ 02.640.76.12

Hôtel des Ventes Vanderkindere
685–687 chaussée d'Alsemberg, St-Gilles ☎ 02.344.54.46

Salle de Ventes au Palais des Beaux-Arts
10 rue Royale, Central ☎ 02.513.60.80

chocolates

Belgium's greatest gift to the world is all over Brussels. **Neuhaus** [→13], **Godiva** [→22] and **Léonidas** [→14] might have branches worldwide and are household names in connoisseur circles, but you'll find plenty of pralines they don't export. Belgians can argue for hours as to which of the famous trio is best... and there's no definitive answer. Léonidas' are cheapest and sweetest, Godiva's are expensive, while Neuhaus is the oldest kid on the block.

Swissman Jean Neuhaus opened a pharmacy in 1857 in Galerie de la Reine – now the flagship – selling marshmallows, liquorice, and the odd piece of chocolate. When his son Frédéric got involved, they started Confiserie et Chocolaterie Neuhaus-Perrin. Since the day Neuhaus senior's grandson came up with the first praline and a protective box, there's been no looking back. Family-run **Wittamer** [→22] has been around for almost as long. It takes a more elitist approach by keeping small and to trad methods. **Mary's** [→14 & 39] is as exclusive – it's the official supplier to the royal family. New-wave fave is thirtysomething **Pierre Marcolini** [→22]. He focuses on bittersweet chocolate sculptures for sophisticates. Subtle flavours like jasmine and bergamot are used to flavour his pralines, among the most expensive in Belgium. Also newish is **Planète Chocolat** [→14], run by Frank Duval, who commissions local sculptors to design the chocolate moulds into which he pours his delicately flavoured high cocoa-content chocolate. For a potted history of chocolate-making, there's a tiny museum at the back. Brussels' official museum, however, is on the Grand' Place.

linen

They say once you've slept between fine linen sheets, nothing else will do. The real expensive stuff made of flax yarns is synonymous with Flanders – and has been for centuries. Contemporary designers charge serious money for their hand-crafted linen. **Martine Doly** [→33] is the Belgian queen when it comes to cutting-edge table and bed linen. Her massive shop is evidence of demand. Hand-finished touches like embroidery and fab buttons make them hard to resist. **Cinabre** [→35] – a mecca for trendy ceramics and glassware – sells household linen supplies for committed lifestylers. The designers' names are obscure, but the quality of pieces is unbeatable. **Scènes de Ménage** [→35] sells a mix of new and antique linen (including pyjamas), a bit pricey, but good quality. Don't overlook the Sablon's traditional-style **Linen House** [→22] which makes and sells an impressive line of sheets, tablecloths and cushion covers. Pristine turn-of-last-century household linen can easily be found in Brussels. Prices are better if you trawl markets such as the **place du Jeu de Balle** [→25]. Vintage clothes shop **Modes** [→26] is worth a scout too – they have a small selection of specialized table linen.

bande dessinée

Comic strip (*bandes dessinées* in French and *beeldverhaal* in Flemish) murals brighten the walls of many downtown buildings. The TIB have planned a Comic Strip Route to celebrate Belgium's best-loved of the so-called 'eighth art'. Album characters like Tintin and Snowy, The Smurfs, Bob and Bobette (Willy and Wanda in the US), Lucky Luke and *Le Chat* – all by home-grown artists – are given hero status. It's not surprising, as BD is one of Belgium's mega exports, in the same league as beer and chocs. Free route maps for this enjoyable walk can be picked up at the Centre Belge de la Bande Dessinée [→64] or the TIB [→134] – the former is the best kick-off spot for background history of, and original illustrations by the likes of Hergé, Peyo, Willy Vandersteen and Morris. The shop here is handy for a line-up of new albums, limited-edition figurines of cartoon greats and other memorabilia, but there's much better... Unbeatable for new albums and objects are **Schlirf Book** and **Ziggourat** [→30]; or, for a more central address, try **Multi BD**. Serious collectors of vintage albums, pre or post war, however, should hotfoot it to leaders of the pack **La Bande des Six Nez** or **Le Deuxième Souffle** [→46]. Both have been on the scene for two decades. **Bédémania**, meanwhile, can't fail to please Hergé fans. It's a smallish store, but there's plenty of vintage greats – including albums and figurines.

La Bande des Six Nez
179 chaussée de Wavre, Ixelles (East) ☎ 02.513.72.58

Bédémania
169 chaussée de Waterloo, St-Gilles ☎ 02.537.96.20

Multi BD
126 boulevard Anspach, Central ☎ 02.513.01.86

Schlirf Book
752 chaussée de Waterloo, Uccle

top shops

markets

There's no better insight into the soul of Brussels and its people than a trip to the massive street market at **Marché du Midi** [→29], right next to the Eurostar terminal around place de la Constitution. Foods from North Africa and other Med hot spots are best; handfuls of fresh mint and coriander are dirt cheap, and slabs of marinated lamb are a bargain. Belgian Trappist-made cheeses like Orval and Chimay and hard goat's milk cheeses mixed with herbs are also recommended. Kick-off is early Sunday morning – dawnish – and it all winds down at midday.

Less sprawling is the Wednesday afternoon market at **place du Châtelain** [→34]. This is more geared to busy professionals – delish quiches, pittas stuffed with falafels and wickedly good tarts for easy bites. It's a cozy set-up in winter, with stalls selling mulled wine, mussels, and snails. For a local, no-frills daily affair, try **place Flagey** [→38]. In the heart of the Portuguese community, it's fab for stalls selling salt cod, cured meats and regional cheeses. Same style, but closer to downtown Brussels and with more North African influences, is the marché St-Gilles morning gathering on **parvis St-Gilles** [→29]. But save time for a trip to Brussels' daily flea market on **place du Jeu de Balle** [→25]. It's in downtown Marolles, and is a melting pot of cultures, with all sorts of junk on sale. Old books, vintage clothes, and grungy brocante are permanents. Get there at the crack of dawn along with the antiques dealers when true bargains are easy to come by.

getting your bearings

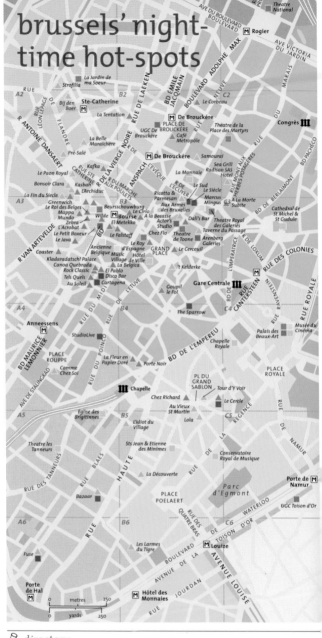

brussels' night-time hot-spots

Map labels:

A1 · B1 · Magasin · C1
AVE DU BOULEVARD
RUE DU PROGRÈS
Theatre National
BOULEVARD
ADOLPHE MAX
Rogier
AVE VICTORIA DU JARDIN
La Jardin de ma Soeur
Strofilia
Bij den Boer
Ste-Catherine
BD ÉMILE JACQMAIN
RUE NEUVE
Le Corbeau
C2
RUE DU MARAIS
De Brouckère
Théâtre de la Place des Martyrs
Congrès
La Tentation
RUE DE LAEKEN
UGC De Brouckère
PLACE DE BROUCKÈRE
Café Métropole
BD PACHECO
La Belle Maraîchère
Pré-Salé
De Brouckère
Samourai
Sea Grill
Radisson SAS Hotel
Kafka
Le Paon Royal
RUE STE CATHERINE
RUE DE LA VIERGE NOIRE
RUE DU MARCHE AUX POULETS
La Monnaie
R DE L'ÉCUYER
Le Sud
Le Siècle
Marcus Mingus
A la Morte Subite
BD DE BERLAIMONT
Bonsoir Clara
Kasbah
L'Archiduc
Ricotta & Parmesan
A la Beasse
Cathedral of St Michel & St Gudule
La Fin du Siècle
Greenwich
Le Roi des Belges
Mappa
Mundo
Zebra
Beursschouwburg
Le Cirio
Wilde
Bourse
El Metekko
Aux Armes des Bruxelles
Actor's Studio
Dali's Bar
Théâtre Royal des Galeries
Taverne du Passage
RUE DE LOKUM
RUE DES COLONIES
L'Acrobat
Le Petit Boxeur
Le Java
Chez Flo
Théâtre de Toone
Arenberg Galeries
Ancienne Belgique
Music Village
Hôtel de Ville
La Belgica
Le Roy d'Espagne
GRAND PLACE
Le Cerceuil
Coaster
Kladaradatsch! Palace
Canoa Quebrada
Rock Classic
Tels Quels
Au Soleil
El Pablo Disco Bar
Cartagena
't Kelderke
Gare Centrale
RUE CANTERSTEEN
RUE RAVENSTEIN
RUE ROYALE
Goupil le Fol
Anneessens
BD MAURICE LEMONNIER
StudioLive
The Sparrow
C4
Musée du Cinéma
Palais des Beaux-Art
PLACE ROYALE
PLACE ROUPPE
Comme Chez Soi
RUE DU POINÇON
La Fleur en Papier Doré
Porte Noir
BD DE L'EMPEREUR
Chapelle Royale
AVE DE STALINGRAD
Chapelle
PL DU GRAND SABLON
Tour d'Y Voir
Chez Richard
Le Cercle
RUE DE LA RÉGENCE
Église des Brigittines
Au Vieux St Martin
Lola
C5
RUE DE NAMUR
L'Idiot du Village
Théâtre les Tanneurs
RUE DES TANNEURS
RUE BLAES
RUE HAUTE
Sts Jean & Étienne des Minimes
Conservatoire Royal de Musique
Porte de Namur
La Découverte
Parc d'Egmont
UGC Toison d'Or
Bazaar
PLACE POELAERT
C6
Fuse
Les Larmes du Tigre
BOULEVARD DE LA
RUE DES QUATRE BRAS
DE TOISON D'OR
Louize
WATERLOO
AVENUE LOUISE
Porte de Hal
metres 250
yards 250
Hôtel des Monnaies
AVENUE DE LA JOURDAN

♪ directory

bars & cafés

A la Bécasse ♪B3 [→105]
L'Acrobat ♪A3 [→107]
A la Morte Subite ♪C3 [→105]
L'Archiduc ♪A2 [→103]
Au Soleil ♪A3 [→103]
Le Belgica ♪B3 [→106]
Beursschouwburg ♪A3 [→103]

Café Metropole ♪B2 [→105]
Canoa Quebrada ♪A3 [→107]
Cartagena ♪A3 [→107]
Le Cercle ♪B4 [→107]
Le Cerceuil ♪B3 [→104]
Le Cirio ♪B3 [→105]
Coaster ♪A3 [→106]
Le Corbeau ♪B2 [→106]
Dali's ♪B3 [→104]

El Pablo Disco Bar ♪A3 [→107]
El Metekko ♪A3 [→104]
Le Falstaff ♪A3 [→105]
La Fleur en Papier Doré ♪B4 [→104]
Goupil le Fol ♪B3 [→104]
Le Greenwich ♪A3 [→105]
Le Java ♪A3 [→103]
Kafka ♪A2 [→105]

In the map:
Ste-Catherine [→6–12]
Central [→13–19]
Le Sablon [→20–24]
Les Marolles [→25–28]
St-Gilles [→29–32]
Ixelles (West) [→33–37]
Ixelles (East) [→38–41]
Quartier Européen [→42–44]
St-Josse & Schaerbeek [→45–47]
▲ restaurants
▲ bars & cafés
■ clubs
■ cinemas
■ music venues
■ theatre
■ dance & classical music venues
Ⓜ Metro/Pre-Metro station
train station

top restaurants, bars, cafés & clubs

what's where

↓ anderlecht

Brasserie La Paix | ⊚⊚–⊚⊚⊚ [→95] ⌀

Orientalia | ⊚ [→102] ⌀

↓ central

À la Bécasse [→105] ⎕

À la Mort Subite [→105] ⎕

Au Soleil [→103] ⎕

Aux Armes de Bruxelles | ⊚⊚–⊚⊚⊚⊚
[→101] ⌀

Le Belgica [→106] ⎕

Café Métropole [→105] ⎕

Canoa Quebrada [→107] ⎕

Cartagena [→107] ⎕

Le Cerceuil [→104] ⎕

Le Cirio [→105] ⎕

Comme Chez Soi | ⊚–⊚⊚⊚⊚ [→97] ⌀

Le Corbeau [→106] ⎕

Dali's Bar [→104] ⎕

Le Falstaff [→105] ⎕

Goupil le Fol [→104] ⎕

't Kelderke | ⊚–⊚⊚⊚ [→97] ⌀

El Metekko [→103] ⎕

El Pablo Disco Bar [→107] ⎕

Ricotta & Parmesan | ⊚–⊚⊚ [→102] ⌀

Rock Classic [→106] ⎕

Le Roy d'Espagne [→105] ⎕

Samourai | ⊚⊚–⊚⊚⊚ [→101] ⌀

Sea Grill | ⊚⊚⊚ [→102] ⌀

Le Sparrow [→108] ◓

StudioLive [→109] ◓

Le Sud [→109] ◓

La Taverne du Passage | ⊚–⊚⊚⊚⊚
[→96] ⌀

Tels Quels [→107] ⎕

Wilde [→104] ⎕

↓ ixelles (east)

L'Amour Fou [→107] ⎕

L'Atelier [→106] ⎕

Canterbury | ⊚⊚–⊚⊚⊚ [→95] ⌀

Chez Marie | ⊚⊚–⊚⊚⊚ [→97] ⌀

De la Vigne à l'Assiette | ⊚⊚–⊚⊚⊚
[→96] ⌀

Dolma | ⊚–⊚⊚ [→102] ⌀

El Yasmine | ⊚–⊚⊚ [→98] ⌀

L112 | ⊚⊚ [→95] ⌀

Poussières d'Étoile | ⊚ [→101] ⌀

Les Pyramides | ⊚–⊚⊚ [→99] ⌀

L'Ultime Atome [→107] ⎕

Yamayu Santatsu | ⊚–⊚⊚⊚ [→101] ⌀

ixelles (west)

L'Amadeus | ⊚⊚–⊚⊚⊚⊚ [→95] ⌀

The Bank [→106] ⎕

Les Brasseries Georges | ⊚⊚–⊚⊚⊚⊚
[→96] ⌀

La Cantonnaise | ⊚–⊚⊚ [→102] ⌀

EAT | ⊚ [→94] ⌀

Le Fils de Jules | ⊚⊚ [→99] ⌀

La Fin de Siècle | ⊚–⊚⊚ [→99] ⌀

La Porte des Indes | ⊚⊚–⊚⊚⊚
[→100] ⌀

La Quincaillerie | ⊚⊚–⊚⊚⊚⊚ [→98] ⌀

Monkey Business [→104] ⎕

Sports Avenue [→104] ⎕

La Tsampa | ⊚–⊚⊚ [→102] ⌀

↓ les marolles

La Fleur en Papier Doré [→104] ⎕

Fuse [→108] ◓

Het Warm Water | ⊚ [→99] ⌀

L'Idiot du Village | ⊚⊚–⊚⊚⊚⊚ [→97] ⌀

Les Larmes du Tigre | ⊚⊚ [→100] ⌀

Porte Noire [→106] ⎕

↓ quartier européen

Maison d'Antoine | ⊚ [→95] ⌀

Wild Geese [→106] ⎕

↓ le sablon

Au Vieux St-Martin | ⊚–⊚⊚⊚⊚ [→96] ⌀

Le Cercle [→107] ⎕

Chez Richard [→106] ⎕

La Découverte | ⊚–⊚⊚⊚ [→99] ⌀

Lola | ⓜⓜ [→100] ♐°

Tour d'y Voir | ⓜⓜ–ⓜⓜⓜ [→98] ♐°

↓ ste-catherine

L'Acrobat [→107] ⓑ

L'Archiduc [→103] ⓑ

Beursschouwburg [→103] ⓑ

La Belle Maraichère | ⓜⓜ–ⓜⓜⓜ [→101] ♐°

Bij den Boer | ⓜⓜ–ⓜⓜⓜ [→96] ♐°

Bonsoir Clara | ⓜⓜ–ⓜⓜⓜ [→94] ♐°

Coaster [→106] ⓑ

La Fin de Siècle | ⓜ–ⓜⓜ [→99] ♐°

Le Greenwich [→105] ⓑ

Le Java [→103] ⓑ

Kafka [→104] ⓑ

Kasbah | ⓜ–ⓜⓜ [→98] ♐°

Mappa Mundo [→103] ⓑ

La Marée | ⓜⓜ [→96] ♐°

O'Reilly's [→106] ⓑ

Le Pain Quotidien | ⓜ [→99] ♐°

Le Paon Royal | ⓜ [→102] ♐°

Le Petit Boxeur | ⓜⓜ–ⓜⓜⓜ [→98] ♐°

Pré Salé | ⓜⓜ [→96] ♐°

Le Roi des Belges [→103] ⓑ

Strofilia | ⓜ–ⓜⓜⓜ [→100] ♐°

Den Teepot | ⓜ [→102] ♐°

La Tentation [→105] ⓑ

Zebra [→104] ⓑ

↓ st-gilles

La Barrière St-Gilles | ⓜ [→95] ♐°

Brasserie Verscheuren [→107] ⓑ

Chelsea | ⓜ–ⓜⓜⓜ [→94] ♐°

Le Living Room | ⓜⓜ–ⓜⓜⓜ [→94] ♐°

Moeder Lambic [→107] ⓑ

↓ st-josse & schaerbeek

La Bonne Humeur | ⓜⓜ [→96] ♐°

Chez Johnny [→108] ⓞ

L'École Buissonnière | ⓜ–ⓜⓜ [→97] ♐°

Mirano Continental [→108] ⓞ

Senza Nome | ⓜⓜ–ⓜⓜⓜ [→100] ♐°

De Ultieme Hallucinatie [→104] ⓑ

↓ uccle

Le Pain et le Vin | ⓜⓜ–ⓜⓜⓜ [→98] ♐°

Les Deux Frères | ⓜⓜ [→97] ♐°

key

ⓜ   main courses up to 400BF

ⓜⓜ   main courses between 400BF–800BF

ⓜⓜⓜ main courses over 800BF

♐°   restaurant

ⓑ   bar

ⓞ   club

belgian beer: the lowdown

With more than 400 ales and a fistful of world classics, Belgium's reputation as a beer paradise is a) well deserved and b) second to none. But not everything brewed in le plat pays is perfect – as Belgian beer has gone global, big businesses have squeezed out traditional brewers or bought up their products and bastardized them. Ones to beware of are often called 'abbey beers' – modelled on Trappist ales but all too often lacking their true qualities – and most of the once-great fruit beers. But the good news is you're still spoilt for choice. Gentlemen who prefer blondes should sample Westmalle Tripel, while those drawn to the dark side will love Chimay Bleu, Rochefort Ten, and Gauloise Brune. In between are the knife-sharp gueuzes, the hop-heavy Orval and Hommelbier, the refreshing Palm and De Koninck, and the wheaty, spicy blanches/witbiers, of which Hoegaarden is still the yardstick by which all the others are measured. A word of warning, however: darkness or lightness of colour is no indication of strength, as the cheerful-looking Duvel demonstrates (with its powerful 8.5% alcohol levels, this straw-coloured brew is double the strength of your average European lager). Finding your favourite beer in Belgium is a long, pleasurable process; but remembering the name the next morning might be more of a struggle. Against expectations, there aren't that many bars with commendable beer lists, so dedicated beer-hunters should head for Bier Circus [→17], Moeder Lambic [→107] or L'Atelier [→105] for a true brew experience.

Brussels' restaurants may not have the style of London or the culinary fame of Paris, but they sure make up for it in number and variety. Whether it's a *Belge* brasserie, a North African caff, or a modern fusion hangout, it's all good.

à table

↓ trendy

Bonsoir Clara 22–26 rue Antoine Dansaert, Ste-Catherine

This restaurant's cutting-edge interior makes it worth a visit in itself. Set smack in the middle of trendy Ste-Catherine, stylish and arty types squabble over the tightly squeezed tables, thanks to the excellent modern French and Italian cuisine. Maybe that's why the little metal tables are put together just a bit too tightly. Don't leave without trying the puff pastry filled with a spiced biscuit mousse or the oven-baked apples. It's far better than most Brussels' restaurants for vegetarians. Book ahead at weekends.

☎ 02.502.09.90 Ⓜ Bourse ◑ *12–2.30pm & 7–11.30pm Mon–Sat (to midnight Fri–Sat).* ♠ 120 ▯ ⇨✕ Ⓥ Ⓡ ⊟ AE/MC/V ⑩–⑩ ⑩

Chelsea 85 chaussée de Charleroi, St-Gilles

Supporters of its footballing namesake are probably the last people you'll encounter in this restaurant-cum-wine bar. Decorated with a curious mix of oriental carpets and minimalist modern paintings, it is capped by a smoking room (a wide range of Cuban cigars is available), where patrons are welcome to unwind after a hefty feed. The menu is French, with foie gras, beef (from Argentina) and salmon (from Scotland) featuring heavily.

☎ 02.544.19.77 🚌 92 ◑ *12–2pm & 7–11pm Mon–Sat (to midnight Fri–Sat).* ♠ 80 ♿ ▯ ▤ ⚿ Ⓡ ⊟ AE/DC/MC/V ⑩–⑩ ⑩

EAT 103 rue de L'Aqueduc, Ixelles (West)

Specializing in substantial salads, this young, funky eatery feeds the hungry lunchtime crowds. Menus written up on blackboards avoid commitment to paper, allowing daily changes to benefit from fresh produce. Classic salad combinations, like deep-fried brie and plum salad, are imaginative enough to elevate them from the bog standard. Good intentions of just a light lunch are then efficiently dispelled by a tempting array of home-made cakes and tarts, which you can also take away.

☎ 02.537.22.90 🚌 93, 94 ◑ *8am–4pm daily (from 10am Sat; to 10pm Wed).* ♠ 50 ⇨✕ Ⓥ Ⓡ ⊟ none ⑩

Le Living Room 50 chaussée de Charleroi, St-Gilles

With its fantasy baroque decor, low tables with armchairs, candelabras, seductive lighting, and blood red and purple walls, you'd be forgiven for thinking you'd just stepped into a Peter Greenaway film set. Le Living Room is worth a visit for the interior alone, but the menu is also a bit of a wow, ranging from sushi and pasta to beef carpaccio, and goat's cheese cake with crushed tomatoes. And if that's not eclectic enough, you can finish with an assorted dish of Le Living Room desserts (think tiramisu with strawberries, or home-made upside-down apple pie).

☎ 02.534.44.34 🚌 92 ◑ *7pm–midnight daily.* ♠ 140 ♿ ▯ ▤ Ⓥ Ⓡ ⊟ AE ⑩ ⑩–⑩ ⑩

L112 112 rue Lesbroussart, Ixelles (East)

A hidden jewel on the Brussels restaurant trail, and an easy one to miss if you're not in the know. This simple, small, minimal-fuss restaurant gives few clues as to the riches of its kitchen, although the backlit pictures, warm earth-toned walls, bamboo bar, and beautiful fragrant garden area do hint at an individual spirit. This charm is reflected in the cuisine, prepared by chef Bernard André. A delicate alchemy of flavours is in every dish: grilled prawns with saffron and red peppercorns, chicken with lemon and honey, or chocolate mousse with a hint of cinnamon, served with bittersweet redcurrants.

☎ 02.640.83.43 🚌 92, 93, 94 🕐 12–2.30pm & 7–10pm Mon–Sat (to 11pm Fri & Sat; closed Mon eve & Sat lunch). 👤 35 🍷 🔲 🍴 Ⓥ Ⓡ 🍽 all ⓖⓟ ⓖⓟ

↓ brasseries & bistros

L'Amadeus 13 rue Veydt, Ixelles (West)

It may be noisy, pricey, and a little yuppie, but a visit here is still a bit of an event: from the dark, candlelit conservatory (a former Rodin workshop) to the even darker 'cozies' near the kitchens. The menu is respectable brasserie fare (like goat's cheese and basil tart) without much flourish, but with a good choice of wines, and a sommelier on hand if you're really stuck. The yuppie community comes here in groups, but it's not averse to couples on a romantic night out.

☎ 02.538.34.27 Ⓜ Louise 🕐 6.30pm–1am Mon–Sun. 👤 80 🍷 🍴 Ⓥ Ⓡ 🍽 AE/DC/V ⓖⓟ ⓖⓟ–ⓖⓟ ⓖⓟ ⓖⓟ

Brasserie La Paix 49 rue Ropsy-Chaudron, Anderlecht

A Brussels institution – this family restaurant has been opposite the beautiful glass structure of the old abattoirs (now a market) since 1882. It's Belgian in every possible way, from the richly sauced meat dishes to the blown up photos of family weddings on the walls. Friendly and familiar; the maître d' may just sit down and have a chat and cigarette break at your table.

☎ 02.523.09.58 Ⓜ Clemenceau 🕐 12–3pm & 6–9pm Mon–Sat. 👤 70 🍷 🔲 🍽 AE/MC/V ⓖⓟ–ⓖⓟ ⓖⓟ

Canterbury 2 avenue de l'Hippodrome, Ixelles (East)

This constantly busy modern brasserie is popular with families, business people and locals. Everyone's welcome, even dogs – bowls of water are provided for them on the leafy terrace. Staff are friendly and efficient, food is of a high quality, and the portions are generous. Specialities include chicken *waterzooi* (a thick creamy chicken soup with vegetables and potato). Try the *fish & chips comme à Liverpool* (the likes of which you'll never taste again, even in Liverpool), or the Irish entrecôte steak with red wine-flavoured butter. There's a good selection of Belgian beers, aperitifs, and spirits, or try a glass of peach-flavoured champagne – the house favourite. It's very expensive.

☎ 02.646.83.93 🚌 71 🕐 12pm–midnight Mon–Sat. 👤75 ♿ 🔲 🍴 Ⓡ Ⓑ🄵 🍽 none ⓖⓟ ⓖⓟ–ⓖⓟ ⓖⓟ ⓖⓟ

↓ frites

La Barrière St-Gilles 3 chaussée d'Alsemberg, St-Gilles
Bruxellois always opt for the *friterie* on the Barrière.
☎ 02.538.34.48 Ⓜ Horta 🕐 12–6pm Mon–Sat. ⓖⓟ

Maison d'Antoine 1 place Jourdan, Quartier Européen
The best chips in Brussels? Expats certainly seem to think so.
☎ 02.230.54.56 🚌 80 🕐 12–6pm daily (to 4pm Sun). ⓖⓟ

Price codes [→144]

De la Vigne à l'Assiette 51 rue de la Longue Haie, Ixelles (East)

Sitting alone in a residential street, this fine little restaurant is a fave with the business crowd at lunch and those in-the-know in the evenings. Simply but carefully designed, the wooden tables are scrubbed up a treat along with pale lemon chairs to match the walls. Cloudy glass globes complete the flung-together look. The menu is small but intense, combining flavour and texture to produce memorable combinations such as lamb with Chinese five-spice. Co-owner Eddy Dandrimont is a sommelier at heart (Belgium's No. 1 in 1995) and is rightly proud of his reassuringly well-priced wine list.

☎ 02.647.68.03 93, 94 *12–2.30pm & 7–11pm Tue–Sat (to midnight Fri–Sat; closed Sat lunch).* 35–40 AE/DC/MC/V (BF)(BF)–(BF)(BF)(BF)

Taverne du Passage 30 galerie de la Reine, Central

The hint of formality in the Taverne's 1920s setting makes it a favourite with a slightly older crowd. The food is every bit as crisp and well presented as the waiters' shirts, and trad French and Belgian cooking is *de rigueur* (*waterzooi* is on the menu, as are *moules*). The service is friendly and professional, and if you can overcome the feeling of being a bit-part in an Orient Express re-run, you'll enjoy the genteel atmosphere and fine food.

☎ 02.512.37.32 Bourse *12pm–midnight daily.* 150 all (BF)–(BF)(BF)(BF)

↓ belgian & french

Au Vieux St-Martin 38 place du Grand Sablon, Le Sablon

Atypique Belgian food on a stacked plate. Local dishes like *waterzooi* (creamy fish stew) and *stoemp* (vegetable mash) come alongside better-known exports like steak, *frites*, and pâté salads. Fresh produce and cream rule in the kitchen, while in the dining room, equal numbers of pampered Belgians and tourists pig out. Cheeky calorie cards are provided and doggy bags are common. Lingering is encouraged – a rack of magazines caters for art lovers and *Playboy* readers alike. But the decor and prices are definitely not so *atypique*.

☎ 02.512.64.76 92, 93, 94 *12pm–midnight daily.* 70 MC/V (BF)–(BF)(BF)(BF)

Les Brasseries Georges 259 avenue Winston Churchill, Ixelles (West)

The red velvet curtains at its entrance set the affected tone of this Paris-style brasserie. Not surprisingly then, its clientele mainly comprises the well-heeled professionals living in Uccle, just to the south. Red meat features strongly on the menu, although shellfish, oysters, and other *fruits de mer* are also recommended. Vegetarians beware: you might have to make do with a plate of mushrooms and chips.

☎ 02.647.21.00 23, 90 *12–12.30am Sun–Thu, 12–1am Fri–Sat.* 400 all (BF)(BF)–(BF)(BF)(BF)

↓ moules

Bij den Boer 60 quai aux Briques, Ste-Catherine

Red-clothed tables in rows, panelled walls, and mussels in steaming casseroles. A classic.

☎ 02.512.61.22 Ste-Catherine; Yser *12–3pm & 6–11pm Mon–Sat.* (BF)(BF)–(BF)(BF)(BF)

La Bonne Humeur 244 chaussée de Louvain, St-Josse & Scharbeek

When you see *Spécialité de Moules* hand-painted in a window, you know you've arrived. 1960s Formica furniture – for real, not retro chic.

☎ 02.230.71.69 59 *12–2pm & 6.30–9.30pm Thu–Mon.* (BF)(BF)

La Marée 99 rue de Flandre, Ste-Catherine

Scrubbed-pine interior and fish tanks. A tad more expensive than others, but *moules* afficionados don't care.

☎ 02.511.00.40 63 *12–2.30pm & 6–11pm Tue–Sun.* (BF)(BF)

Pré Salé 20 rue de Flandre, Ste-Catherine

Tiled walls, globe lights, 1ère qualité moules-golden. An institution.

☎ 02.513.43.23 63 *12–2.30pm & 6.30–11pm Tue–Sun.* (BF)(BF)

Chez Marie 40 rue Alphonse de Witte, Ixelles (East)

The standards of stylishly good food in a small, elegant room draw in a finely blended mix of expats and locals. Dishes often seen in cookery books but rarely attempted at home, such as stuffed baby courgette flowers, are efficiently dispatched to tables. Whether it's people or food you're into watching, the mirrors over each table give great cover, avoiding having to stare openly.

☎ 02.644.30.31 🚌 71, 36 🕐 12–2.30pm Mon–Fri; 7–10.30pm Mon–Sat. 👤 42 🖥 Ⓡ BF 💳 AE/V ⑬⑬–⑬⑬⑬

Comme Chez Soi 23 place Rouppé, Central

Brussels' only three-Michelin-star restaurant revels in its reputation. Chef Pierre Wynants and his team ensure that this is one of those places everyone wants to go to, but getting a hip operation is quicker than securing a table here. Whether in the opulent Art Nouveau dining room or at the Chef's Table – just a truffle's throw from the kitchen – the French food is without blemish. If it's haute cuisine you're after, you can't get any hauter. For expense accounts, special occasions and pure hedonism, this is quite simply the best.

☎ 02.512.29.21 F 02.511.80.52 Ⓜ Anneessens 🕐 12–1.30pm & 7–9.30pm Tue–Sat. 👤 40 ♿ ✗ 🖥 Ⓡ BF 💳 all ⑬⑬–⑬⑬⑬

Les Deux Frères 2 avenue Vanderaey, Uccle

Although some distance from the centre, this expensive restaurant is frequently packed, and especially popular for corporate dinner parties. While multi-era images of the female nude cling to its walls, there's nothing seedy about it. Waiters are almost annoyingly helpful, not even allowing you to pour your own wine. Fish, fowl, and beef feature heavily, with all the dishes (like veal sautéed with calamari and olives) immaculately presented.

☎ 02.376.76.06 🚌 55 🕐 12–2.30pm Mon–Fri; 7–11pm Tue–Sat (to midnight Fri–Sat). 👤 70 ♿ ✗ 🖋 Ⓡ BF 💳 AE/DC/MC/V ⑬⑬

L'École Buissonnière 13 rue Traversière, St-Josse & Schaerbeek

This restaurant, whose name means 'playing truant', was once a youth hostel canteen. Its owner, Alain Corbion, has kept up the laid-back vibe, and prides himself on the informal food and atmosphere. Packed with local business folk looking for a quick fix, it's renowned for fast service (a record 17 minutes for the 3-course lunch). Alain gets your measure on the house wine, too, leaving a litre on the table and charging by the centimetre (even emptying the bottle works out cheap). In the evening, a young, international crowd chats across the wooden tables whilst tucking into one of 12 special salads, or a wide range of bargain fish and meat. Playing hooky was never this good.

☎ 02.217.01.65 Ⓜ Botanique 🕐 12–2.30pm & 6.30–10pm Mon–Fri. 👤 80 ✗ 🖋 Ⓥ Ⓡ BF 💳 MC/V ⑬⑬–⑬⑬

L'Idiot du Village 19 rue Notre Seigneur, Les Marolles

Fantastic food and a relaxed atmosphere lead to protracted nights of gossip and laughter in this favoured haunt of celebs. In the scarlet warmth of walls covered with flea-market paintings, relaxed staff hum along to French film soundtracks. The food, while elaborate, remains earthy. The rabbit and leek stew respects its ingredients and, bizarrely, a lightly salted meringue with ice cream and caramel sauce works blissfully.

☎ 02.502.55.82 Ⓜ Hôtel des Monnaies 🕐 12–2pm & 7.15–11pm Mon–Fri. 👤 30 ♿ Ⓥ Ⓡ 💳 AE/DC/MC/V ⑬⑬–⑬⑬⑬

't Kelderke 15 Grand' Place, Central

Long wooden benches and a vaulted ceiling give the 'little cellar' a suitably homely feel. This is unfussy home cooking with a very definite Belgian twist. Go overboard on *stoemp* (mashed potatoes and vegetables) served with black pudding or enormous sausages – and wash it all down with a cool beer. Otherwise, go even more local on the steaks or *moules*. Always busy, so book ahead or be prepared to wait.

☎ 02.513.73.44 Ⓜ Bourse; De Brouckère 🕐 12pm–2am daily. 👤 48 🚻 💳 all ⑬⑬–⑬⑬

Price codes [→144]

top restaurants

Le Pain et le Vin 812 chaussée d'Alsemberg, Uccle

The trail to suburbia ends, in summertime, with aperitifs on Le Pain et le Vin's leafy terrace. Heading inside to eat, the sparsely stylish dining room purrs with happily munching Belgians. Light courgette mousse, foie gras with a quince chutney, and classic steaks infuse the menu with creativity and breadth. The wine list spans the globe and there's something for all pockets. Savvy staff offer decent drinking advice, fuelling speculation that their friendliness stems from obligatory wine-tasting.

☎ 02.332.37.74 🚋 55 🌓 12–2.30pm & 7–10.30pm Mon–Fri; 7–10.30pm Sat. ♦ 44 🍴 Ⅴ Ⓡ BF 🗀 AE/DC/MC/V ⒽⓅ–ⒽⓅ ⒽⓅ

Le Petit Boxeur 3 rue Borgval, Ste-Catherine

It's hard to find anything to dislike about this quaint renovated restaurant near trendy place St-Géry. Innovative dishes like mushroom terrine and squid lasagne are sure to liven up palates bored with trad Belgian fare. Starters and main courses are just the right size, but beware of industrial-strength rich desserts. Warmed by candlelight and mellow jazz, it's the perfect place for a romantic meal.

☎ 02.511.40.00 Ⓜ Bourse 🌓 7.30–11pm Tue–Sat. ♦ 35 ⚊✗ Ⅴ ✎ occasionally Ⓡ 🗀 AE/V ⒽⓅ–ⒽⓅ

La Quincaillerie 45 rue du Page, Ixelles (West)

From the two tiers of balconies, smaller parties can look down on the meals of other eaters in this converted hardware shop, the refurbishment of which was overseen by Antonio Pinto. Plates of fresh seafood, huge salads, steaks and other traditional dishes are prepared masterfully without sticking to the culinary staight-and-narrow. With an oyster bar downstairs, and four dining rooms, booking is rarely necessary, but service can be impersona° – the lone diner can be forgotten on the upper balcony.

☎ 02.538.25.53 🚋 81, 82 🌓 12–2.30pm & 7.15–11pm Mon–Fri; 7.15–11pm Sat & Sun. ♦ 220 ▤ Ⅴ Ⓡ BF 🗀 AE/DC/V ⒽⓅ–ⒽⓅ

Tour d'y Voir 6 place du Grand' Sablon, Le Sablon

Stained-glass windows and cherubic paintings lend an ecclesiastic feel to this luxurious restaurant, where diners often sport the latest Gucci or Armani numbers. Staff are cordial, if a little slow. Duck, beef, pork, salmon – even walrus – are among the varied delights on the menu. No vegetarian options are listed as main courses on the menu, although meat-free dishes can be prepared on request. The wine list is superb, though pricey.

☎ 02.511.40.43 🚋 92, 93, 94 🌓 12–2pm & 7–11pm Tues–Sun (to midnight Fri–Sat). ♦ 80 ⚊✗ ▤ Ⅴ Ⓡ BF 🗀 all ⒽⓅ–ⒽⓅ

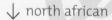

↓ north african

El Yasmine 7 rue Defacqz, Ixelles (East)

It's hard to know what to put top of the list at this Moroccan/Tunisian restaurant: good prices, tasty food, the Bedouin decor, or the friendly service. El Yasmine offers all this in a picture-postcard setting. It's tasty, it's fun (with great music) and even the plates are for sale (they'll provide clean ones). Since moving to this new location, the *tajines*, couscous, and delightfully fresh salads seem even tastier. Finish off with an invigorating mint tea.

☎ 02.647.51.81 🚋 92, 93, 94 🌓 12–2pm & 7–10pm Mon–Sat (closed Sat lunch). ♦ 50 ♿ ⚊✗ 🍴 Ⅴ Ⓡ BF 🗀 AE/MC/V ⒽⓅ–ⒽⓅ

Kasbah 20 rue Antoine Dansaert, Ste-Catherine

The Kasbah would be a dark, romantic place to mull over the fine food of North Africa (like couscous *merguez* or chicken *tajine* with lemon) if it wasn't so crowded. Being reasonably priced, and in the trendiest street in town, means that elbows have to be tucked in. There's buckets of atmosphere, thanks to the trad Moorish lighting. But it's not very authentic.

☎ 02.502.40.26 Ⓜ Bourse 🌓 12–2pm & 7–11pm daily (to 12.30am Fri & Sat). ♦ 110 ♿ ▤ Ⅴ Ⓡ 🗀 AE/MC/V ⒽⓅ–ⒽⓅ

Les Pyramides 298 chaussée d'Ixelles, Ixelles (East)

Despite the tacky images adorning its window, this is an excellent place for Egyptian and Lebanese food. Couscous and mixed grills are among the main-course specialities; but the meze is the best option. It tends to get crowded on weekend evenings, when a live belly dancer delights diners with her graceful shimmying, but service still remains efficient and friendly.

☎ 02.644.03.55 🚌 71 ◑ 6pm–midnight daily. 👥 100 ⚄ Ⓥ Ⓡ BF 🖬 MC/V ⑰–⑰⑰

↓ mediterranean

La Découverte 26 rue de L'Epée, Le Sablon

As tiny and friendly as Mum's front room; you get what you're given and don't complain at this intimate joint. Not that there'd be reason to – the set menu is pieced together from the best that markets and farms have to offer that day. Where choice is lacking, quality and imagination step in. Raspberries on tender duck, for example, are gob-smackingly good. Vegetarians are not a problem to the chefs-cum-waiters, amazingly for Brussels. Phone, ask what's on today, and reserve your table.

☎ 02.513.43.11 🚌 20, 48 ◑ 12–3pm Mon–Fri; 6–10.30pm Fri & Sat. 👥 70 ▤ Ⓥ Ⓡ BF 🖬 MC/V ⑰–⑰⑰

Le Fils de Jules 35 rue du Page, Ixelles (West)

New York hits Brussels via France and Spain in this trendy 1930s retro resto. Sporting the latest in black, the staff bring Basque influences to the tables set with knife, fork, and (often) mobile phone. Impenetrable names for dishes belie the honesty and flair in the cooking (which is big on foie gras and fish). At lunch, business folk do their deals; in the evening, a disposable-income set takes over. All ages, all professional, all-inspiring.

☎ 02.534.00.57 🚌 92, 93, 94 ◑ 12–2pm & 7–11pm Mon–Sat (to midnight Fri–Sat). 👥 60 ▱ ▤ ⌀ Ⓥ Ⓡ BF 🖬 all ⑰⑰

La Fin de Siècle 9 rue des Chartreux, Ste-Catherine

La Fin de Siècle is the place to head for if you want home-grown atmosphere in this area of high trend. In the afternoon, locals play chess; in the evenings, this rustic bistro with roughly painted walls and old wooden tables can fill to bursting point with all types. The menu is varied, offering tandoori chicken alongside *tabouli*. Belgian specialities include rabbit with cherry beer and *stoemp* (potato and vegetable mash with country sausages). No relation to the La Fin de Siècle on avenue Louise.

☎ 02.513.51.23 Ⓜ Bourse ◑ 4.30pm–3am Tue–Sun. 👥 100 ▱ ▱ Ⓡ 🖬 MC/V ⑰–⑰⑰

La Fin de Siècle 423 avenue Louise, Ixelles (West)

Baroque rules in this candlelit, red-velvet-decked townhouse. But don't let this mislead you – there's no need to get out your gold card. A young and stylish crowd gathers for fine Italian dishes (think aubergines and parmesan with a tomato coulis), topped off with exquisite *gelatos*. In summer, a tranquil garden serves as the perfect background for romantic endeavours. If you don't book ahead, you'll be shown the door, so try its sister on avenue de l'Armée.

☎ 02.648.80.41 🚌 92, 93, 94 ◑ 12–2.30pm & 7–11pm Mon–Sat (closed Sat lunch). 👥 50 ▱ ▤ ⌀ Ⓥ Ⓡ 🖬 MC/V ⑰–⑰⑰

↓ breakfast & brunch

Het Warm Water 19 rue des Renards, Les Marolles
Veggie snackery that suits the mood after a ramble through the flea market [→28].
☎ 02.513.91.59 🚌 20, 48 ◑ 10am–7pm Thu–Tue. ⑰

Le Pain Quotidien 16 rue Antoine Dansaert, Ste-Catherine
Breakfast and brunch continental-style are always on offer in the mornings at any of the city-wide branches of this café chain. The croissants and breads are divine, and the java nice and strong. There are lots of chocolate spreads to choose from.
☎ 02.502.23.61 Ⓜ Bourse ◑ 7am–7pm daily. ⑰

Price codes [→144]

top restaurants

Lola 33 place du Grand Sablon, Le Sablon

This elegant, long-roomed restaurant serves French brasserie-style cuisine with a lightness and delicacy that seems fitting for its stylish clientele. Rumour has it that this was Georgio Armani's regular lunchtime spot when he was overseeing the finishing touches of his Emporio Armani store a couple of doors down. Brasserie classics like rabbit and duck are served with a creative twist and delicate fragrant sauces. Mouth-watering salads and fish dishes, as well as some vegetarian options, are also available.

☎ 02.514.24.60 🚌 92, 93, 94 🕐 12–3pm & 6.30–11.30pm Mon–Fri (12.30–4pm & 6.30–11.30pm Sat–Sun). 🪑 60 ⚤ 🍽 🅥 🆁 🗆 AE/MC/V ⓖⓟ ⓑⓕ

Senza Nome 22 rue Royale Ste-Marie, St-Josse & Schaerbeek

Reserve a table before trekking to this cozy St-Josse restaurant – it gets very busy, especially when audiences from the nearby Halles de Schaerbeek [→117] come for a post-show feed. The menu changes regularly and depends on the freshest ingredients available (try the sautéed mushrooms for a full-on taste sensation), resulting in a wide selection of light, tangy dishes bursting with flavour (like the veal in the *tagliata di filetto*). Tomato heaven. But a non-smoker's hell.

☎ 02.223.16.17 🚌 92, 93 🕐 12–2.30pm & 7–10.30pm Mon–Fri; 7–10.30pm Sat. 🪑 42 ♿ ⚤ 🍽 🅥 🆁 🗆 MC/V ⓖⓟ–ⓖⓟⓑⓕ

Strofilia 13 rue du Marché aux Porcs, Ste-Catherine

Stefanos Svanias had already established his reputation with the Ouzerie [→41]. But not content to rest on his vine leaves, he now runs this stunner of a Greek restaurant. Built in the remnants of an old pig market, the tiled and terracotta'd front room gives way to a New York-style brick and stone floor loft at the back. The menu is heavy on meze (although there is a small selection of large main courses available), encouraging sharing among friends. And the wines are all Greek – no cheapo retsinas here, these vintages are handpicked. Efficient service and a pride in pleasing the punters make this restaurant popular with a relaxed, youngish crowd in the evenings.

☎ 02.512.32.93 Ⓜ Ste-Catherine 🕐 5pm–midnight daily. 🪑 110 🚭 ⚤ 🍽 🅥 🆁 ⓑⓕ 🗆 AE/MC/V ⓖⓟ–ⓖⓟⓑⓕ

↓ asian

Les Larmes du Tigre 21 rue Wynants, Les Marolles

Marc Beukers and sibling Muriel have established this Thai restaurant as one of Brussels' best. Walk into the classic townhouse and admire the hundreds of parasols hanging from the ceiling above the clean, white interior. It's all about sleek service and intensely authentic food, with the giant prawns in red curry sauce proving that size really does matter. The lunchtime crowd is professional with a hint of legal; in the evening, there's more of an international buzz. Perfect for hotting up those post-acquittal celebrations.

☎ 02.512.18.77 Ⓜ Louise 🕐 12–2.30pm & 7–10.30pm daily (to 11pm Fri–Sun; closed Sat lunch). 🪑 70 ⚤ 🍽 🅥 🆁 ⓑⓕ 🗆 all ⓖⓟ

La Porte des Indes 455 avenue Louise, Ixelles (West)

Run by the well-established Blue Elephant chain of Thai restaurants, La Porte des Indes equals its sister restaurants in quality (and cost). The menu boasts dishes from the former French colonies of South India, with an inclination towards seafood rather than curry. Like most of the restaurants along avenue Louise, it attracts a bourgeois clientele, with no expense spared on decorative canopies and gilded images of Hindu deities. Buffets are laid on every Thursday and Saturday evenings for the less well-banked to sample the finer side of life.

☎ 02.647.86.51 🚌 93, 94 🕐 12–2.30pm & 7–10.30pm daily (to 11.30pm Fri–Sun; closed Sun lunch). 🪑 100 🚭 ⚤ 🍽 🅥 🆁 ⓑⓕ 🗆 AE/DC/V ⓖⓟ–ⓖⓟⓑⓕ

Poussières d'Etoile 437 chaussée de Boondael, Ixelles (East)

Twinkling lanterns (normal ones as well as those made out of old oil cans) are everywhere – and it's not only the painstakingly detailed interior that puts this head and shoulders above the rest of a row of Vietnamese restaurants on this street. Lightly steamed raviolis reveal spiced tender strips of meat, and the shock of finding deep-fried coconut balls with banana ice cream is actually delicious takes a bit of getting over. There are further surprises at the cash desk – this place is really, really cheap.

☎ 02.640.71.58 🚋 93, 94 🌓 12–2.30pm & 6–11.30pm daily. 🍴 70 ▤ ✍ Ⓡ BF 🍽 none ⓖⓟ

Samourai 28 rue du Fossé aux Loups, Central

Opinion varies on whether the interior of this Japanese restaurant is Zen minimalist or just plain unimaginative. Three small rooms stacked on top of each other mean you have to tuck your elbows in. But despite its size, the restaurant is crammed with a raft of chefs who turn out the freshest sushi, tempura and sashimi, with imaginative menu combinations. An impressive French wine list at even more impressive prices should entice you to go native and stick with the saké. Tucked into a passageway, Samourai has a loyal following of local regulars.

☎ 02.217.56.39 Ⓜ De Brouckère 🌓 12–2pm & 7–9pm Wed–Mon. 🍴 60 ♿ ✍× ▤ Ⓥ Ⓡ 🍽 all ⓖⓟ–ⓖⓟ

Yamayu Santatsu 141 chaussée d'Ixelles, Ixelles (East)

There's no messing around with Chef Yu Aoki. After all, you are in one of the best sushi restaurants in Belgium. The Brussels-based Japanese community spreads its wings here: just check out the whisky bottles labelled with the company's names. Have Yo Sushi followed by a Japanese ice cream for dessert – and don't forget the saké. Book your table ahead or sit at the counter.

☎ 02.513.53.12 Ⓜ Porte de Namur 🌓 12–2pm & 7–10pm daily (closed Sun–Mon lunch). 🍴 100 Ⓡ BF 🍽 AE/MC/V ⓖⓟ–ⓖⓟ

↓ fish & seafood

Aux Armes de Bruxelles 13 rue des Bouchers, Central

In a street overflowing with fish restaurants ready and waiting for the constant flow of tourists, and many eateries overpriced for what they offer, Aux Armes de Bruxelles stands alone. With its old-world charm, high-quality service and cuisine – try baked cod served with spinach, or lobster bisque (the best in town) – it doesn't need to throw the line out. This really is one of Brussels' best fish restaurants, and the one to head for if you find yourself washed up on the shores of rue des Bouchers. Of course, *moules* are on the menu, and you can even have them with mustard sauce.

☎ 02.511.55.98 Ⓜ De Brouckère 🌓 12–11.30pm Tue–Sun. 🍴 140 ♿ ✍× ▤ ✍ Ⓡ BF 🍽 all ⓖⓟ–ⓖⓟⓟ

La Belle Maraîchère 11 place Ste-Catherine, Ste-Catherine

Slap bang in the middle of the fish district around place Ste-Catherine, this big fish restaurant is run by brothers Freddy and Eddy Devreker, both officially Master Chefs of Belgium. Still a family affair, Freddy's son now does the cooking deeds, which includes a magnificent *marmite des pêcheurs*. Unfettered by fashion, the decor doesn't seem to have changed in 30 years, nor the style of cooking, which is no bad thing. Waiters, young and old, are on hand with seamless service. Serious eating, serious punters, serious prices. A Brussels institution.

☎ 02.512.97.59 Ⓜ Ste-Catherine 🌓 12–2.30pm & 6–9.30pm Fri–Tue. 🍴 90 ♿ ✍× ▤ Ⓡ BF 🍽 all ⓖⓟ–ⓖⓟⓟ

top restaurants

Sea Grill Radisson SAS Hotel, 47 rue du Fossé aux Loups, Central

Purists balk at the idea of going to a 5-star hotel to eat, but push all principles aside just once and make this place a must-go. Sit in utter luxury among glass-etched Norwegian fjords. Then marvel at the Christoffle lobster press as it squeezes your *Homard Breton à la Presse* to a mere shadow of its former self. Fêted chef Yves Mattagne, heavily laden with medals, will even sell you his recipes and 2500 pictures on CD-Rom. Cushioned waiters, unashamed elegance, two Michelin stars (earned on the back of innovative cooking where fish is prepared to trad meat recipes), and an affordable set menu. Sounds like heaven? It is.

☎ 02.219.28.28 Ⓜ De Brouckère ◑ *12–2pm & 7–10pm daily.* ♞ 80 ♿ 🖥 ⌗ ▤ Ⓡ ʙꜰ
🗀 all ⑱–⑱⑱

↓ vegetarian

Dolma 331 chaussée d'Ixelles, Ixelles (East)

If you accept that quorn and tofu don't have to be bland, then Dolma could prove a treat. Next to a health food shop, its main attraction is a buffet where you can pile your plate with as much pasta, salad, and savoury pastries as you like, while still keeping the calorie count low. The choice of puddings is more limited, with chocolate cake and fruit salad the staple fare. Photographs of Tibet add to its Eastern feel. The only major flaw is a pianist who makes elevator music sound lively by comparison.

☎ 02.649.89.81 🚌 71, 81, 82, 366 ◑ *12–2pm & 7–9pm Mon–Sat.* ♞ 70 🖥 ✗ Ⓥ ✎ Ⓡ ʙꜰ
🗀 AE/DC/MC/V ⑱–⑱⑱

La Tsampa 109 rue de Livourne, Ixelles (West)

This is where Yin meets Yang on a plate. Chef Silva Jorge dazzles your taste buds with dishes from all over the world in a down-to-earth setting behind an organic food shop. Have the Tibetan ravioli followed by a Japanese *pot-au-feu*; or why not try the *pirojki* (vegetable and yoghurt in puff pastry)? And don't skip the puddings – the raspberry soufflé or chocolate chestnut cake are just too good to be true. Wash it all down with one of the organic wines.

☎ 02.647.03.67 🚌 93, 94 ◑ *12–2pm & 7–9.30pm Mon–Sat.* ♞ 50 ✗ 🏷 Ⓥ ʙꜰ 🗀 all
⑱–⑱⑱

↓ cheap eats & snackbars

La Cantonnaise 110 rue Tenbosch, Ixelles (West)
Fast but still special, this lunchtime favourite hums in the evening, serving quality Chinese tasties.
☎ 02.344.70.42 🚌 93, 94 ◑ *11.30am–3pm & 5–11pm Mon–Sat (closed Sat lunch).*
⑱–⑱⑱

Den Teepot 66 rue des Chartreux, Ste-Catherine
Veggie in the bean-and-lentil order of evolution. While wholesomely fibrous, tastiness isn't relinquished.
☎ 02.511.94.02 Ⓜ Ste-Catherine ◑ *12–6pm Mon–Sat.* ⑱

Orientalia 129 chaussée de Mons, Anderlecht
Some say this is the best Lebanese in Europe. Others just appreciate the range of cheap tasty dishes.
☎ 02.520.75.75 🚌 57 ◑ *9.30am–7.30pm Mon–Sat.* ⑱

Le Paon Royal 6 rue du Vieux Marché aux Grains, Ste-Catherine
Great choice of beers, some becoming ingredients in this rustic, traditional tavern that's a favourite of local notables.
☎ 02.513.08.68 🚌 34, 95, 96 ◑ *11.30am–2.30pm & 6–9.30pm Tue–Sat.* ⑱–⑱⑱

Ricotta & Parmesan 31 rue de l'Ecuyer, Central
Cheap and cheerful trattoria that makes use of of its Art Nouveau space with originality and care.
☎ 02.502.80.82 Ⓜ Centrale ◑ *12–3.30pm & 6.30pm–1am Mon–Sat.* ⑱–⑱⑱

Drinking in Brussels is one of life's pure, unadulterated joys – the variety of bars is dizzying, the opening hours elastic, the price of drinks cheap for a major city, and the beers arguably the best in the world. In fact, the only real dilemma is which watering hole to stagger to next.

holy ale

top bars & cafés

hip hangouts

L'Archiduc

Sumptuous Art Deco lounge-bar with slinky stairwell and curvaceous balcony. Try the Georges Simenon cocktail (mainly grapefruit, gin, campari) in a vibe reminiscent of his *noir* pennings. Sometimes piano players and jazz bands keep punters happy late into the night. At peak times, ring the bell to enter.

6 rue Antoine Dansaert, Ste-Catherine ☎ 02.512.06.52 Ⓜ Bourse ◐ 4pm–3/5am daily. ♿ ⌣ ⚲ Sat–Sun

Beursschouwburg

This cavernous drinking hall is downtown central for a hip Flemish crowd. It hosts concerts and DJs, with everything from drum'n' bass to tea dances playing Belgian *chansons*. Low-maintenance decor contributes to the alternative vibe. Grab a *witbier* and fight for a trestle table.

20–28 rue August Orts, Ste-Catherine ☎ 02.513.82.90 Ⓜ Bourse ◐ 7.30pm–4am Mon–Sat. ⌣ ⚲

El Metekko

In spite of its makeover, this trad bar next to the Stock Exchange still attracts chain-smoking intellectual types. Always lively, and with a fine selection of pasta dishes on offer, El Metekko is a perfect starting point for a night on the tiles.

86–88 boulevard Anspach, Central ☎ 02.512.46.48 Ⓜ De Brouckère ◐ 9–1am Mon–Fri; 10–3am Sat–Sun (from 11am Sun). ⚲ ⌣ ◑

Le Java

A snaking mosaic-encrusted bar takes up over half the space in this tiny café, making contact between trendy expats and local artistes that much easier. Famed for its cocktails (all the usual suspects), the Java has a small Brazilian restaurant upstairs.

31 rue St Géry, Ste-Catherine ☎ 02.512.37.16 Ⓜ Bourse ◐ 8am–3am Mon–Sat. ♿ ⚲ ⌣ ⚲ ⚲ ◯ Fri–Sat

Mappa Mundo

With music ranging from raï to rap, food spanning bagels to bolognese, and young hipsters hailing from all four corners of the globe, Mappa is the most international of the place St-Géry bars. It is also the most laid-back – people come here to enjoy themselves, not to pose.

2 rue du Pont de la Carpe, Ste-Catherine ☎ 02.514.35.55 Ⓜ Bourse ◐ 11–2am daily (to 3am Fri–Sat). ⚲ ⌣ ⚲

Le Roi des Belges

With Zebra and Mappa Mundo on either side, it was only a matter of time before the brushed steel and cherry wood fittings in this former Indian store became a bar. Downstairs is warm and smoky, while the 1970s-style salon upstairs is very Austin Powers.

35 rue Jules van Praet, Ste-Catherine ☎ 02.503.43.00 Ⓜ Bourse ◐ 12pm–2am daily (to 3am Fri–Sat). ⚲ ⌣ ⚲ ⚲ ◯ Fri–Sat

Au Soleil

During the day, this former clothes store is a quiet place to sample local brews and read the paper. But at night a mixed crowd of barflies and artsy locals spills out onto the bar's sprawling terrace on one of the city's liveliest streets.

86 rue du Marché au Charbon, Central ☎ 02.513.34.30 Ⓜ Bourse ◐ 10–1am daily (to 2am Fri–Sat; from 11am Sun). ♿ ⚲ ⚲

De Ultieme Hallucinatie

Stepping into 'The Ultimate Hall-ucination' from this drab street is like entering a dreamworld. The unassuming entrance hides one of the finest examples of Art Nouveau in Brussels, with rich wood furni-ture and pale green ironwork. First-rate grub is served in the bar, and there's a swanky restaurant too.

316 rue Royale, St-Josse & Schaerbeek
☎ 02.217.06.14 🚌 92, 93, 94 ◑ 11am–2am Mon–Sat (from 4pm Sat). ☜ ◢ ✇

Wilde

Although this spanking new lounge- bar is owned by an Irish-man and serves a mean Kilkenny, there are no false nicotine-stained ceilings in this studiously cool hangout. The decor may be 1950s retro, but the tunes spun by the resident DJs are definitely up-to-the-minute.

79 boulevard Anspach, Central
☎ 02.514.30.69? Ⓜ Bourse ◑11am–2am daily. ◢ ◐ daily ◗

Zebra

With its cool metallic fittings and sprawling terrace, the Zebra helped turn place St-Géry from a sleepy backwater into Brussels' most hip and happening place to go out. Six years on, it's still the place to be seen downtown, as anyone who has ever tried to find a table here will vouch.

33 place St Géry, Ste-Catherine
☎ 02.511.09.01 Ⓜ Bourse ◑ 12pm–2am daily (to 3am Fri–Sat). ☜ ◢ ✇

weird & wild

Le Cerceuil

With coffins serving as tables, the beer served in skull-shaped mugs and skeletons hanging from the ceiling, this dark and dingy bar is something of a goths'

paradise. Wear black and make sure your wallet's full, as the pricey beers are enough to make Count Dracula turn in his grave.

10–12 rue des Harengs, Central
☎ 02.512.30.77 Ⓜ Bourse ◑ 11–2am daily (to 4am Fri–Sat). ☜/

Dali's Bar

With its easel-shaped settees, melted clocks, and brightly coloured walls, Dali's pays homage to the Spanish Surrealist painter. Downstairs there's a dance floor and chill-out room, with regular live jungle, trip-hop, and acid jazz sessions.

35 Petite rue des Bouchers, Central
☎ 02.511.54.67 Ⓜ Bourse; De Brouckère ◑ 10am–4pm Mon–Fri; 9am–dawn week-ends. ◢ ✎ ◐ nightly

La Fleur en Papier Doré

'Every man has the right to 24 hours of freedom a day,' a Dadaist poet wrote above the entrance to this thesps' hangout. Regulars Magritte and Delvaux certainly thought so (check out their doodlings on the walls). These days there are more tourists than artists, but there's still a surreal feel to the place.

53 rue des Alexiens, Les Marolles ☎ 02.511.16.59 Ⓜ Anneessens ◑ 11–1am daily (to 3am Fri–Sat). ☜ ◢ ✇ ✎ sometimes

Goupil le Fol

Chances are that Piaf or Brel will be crooning on the jukebox when you enter this former brothel, a boho bar with deep, battered sofas and junk shop bric-a-brac. There'll also probably be an intellectual reading Rimbaud, and a group of bemused Japanese tourists sipping the café's famed fruit wine. Unmissable.

22 rue de la Violette, Central
☎ 02.511.13.96 Ⓜ Bourse ◑ 7.30pm–dawn daily. ♿ ◢

sports bars

Monkey Business 30 rue Defacqz, Ixelles (East)
A good-time beer bar popular with Americans and young Brits. Shows major sporting events and serves damn fine Tex-Mex food.

☎ 02.538.69.34 🚌 92, 93, 94 ◑ 12–3pm & 6pm–3.30am Mon–Sat; 11am–late Sun. ♿ ☜ ◢ ▤ ✇ ✎ Thu ◗

Sports Avenue 4–5 avenue de la Toison d'Or, Ixelles (West)
High-tech sports bar with basketball memorabilia and a gigantic screen.

☎ 02.500.78.38 Ⓜ Porte de Namur; Louise ◑ 10am–1am daily. ♿ ☜ ◢ ▤ ✇ ◗

top bars & cafés

Kafka

Quirky downtown bar filled with Kafka memorabilia and Flemish intellectuals. A stone's throw from the UGC De Brouckère cinema, it's just the place to discuss the night's movie over a Trappist ale or one of the bar's impressive array of Russian vodkas. Franz would have loved it.

6 rue de la Vierge Noire, Ste-Catherine ☎ 02.513.54.89 Ⓜ De Brouckère ◑ 4pm–3am daily (to later Fri–Sat). ♿ ◢ 🎱 ✎ Sun

La Tentation

Don't be surprised to see bagpipers or whirling Celtic dancers here, as this gloriously restored red-brick building is home to the city's large Galician diaspora. Entrance fees are charged when bands are on.

28 rue de Laeken, Ste-Catherine ☎ 02.223.22.75 Ⓜ De Brouckère ◑ 10.30am–late Mon–Sat (from 6.30pm Sat). 🎱 ◢ ✎ Wed & Fri

trad bars

À la Bécasse

Down a narrow alley lies a bar which doesn't seem to have changed since Brueghel's days. The waiters look like monks, the food is served on wooden platters, and the local Lambic beers come in ceramic jugs. Very medieval.

11 rue de Tabora, Central ☎ 02.511.00.06 Ⓜ Bourse ◑ 11am–1am daily (to 2am Fri–Sat; to midnight Sun). ♿ 🎱 ◢ 🖥

À la Mort Subite

Mort subite means 'sudden death', and if you drink enough of this legendary bar's fruit beers, such a fate might befall you. Smoke-stained ceilings and surly waitresses add to this institution's charm.

7 rue des Montagnes aux Herbes Potagères, Central ☎ 02.513.13.18 Ⓜ De Brouckère ◑ 10.30–1am daily (from 12.30pm Sun). ♿ 🎱 ◢

Café Métropole

Treat yourself to a drink in the city's most sumptuous hotel café. It's all about aesthetics: plush upholstery, antique furniture, and a *fin de siècle* ceiling with huge chandelier. Beers are available, along with an impressive range of whiskies and cognacs.

31 place de Brouckère, Central ☎ 02.219.23.84 Ⓜ De Brouckère ◑ 9am–1am daily (to 2am Sat & Sun). ♿ 🎱 ◢ 🎱

Le Cirio

Coiffured old ladies and their well-trimmed dogs come here to drink strong Trappist ales and *half en half* – a champagne/ white wine mix. A beautiful oasis of calm in one of the city's most bustling areas.

18 rue de la Bourse, Central ☎ 02.512.13.95 Ⓜ Bourse ◑ 10am–11pm daily. ♿ 🎱 ◢ 🎱

Le Falstaff

A beautifully ornate Art Nouveau café, Le Falstaff is a great place to soak up the atmosphere of turn-of-the-century Brussels. Liveried waiters glide between potted palms, while silver-haired ladies tuck into classic Belgian fodder. The attached Monte Christo bar has regular latin DJs.

17–21 rue Henri Maus, Central ☎ 02.511.87.89 Ⓜ Bourse ◑ 9–1am daily (to 3am Fri–Sat). 🎱 ◢ 🖥 🎱

Le Greenwich

Unfazed by the yuppification taking place around it, Le Greenwich remains the same as when Magritte tried to hawk his paintings here in the 1920s. The only sound you're likely to hear in this graceful mirrored establishment is that of chess players' slapping their stop-clocks.

7 rue des Chartreux, Ste-Catherine ☎ 02.511.41.67 Ⓜ Bourse ◑ 10.30–1am Mon–Sat (to 2am Fri–Sat). ♿ 🎱 ◢ 🎱

Le Roy d'Espagne

Karl Marx and Engels are said to have supped a few here while taking breaks from penning the Communist Manifesto. The only revolutionary thing about it these days is the stuffed horse. With a roaring fire in winter, and sunny terrace in summer, it's the best place to watch the comings and goings on the Grand' Place.

1 Grand' Place, Central ☎ 02.513.08.07 Ⓜ De Brouckère ◑ 10–1am daily. 🎱 ◢ 🎱

drinking dens

L'Atelier

Legendary student hangout (it's next to the University, ULB), with over 200 types of beer, loud music and even louder chit-chat. Sometimes there's live music on; but if not, there are always animated discussions of life and love to get involved in, or games of pinball and table football to watch.

77 rue Elise, Ixelles (East) ☎ 02.649.19.53 🚋 93.94 🚌 74 ◑ 6pm–8am daily.

The Bank 79 rue du Bailli, Ixelles (West)
Tastefully decorated uptown joint catering to an expat crowd.
☎ 02.537.52.65 🚊 93, 94 ◐ 11–1am daily (to 2am Fri–Sun). ♿ ☕ 🍴 📖 🗇 ⚲ ☟

O'Reilly's 1 place de la Bourse, Central
Cavernous and often raucous pub. Excellent country cooking.
☎ 02.552.04.80 Ⓜ Bourse ◐ 11–2am daily (to 4am Fri–Sat). ☕ 🍴 📖 🗇 ☟

Wild Geese 2–4 avenue Livingstone, Quartier Européen
This ever-popular watering hole brings some much-needed *craic* to an otherwise soulless office area. Popular with wannabe Eurocrats on the pull.
☎ 02.230.19.90 Ⓜ Maelbeek ◐ 7–8am & 10.30–1am daily (to 3am Fri–Sat).
♿ ☕ 📖 🗇 🗇 ☟

Chez Richard

A bite-size slice of madness on an
otherwise sedate square, Chez
Richard is something of an institution for thirtysomething party-goers
who still dance on tables and sing
along to soppy ballads and rock
classics until the wee small hours
of the morning. *Très* French indeed.

2 rue des Minimes, Le Sablon
☎ 02.512.14.06 Ⓜ Centrale ◐ 7–3/4am
daily. ☕ 🍴 📖 ⚲ ☟

Coaster

The centrepiece of this small but
perfectly formed bar is a giant
operating-theatre lamp – and after
a boozy night in this barfly's hangout, it might come in handy. Your
stamina (and liver) is put to the test
by the regulars. Fun-loving DJs and
a local crowd who like to party till
dawn (it's been known to stay open
until gone 8am) make this buzzing
bar one of Brussels' best-kept secrets.

28 rue des Riches Claires, Ste-Catherine
☎ 02.512.08.47 Ⓜ Bourse ◐ 8–11pm daily.
📖 ◓ Fri–Sat

Le Corbeau

If you're after a quiet drink, it's best
to avoid this boozers' paradise. The
music is ear-splitting, the customers
young and rowdy, and the beer
comes in a *chevalier*, a half-metre
glass that make taking a sip challenging. If you've never danced on a
table to Bonnie Tyler before, this may
be the place to make your debut.

18–20 rue St Michel, Central ☎ 02.219.
52.46 Ⓜ De Brouckère ◐ 9.30am– midnight daily. ♿ ☕ 🍴 ⚲ ◓ Fri–Sat

Porte Noire

For a crash course in Belgian beers,
let the barman of this smoky, dimly
lit bar be your guide. With a dozen
local brews on tap and over 120 in

the fridge, your only headache (until
the next morning, of course) will be
deciding which one to sample first.

67 rue des Alexiens, Les Marolles
☎ 02.511.78.37 Ⓜ Anneessens ◐ 11.30–
2.30pm Mon–Thu; 11.30am–late Fri–Sat
(from 4pm Sat). ☕ 🍴

Rock Classic

Though this good-time bar blasts
out hard-core music, the atmosphere inside is much gentler.
A huge portrait of David Bowie,
guards the entrance to the black-
and-white tiled toilets and most of
the customers seem more interest-
ed in playing pinball, table football,
or chess than playing air guitar to
AC/DC. Not as tough as it thinks it is.

55 rue Marché aux Charbons, Central
☎ 02.512.15.42 Ⓜ Bourse ◐ hours vary,
ring for details. ♿

gay thirst

Le Belgica

Situated opposite Brussels' central
police station, this loud and
proud gay bar has always raised
a metaphorical finger at authority
and continues to do so. Its selection
of fruit-flavoured *jenevers* (gin) is
unrivalled in Brussels.

rue Marché aux Charbon, Central
☎ no phone Ⓜ Bourse ◐ 10pm–3am
Thu–Sun. 🍴 ◓ occasionally

Tels Quels

There's a relaxed feel to this hub of
Brussels' lively gay and lesbian scene.
People drift in and out for a beer and
a chat, a game of pinball, or simply
to find out what's going on else-
where from the bar's noticeboard.

81 rue du Marché au Charbon, Central
☎ 02.512.32.34 Ⓜ Bourse ◐ 5pm–2am
daily (from 2pm Wed & Sat; to 4am
Fri–Sat). ☕ 🍴 ◓ daily

neighbourhood caffs

L'Amour Fou

Although the decor of this uptown bar has changed more times than its menu, the clientele of students and young professionals has remained faithful. And with its cheap and cheerful grub, backroom lounge-bar and internet access, you can see why.

185 chaussée d'Ixelles, Ixelles (East) ☎ 02.514.27.09 Ⓜ Porte de Namur ◗ 9–1am daily (to 2am Fri–Sat; from 10am Sun). ♨ ⌑

Brasserie Verschueren

There's always a lively scene in this unpretentious neighbourhood café. It may be due to the bar's graceful Art Deco curves or the cheery music, but it's more likely because of the locals who return night after night to do what *les Bruxellois* do best – chill out over a cool beer.

11–13 parvis St-Gilles, St-Gilles ☎ 02.539.40.68 Ⓜ Porte de Hal ◗ 8–1am daily (to 2am Fri–Sat). ♿ ♨ ⌑ ♨

Moeder Lambic

Although the neighbourhood has seen better days, and the decor inside is tatty, this tiny bar probably has more beers on offer – between 800 and 1000 – than any other in town. So pluck a comic from the shelves, order a platter of Belgian cheese and get to work.

68 rue de Savoie, St-Gilles ☎ 02.539.14.19 Ⓜ Albert ◗ 4pm–4am daily. ♿ ♨ ⌑ ♨

L'Ultime Atome

In the heart of Brussels' lively African neighbourhood, L'Ultime Atome draws a mixed crowd of local students and expat yuppies. Some come to people watch, others to tuck into value-for-money grub, all to soak up the café's easy-going vibes.

14 rue St Boniface, Ixelles (East) ☎ 02.511.13.67 Ⓜ Porte de Namur ◗ 9am–midnight/1am daily. ♿ ♨ ⌑

club/bars

L'Acrobat

This self-styled speakeasy plays everything from bossa nova to vintage Michael Jackson. The interior is multicultural kitsch: Indian murals, twinkly lights, and papier mâché squid. Dress to sweat when the dance floor in the back is open (Fri–Sat); it's as well-ventilated as a Turkish steambath.

14 rue Borgval, Ste-Catherine ☎ 02.513.73.08 Ⓜ Bourse ◗ 8–3am Mon–Thu; 11–6am Fri–Sat. ♿ ⌑ ♨ ⚒ Thu ◉ Fri–Sat

Canoa Quebrada

Latinos, Africans and pasty-faced north Europeans all throng to this Brazilian bar to dance samba and down the meanest (and maybe the priciest) *caipirinhas* this side of Rio.

53 Rue du Marché au Charbon, Central ☎ 02.511.13.54 Ⓜ Bourse ◗ 9.30pm–5am Tue–Sun ♿ ⌑ 目 ◉ Fri–Sat

Cartagena

If you know how to dance salsa and merengue, this tiny Columbian joint is the best place to practice. If you don't, sit at the bar with a *mojito* in your hand and feast your eyes.

70 rue du Marché au Charbon, Central ☎ 02.502.59.08 Ⓜ Bourse ◗ 11pm–4/5am Fri–Sat 目 ◉ Fri–Sat ◖

Le Cercle

There's something for everyone in this Sablon bar. Sounds of salsa and the Congo keep the dance floor full at weekends. Other nights run the gamut from world music to jazz, with Sunday afternoons dedicated to Café Philo, excursions into Sartre, Nietzsche, and other deep thinkers.

20–22 rue Ste-Anne, Le Sablon ☎ 02.514.03.53 Ⓜ Gare Centrale 🚌 92, 93, 94 ◗ Bar: 10.30am–late Thu–Sun (from 7.30pm Fri; from 6.30pm Sun); Club: 7.30pm–late Mon–Wed & 10.30pm–late Fri–Sat (closed late Jul–early Aug). 目 ⚒ ◉ daily ◖

El Pablo Disco Bar

Major DJs spin a mix of house, ambient and garage at this hyper-trendy bar, but you won't see much dancing. Punters are too busy tucking into shakes, cocktails and 60 kinds of vodka. A lot of Red Bull is drunk as Brussels' beautiful young things liven themselves up for a dance.

60 rue du Marché au Charbon, Central ☎ 02.514.51.49 Ⓜ Bourse ◗ 10pm–3am Tue–Sat. ♿ ⌑ ⚒ occasionally ◉ nightly ◖

The Brussels-Antwerp clubbing scene is international in flavour. The children of Europe meet on the dancefloor, with casual as the dress code and relaxed as the mood; there's no point in breaking out your Gucci here – unless you want to feel over-dressed, that is. Whether you're up for hip-hop, drum 'n' bass, deep house or sassy salsa, the vibe is always *très* laid back.

c'est la fête

↓ top venues

brussels

Chez Johnny

The Belgian answer to an Essex boy (or Guido), a Johnny wears his gold jewellery with pride, loves his car and leaves a whiff of Brut trailing after him wherever he goes. This club is his home. Sort of a joke, actually, as the club is long on kitsch appeal: loads of Abba and French pop music from all decades, with the legendary Claude François – the francophone Cliff Richard – being a real favourite. Carnavalesque decor and a very packed house, it handles the not-so-chic overflow from the Mirano next door well.

24 chaussée de Louvain, St-Josse & Schaerbeek ☎ 02.227.39.99 Ⓜ Madou ⒝⒡ 200BF ◑ 11pm–5am Fri–Sat. ⍭ casual ❑

Fuse

Kevin Saunderson, Stacey Pullen, and Dave Clarke are just some of the big-name DJs who've put the needle on the record at Brussels' temple of techno. Paris's famed Respect is Burning party series often takes up residence, as do other party nights, like Fuse (every Saturday) and La Démence. People come from all over Europe for the no-nonsense, hard-edge trance/techno. No prizes for the interior, but the punters don't seem to mind.

208 rue Blaes, Les Marolles ☎ 02.511.97.89 Ⓦ www.fuse.be Ⓜ Porte de Hal ⒝⒡ 100BF–600BF ◑ 10pm–7 or 7.30am Tue–Sun. ⋔ ⍭ casual, hip ❑

Mirano Continental

This is the disco that just won't die. Mirano is Brussels' answer to Stringfellows and Studio 54. This former cinema is the club of choice for the city's BCBG – *bon chic bon genre*; in other words, the Ralph Lauren set. It's very Francophone – and all very glam in a *Hello!* magazine kind of way. The music is radio-friendly house, with excursions into funk and garage. The revolving dance floor makes staying sober a very good idea.

38 chaussée de Louvain, St-Josse & Schaerbeek ☎ 02.227.39.70 Ⓜ Madou ⒝⒡ 250BF ◑ 11pm–7.30am Sat. ⋔ ⍭ smart: dress to impress ❑

Le Sparrow

The Sparrow rose from the ashes of the former tourist-trap disco, Le Garage. It's now just about the funkiest dance club in Brussels. The soundtrack consists of the very best hip-hop flavoured soul and R'n'B, mixed with the sounds of Africa. Bring your own partner – this is mostly a couples crowd. The Sparrow's only drawback: the larcenous drinks prices can leave you high and dry.
♧ Salsa takes over Sunday nights.

18 rue Duquesnoy, Central ☎ 02.512.66.22 Ⓜ Centrale ⒝⒡ 200BF–350BF ◑ 11pm–late Wed–Sun. ⍭ casual to smart ❑

Studio Live

This is the new incarnation of the much-lamented former Who's Who's Land. Fierce, groovy house, two-step and other beats bring in the throngs. The decor is recording-studio-meets-Alice-in-Wonderland: huge keyboards and giant mikes provide the backdrop. Less techno than Fuse, bigger beats than Mirano. A winner – if it survives for long enough.

17 rue du Poinçon, Central
☎ 02.512.52.70 Ⓜ Anneessens
🅱🇫 300BF+ ◑ 11pm–4am Sat.
👬 ☜ hip-hop to club gear ❑

Le Sud

Walk Like an Egyptian, anyone? A truly guilty pleasure, this joint serves up sounds of the 1980s for a young crowd who were probably only just teething back then. It's a dingy club, with ramshackle bric-a-brac, musty old sofas, and candle-lights that serve at least to make you look better – no matter how wasted you are. The doormen are some of the dimmest you'll find in Brussels and look like they've a dodgy tale or two to tell.

45 rue de l'Écuyer, Central
Ⓜ De Brouckère
🅱🇫 100BF ◑ 11pm–late Fri–Sat.
☜ as you wish ❑

antwerpen

Café d'Anvers

Smack bang in the middle of Antwerp's red light district, Café d'Anvers used to be a church ministering to the working girls in the area. Bits of the gothic atmos-phere remain intact, but today it serves up chunky house, garage and other club grooves. The crowd is more H&M than VIP, from teens to thirties, and all the better for it. A huge space with cozy corners, low lighting and a second level for getting intimate if you want to.

15 Verversrui ☎ 03.226.38.70
w www.café-d-anvers.be
🚌 from Centraal Station
🅱🇫 free–300BF ◑ 11pm–7.30am Fri–Sat (closes earlier some Friday nights).
👬 ☜ casual/cool ❑

practical information

A few rules for clubbing in Belgium: if you can't speak French or Flemish, use an American accent – America trumps Britain in coolness due to distance – and doormen think Yanks have more money.

◑ Clubs open around 11pm but only hard-up students arrive before midnight – when entrance is usually free. Things hot up around 1am, so pace yourself.

🅱🇫 Tip the doorman on your way out – 50BF is usually the minimum, but the soft hush of a 100BF note paves the way for easy access next time. Bigger clubs take credit cards, but only at the bar.

☜ Generally casual so avoid being over-dressed. Babes have no problem getting in. Guys should avoid arriving in large groups.

❶ To find out about the newest clubs and what's going on, pick up a copy of *Out Soon* at music shops, or check out w www.noctis.com (in English) for up-to-date listings, and w www.café-cool.be (in French and Flemish).

Red & Blue

From muscle boys to hairdressers to common or garden variety gay, Red & Blue handles 'em all on Saturdays. Formerly a supper club, spacious R'n'B kept the faux deco interior of its previous incarnation, with tables and chairs surrounding the dance floor – so you can chill out without being too far from the action. The music ranges from dodgy house to just-shy-of-kitsch disco. But the tunes ain't the drawing card here: it's the mating dance. Up goes the sleaze factor the first Saturday of every month for R'n'B's Club Flesh night.

11–13 Lange Schipperskappelstraat
☎ 03.213.05.55 w www.redandblue.be
🚌 from Centraal Station
🅱🇫 250BF–400BF ◑ 11pm–7.30am Sat.
👬 gay ☜ trashy to classy ❑

Zillion

Four dance floors belching dry ice, four different flavours of house to mess with your mind, and too damned much to deal with just on nature's intended chemicals. Antwerp's mega-club brings in the faux Versace and platform-trainer crowd – although trainers are sup-posedly a no-no at the door. A dance-club monstrosity, Zillion is best enjoyed if you bring your own posse.

4 Jan van Gentstraat
☎ 03.248.15.16 w www.zillion.be
🚌 from Centraal Station
🅱🇫 300BF Thu–Fri; 400BF Sat
◑ 10pm–late Thu–Sat. ☙
👬 ☜ designer knock-offs ❑

↓ best nights

top clubs

brussels

Mad Club @ Fuse

A monthly extravaganza courtesy of DJ Rudy and Brussels' own Cecil B Demille. Beach parties, carnivals, Christmas in July: Rudy & Co push these themes and more to the limit to the sound of commercial house and kitsch disco. It's handbag heaven.

208 rue Blaes, Les Marolles ☎ 02.511.97.89 **w** www.fuse.be 🅼 Porte de Hal
💷 200BF–600BF ◐ 10pm–7.30am Fridays (not every Friday). 🕺🏻 👕 casual, hip ☐

Different @ Sonik

The real deal at Sonik is at Different, a monthly event where gays and lesbians mix it up to vintage disco, soul, and house. The gender blend cancels out the pick-up vibe rampant in boys-only/girls-only clubs. Lousy ventilation keeps you knocking back the drinks – it makes a sauna seem airy.

112 rue du Marché au Charbon, Central 🅼 Anneessens 💷 250BF ◐ 11pm–late 1st Sat of each month. 🕺🏻 gay 👕 casual ☐

Le Cabaret @ Le Siècle

A rarity: a girl-friendly gay night in Belgium (though a gay posse escort is a must). Happening at the otherwise suspect Le Siècle club (yuppie central), weekly Le Cabaret plays diva-powered house with large doses of Gloria Gaynor and Donna Summer. If it's in a drag queen's repertoire, you'll hear it here. Deliciously rank.

41 rue de l'Écuyer, Central ☎ 02.513.08.10 🅼 De Brouckère 💷 200BF ◐ 11pm–5am Sun. 🕺🏻 gay 👕 tight T-shirt & jeans ☐

La Démence @ Fuse

Bus-loads of boys from Amsterdam and Paris flock to Belgium's hottest gay party, held every few Sundays and the night before any major public holiday. Bypass the ground floor's sad techno-house. The real deal is upstairs, with slamming deep garage and stellar house. An amusing side-trip is the lounge outside the darkroom, with all the ambience of a doctor's waiting room.

208 rue Blaes, Les Marolles ☎ 02.511.97.89 **w** www.fuse.be 🅼 Porte de Hal
💷 200BF–600BF ◐ 10pm–7.30am Sundays (not every Sunday). 🕺🏻 gay 👕 fashion victim to muscle stud ☐

antwerpen

Fill Collins Club @ Red & Blue

The name's a joke: Mr Collins of Genesis fame features nowhere on the playlist. Instead, Antwerp's only weekly club night blends funk, raggae, house, garage and almost every other dance flavour for every stripe of club kid. The night recently changed promoters, so the jury's still out on whether the same funky, fierce vibe can be maintained.

11–13 Lange Schipperskappelstraat ☎ 03.213.05.55 **w** www.redandblue.be
🚌 from Centraal Station 💷 250BF–400BF ◐ 11pm–7.30am Sat.
🕺🏻 gay 👕 jeans & polo shirt ☐

clubbing events

Moveable feasts (both location and date-wise) are the norm in the Belgian club scene. Promoters can choose the hottest venues, attract better DJs and provide an enviable variety of events. **Cirque d'Anvers** *(**w** www.café-cool.be) happens twice a year at different locations, but always under the big top: Belgium's best local talent (the likes of Fill Collins' Jan Van Biesen and Café d'Anvers' Sven Van Hees) and international DJs (such as Kevin Saunderson and Monika Krüse) spin house, techno and soul tunes. The circus theme (balloons and jugglers) and 5000 ravers can get on your nerves after a bit; but the music is stellar.* **Kozzmozz** *(**w** www.kozzmozz.com), meanwhile, is a monthly travelling rave from Ghent that sets up in empty factories and old concert halls. It's not big on name-brand talent, but offers good grooves for your money.*

The two biggest techno events of the year are **Ten Days Off** *(**w** www.dma.be/p/5voor12/) and* **I Love Techno** *(**w** www.i-love-techno.org). The former is a summer bash coinciding with Ghent's Gentsefeest, whilst I Love Techno is every November. Since they started six years ago, every DJ worth his slipmat has played one or the other. Last year Joey Negro, Derrick May, Carl Cox, and Dave Clarke entertained the masses: clubheads from all over Europe who came to sample the beats. The only drawback is that acts play on different stages at the same time – you're spoilt for choice.*

Whether you're after clubbing, cinema, dance or cutting-edge sounds, Brussels can supply the goods.

that's entertainment
↓ the inside track

media

tv & radio

An average 30 channels are available on cable, including **Euronews**, **Eurosport**, **BBC1**, **BBC2** and **CNN**. There are two public Flemish channels: **VRT** for light entertainment, and the more upmarket **Ketnet/Canvas** for documentaries and cultural programming. Of the three private Flemish stations, **VTM** is the most commercial; **Kanaal 2** has cartoons and movies; and **VT4** screens mediocre US comedy and movies, as well as soft porn. Both the French public stations, **RTBF1** (La Une) and **RTBF2** (La Deux), show news, documentaries and films, but La Deux is more highbrow. **RTL-TVi**, a Luxembourg-based station, outputs American made-for-TV films and soaps. Meanwhile, **Club RTL** screens cartoons, game shows, and international movies (usually dubbed), and **Télé-Bruxelles** (French)/ **TV Brussel** (Flemish), the twin public-access stations cover local community news and events.

Smaller indie broadcasters compete for the airwaves against public-funded radio stations. The hip **Studio Brussel** (100.6 FM) has an eclectic mix of jazz, acid, African, hip-hop and rock. Real rock fans should check out the French-language **Radio 21** (93.2 FM). Of the three public Flemish stations, **VRT1** (91.7FM) offers political debates, **VRT2** (93.7 FM) middle of the road chart hits, and **VRT3** (89.5 FM) highbrow classical music. On the French side, **RTBF Musique 3** (91.2 FM) plays popular classical numbers and **La Première** (91.5 FM) is a talk station worth tuning into for political debates. Exercise your language skills with **BFM** (107.6 FM), the all-talk French-language station, and the city's news station, **Bruxelles Capitale** (99.3 FM). Neither **Bel RTL** (104 FM) nor **Radio Contact** (102.2 FM) offer anything extraordinary.

the papers

Brussels' newsstands reflect the cultural diversity of the city in the plethora of foreign dailies on offer from *El País* to *Die Welt*. *Le Soir*, the top-selling French-language broadsheet is a more liberal read than its competitor *La Libre Belgique*, once the most influential Catholic daily. For popular Flemish quality reads, check out *De Morgen*, which used to be funded by the Socialist party and has a reputation for political scoops. *De Standaard*, Flanders' biggest-selling broadsheet, is right of centre and has good political and foreign news. Colourful tabloid reads include the French language *La Dernière Heure*, low in eye-candy but high in sports coverage. The sensationalist *Het Laatste Nieuws* is the highest-selling tabloid in Flanders, although *Het Nieuwsblad* has better sports coverage. Top financial reads are the French-language *L'Écho* and the Flemish *De Financieel Economische Tijd*. For an insider's view on EU politics, the English-language weekly, *European Voice*, is best.

listings mags

A must is the English-language expat weekly *The Bulletin*. Its insert, *What's On*, has extensive listings of happenings in Brussels and beyond. The satirical Flemish *Humo* beats any other TV/radio listings mag for its current affairs and cultural coverage (both are out Thursdays). *Télé-moustique* is a French-language TV mag which carries *Mosquito*, a free weekly ents agenda (out Wednesdays). *Kiosque* is the most comprehensive French-language entertainment guide. *The Ticket*, a free music agenda, in French or Flemish, lists events nationwide, as well as club info. French-language *Mofo* features concert dates, band interviews and album reviews. Both are monthly and available in most music stores. One of the best listings is *Mad*, the entertainment and cultural supplement of *Le Soir* (Wednesdays).

websites

There is a plethora of useful Brussels sites: www.bruxelles.irisnet.be (the local government site, with good entertainment links); www.tib.be (tourist info site which lists hotels, events and sports); www.belgiumtourism.net (good info for visitors); timeout.com/brussels (for what's on this month); www.ideartss.com (for more specific cultural and arts info); www.skynet.be (entertainment links and up-to-date travel info); and www.resto.be (for restaurant bookings).

↓ celluloid city

Cinema-going is something of a national pastime in Belgium, not surprisingly given the country's wet and windy weather. Belgians spend more time in front of the silver screen than almost any other nationality.

With over 100 films to choose from on any given day, low-price tickets and state-of-the-art cinemas, movie-buffs will find themselves in celluloid heaven. There is also the added bonus that films are almost always shown in their original language (VO – *version originale*). But Belgium's love affair with watching movies has done little to help its home-grown film-making industry, which hasn't taken off despite successes, such as *Man Bites Dog*, *Toto the Hero* and Palme d'Or winner *Rosetta*.

As in most European cities, the majority of films shown in Brussels are American blockbusters, which tend to arrive six to nine months after they are first screened across the Atlantic. However, *les Bruxellois* are a cosmopolitan lot and it's commonplace to find Danish, Japanese, Iraqi and Spanish flicks alongside the latest Dutch and French releases.

Europe's biggest, and it still has a bit of an aircraft-hangar feel about it. But the double armrest seats and surround sound system make for a sumptuous movie experience. The complex also houses an enormous IMAX screen.

art-house

Luckily, the arrival of industrial-sized cinemas has not squeezed out Brussels' independent theatres, which continue to thrive. An elegant downtown cinema is the **Galeries Arenberg**. Situated in the Galeries St-Hubert, it tends to screen more obscure foreign movies. The best of the uptown indies is the **Vendôme** cinema in the heart of Matongé, the city's lively African district. This comfortable five-screen theatre shows off beat American films alongside more challenging European fare. Two smaller and slightly shabbier arthouse cinemas are the two-screen **Actor's Studio**, close to Grand' Place, and the minute **Styx** theatre in Ixelles. Both mainly screen re-runs and cult films. The **Movy Club**, although a bit out of town, is worth checking out. It's run by an eccen-

tric cineaste and shows quality reruns. Undoubtedly the jewel in the crown of Brussels' cinemas, however, is the **Musée du Cinéma**, situated near the Palais Royal. As well as showing the standard classics at the giveaway price of 60BF, the cinema museum is the only movie hall in the world to project silent films with live piano accompaniment every day .

festivals

The main event in the city's film year is the **Brussels International Film Festival** (☎ 02.227. 39.80) in January, which previews most of Europe's art-house films. Ghent and Flanders also have their own international film festivals later in the year. More bizarre festivals are the slightly eccentric **International Festival of Animated Film** (☎ 02. 218.27.35) (Feb) and the ghoulish **International Festival of Fantasy Film** (☎ 02.201.14.95) (Mar). From June to September **Ecran Total** (☎ 02.512. 80.63) shows a mix of classics and recent releases. There's an annual drive-in movie season in **Parc du Cinquantenaire** (☎ 02. 346.59.49) in July/Aug.

mainstream

Movie-going in Brussels is dominated by two giants of the European film industry – UGC and Kinepolis. The former has two city-centre multiplexes – the 12-screen **UGC De Brouckère**, slap bang in the centre, and the renovated **UCG Toison d'Or** (also known as UGC Acropole), uptown at Porte de Namur. Both tend to focus on mainstream US films, as does the 28-screen **Kinepolis**, on the outskirts of the city. Until recently, this was

tickets & reviews

It's not usually necessary to book ahead for seats, and few cinemas have credit-card booking facilities. The exceptions are: **Kinepolis** ☎ 02.474.26.00 and the two **UGC** cinemas ☎ 0900.104.40 (booking lines in Flemish and French).

🕐 Programmes change on Wednesdays, and most of the larger cinemas show films four times a day – at 2.15–2.45pm, 4–5pm, 7.15–7.45pm and 9–10.15pm. There are usually 20 minutes of adverts and trailers before the feature starts. At midnight on Fridays and Saturdays there are late-night screenings at **De Brouckère**.

[BF] Tickets are cheapish, ranging from 200BF–280BF, with reductions on Mon for students, OAPs and if you pre-pay for four films at once at UGC cinemas.

❶ Check listings in the weekly English-language magazine *The Bulletin* or any national paper on Wednesdays. *Cinebel.be* has scheduling details and reviews of virtually everything that's on, and *www.idearts.com* has general cultural and arts info.

↓ brussels' beats

Its name may not have the same resonance for rock fans as Memphis or Liverpool, but Brussels spawned one of the most important songsmiths of the 20th century: Jacques Brel (1929–1978). Reared in Schaerbeek, the man who penned cabaret standards *Ne me quitte pas* and the bawdy tale *Port of Amsterdam* has influenced everyone from Frank Sinatra to Jarvis Cocker. The closest Brussels gets to invoking Brel's spirit nowadays is through self-proclaimed European cowboy Arno Hintjens. Three of Belgium's biggest successes are: K's Choice, Antwerp's dEUS and Aarschot's Matthew Engelen and his group the Lords of Acid. In 2000, he became the first Belgian to headline the massive Rock Werchter festival.

rock & pop

Because it's easily accessible from other European cities, nearly all major-league acts it's best to buy in Brussels at some stage. Mega-groups such as U2 and the Rolling Stones tend to play at festivals outside the city, although Brussels' **King Baudouin Stadium** has hosted concerts by the likes of Celine Dion and Johnny Hallyday. The city's biggest indoor venue is the 11,000-capacity **Forest-National**, a circular hall that has headlined Tom Jones and Massive Attack. Big-selling acts wanting a more intimate rapport with their audience tend to play the **Ancienne Belgique**. A punk venue in the 1970s, it reopened in the 1990s, and has a top roster of indie, alt, techno and world acts. Round the corner is **Beursschouwburg**, with alt and world music. Another excellent venue is the **Halles de Schaerbeek**, where misfits like Beck and PJ Harvey have played. Those who like to have their eardrums assaulted by more obscure rock bands should check out **Magasin 4**, in the lower town, or **Vaartkapoen** (VK), an endearing, sweaty club west of the centre. Or, for a more offbeat venue try **Espace Catastrophe** in a converted ice factory.

jazz

Brussels is home to a lively and fluid jazz scene – a heady brew of everything from trad swing to Latin grooves. If you're lucky, you might catch a concert by local heroes, like harmonica legend Toots Thielemans or guitarist Philip Catherine, otherwise check out Brussels-based combos Aka Moon or the Brussels Jazz Orchestra. Big-name jazz concerts tend to take place in larger venues such as the **Palais des Beaux-Arts** or **Le Botanique**, but the city's jazz foundations are built on more intimate clubs such as **Sounds**, **The Music Village** and **Marcus Mingus**. Many other bars and cafés also programme occasional jazz: **L'Archiduc** attracts some high-profile touring groups, while **Dolma** often features live jazz.

festivals

In July, there's the fab world music extravaganza **Couleur Café** (☎ 0900. 808.00), and **Klinkende Munt** (☎ 02. 513.82.90), a series of pop/jazz/world/rock concerts in central Brussels locations. As an antidote to the post-summer blues, **Les Nuits Botaniques** (☎ 02.226.12.11) takes place in September; it boasts the best exponents of *chanson*, plus international names. **It's Like a Jungle** (☎ 02.548.24.24) is an annual jamboree for home-spun and world stars of drum 'n' bass and techno (October). For those able to stomach a weekend of camping, and alfresco urinating, the best out-of-town rock festival takes place at **Rock Werchter** (☎ 016.60.04.06), near Leuven, in early July. August brings the **Pukkelpop** festival in Vlaanderen with several

113

music

tickets & reviews

Tickets are generally available on the door, although for popular acts it's best to buy in advance. If you're stuck Brussels' touts are surprisingly altruistic, rarely selling tickets above face value. Among the outlets selling tickets for a wide variety of gigs are **FNAC** ☎ 02.209.22.39 and **Virgin Megastore** ☎ 02.219.90.04.

⏱ There are gigs most nights of the week, and most start between 8pm–9pm (8pm if there's a support act, 9pm if not). Performances tend to be punctual but for sessions in clubs and bars don't bother arriving before 10pm.

💷 Expect to pay 500BF–800BF per ticket for gigs in main venues but for clubs and bars just turn up and pay the cover charge of 200BF–300BF.

❶ For Anglophones, the best rock listings are contained in the weekly *The Bulletin* or *The Ticket* [→xxx]. Those who can understand French should get the MAD supplement of *Le Soir* (Wed), monthly mag *Kiosque*, freebie *Rif-Raf* (available in cafés and record shops), or *The Ticket*, monthly gig guide (also free from most bars and cafés). The Dutch-language newspaper *De Morgen* and magazines *Humo* and *Knack* have good music coverage. For the most up-to-date and comprehensive info on jazz in Brussels check out the excellent website www.jazzinbelgium.org

→directory 117

stages and loads of alternative bands (www.pukkelpop.be). Folksier types should check out **Dranouter** (☎ 05.744.69.33), near Ieper, in August or the **Brosella Festival**'s (☎ 02.548.04.54) outdoor jazz and folk concerts in July, while ravers of the world can unite in Ghent as big-name DJs hit the decks for **10 Days Off** (☎ 03.226.49.63) in July. The highlight of the Brussels jazz calendar is the **Brussels Jazz Marathon** (www.brusselsjazz marathon.be) in late May. Bands cram into the city's bars and squares for a well-attended weekend. The **Audi Jazz Festival** (www.audijazz.be) also brings many international artists to the city (Oct/Nov).

↓ is it harmony?

The city's classical music venues embrace both tradition and innovation. Dvořák devotees and Beethoven boffs can often hear the works of their favourite composers performed in two places in the one day. More daring souls, meanwhile, can listen to Belgian performers like Jos van Immerseel's Anima Eterna, with their reworkings of Mozart and Bach, and new music standard-bearers, the Ictus Ensemble, who interpret contemporary works.

classical music

The nomination of Brussels as the European City of Culture for 2000 provided the impetus for the renovation of the regal Henri Le Boeuf Hall in the **Palais des Beaux-Arts**. The Palais has a varied programme, with visits by top groups like the Pittsburgh Symphony Orchestra. The best emerging Belgian talent can usually be spotted in the city's other main classical venue, the **Conservatoire Royal de Musique**. The heats for the Queen Elisabeth International Music Festival [→119] are held here each spring. For those who feel that classical music is best appreciated in an ecclesiastical setting, the **Cathédrale de St-Michel & St-Gudule** [→119], the Protestant **Chapelle Royale** and the **Sts-Jean-et-Etienne des Minimes** [→71] all hold recitals on a regular basis.

Occasional concerts – particularly in the summer – are held in the open-air splendour of the **Grand' Place** [→61], as well as in the Salle Gothique of the **Hôtel de Ville** [→69]. More avant-garde events tend to take place in smaller venues such as the **Lunatheater** or **Espace Senghor**. The Luna tends to favour experimental forms of classical music, whereas Espace focuses on ethnic-oriented performances.

opera

Brussels doesn't have its own opera company, but there's Vlaamse Opera in Antwerpen and Opera Royal de Wallonie in Liège. Opera aficionados are best advised to check out La Monnaie, first inaugurated in 1700. The talented director, Bernard Foccroulle, mostly imports well-known international acts, and tickets often sell out months in advance.

festivals

March sees the new music event Ars Musica (☎ 02.219.40.44), when the cream of home-spun talent vies for attention with new international stars. Rediscovery is a constant theme of the **Printemps Baroque du Sablon** each May (☎ 02.507.82.00) as forgotten gems get dusted down in the churches and theatres of the area. The Grand' Place, and other venues near the city centre, are filled with symphonic strains in July, when the **Festival d'Eté (Zommerfestival)** (☎ 02.507.82.00) typically attracts international musicians. Strictly speaking, Brussels is not a Walloon city but the **Festival de Wallonie** (☎ 08.173.37.81) features events across both Brussels and the Walloon region in June. There's a relaxed series of outdoor jazz and classical concerts at **Les Dimanches du Bois de la Cambre** (☎ 02.218.40.86).

tickets & reviews

Most venues have their own box office. It is usually possible to buy tickets at the door, but it's best to reserve ahead. The tourist office in the **Grand' Place** ☎ 02.513.89.40 also sells tickets for recitals, or try the book/music store FNAC ☎ 02.209.22.39

⏱ Classical concerts tend to take place Mon–Sat. Curtains normally rise at 8 or 8.30pm, although lunchtime events are not uncommon.

💳 Prices vary widely: in some smaller venues tickets can cost less than 200BF, but opera performances at La Monnaie and recitals in the Palais des Beaux-Arts reach 2500BF.

❶ For listings, it's best to buy the English-language weekly The Bulletin or MAD, the Wednesday supplement to French-language daily Le Soir. The monthly magazine Kiosque is also an excellent source of info. Web sites www.gmn.com and www.agenda.be are also worth checking out for the latest music info.

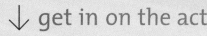

↓ get in on the act

theatre

There are no neon-lit theatre districts here: venues aren't clustered together *à la* Broadway, and the most prestigious are hidden from view with only a hint of what lies inside. Whilst most are within the central ring, some are a bit harder to find.

The two main subsidized theatres are the Flemish **KVS** (Koninklijke Vlaamse Schouwburg) and the French-language **Théâtre National**. The latter is (temporarily) housed in a monstrous tower block, but director Philippe Van Kessel provides an impressive programme of classic French theatre, alongside more contemporary writing in the studio. He also hosts substantial international touring companies such as the RSC. The KVS is currently housed in de Bottelarij, a converted bottling plant-cum-arts-centre in a seedier part of town, whilst its own building undergoes a three-year renovation. The KVS presents new work by Belgian and Dutch writers and looks internationally for inspiration, translating work by writers such as Mark Rouenhill.

Cutting-edge theatre, dance and music from around the world take place in the main house – the **Lunatheater** – and in the **Kaaitheater**, which nestles inside an Art Deco office block. The splendid **Théâtre de la place des Martyrs** offers exciting new takes on French classics and contemporary work, mostly produced by Daniel Scahaise's resident company, Théâtre en Liberté. No signage here; enter through what appears to be a private front door into one of the most modern theatres in Brussels. Only

tickets & reviews

There is no centralized booking facility for theatre tickets; ring individual venues. Credit-card bookings can entail a 3% commission charge. Last-minute tickets are usually available on the door.

☾ There is no hard and fast rule about performance nights, although you can expect Monday and Tuesday nights to be quieter than weekends. Matinée performances are sometimes on offer. There is a definite theatre season, with most closing Jun–early Sep.

BF Prices vary but are cheaper than in other capitals, even for the bigger houses. Expect to pay between 500BF–950BF.

❶ The best place to check for theatre info is the English-language *The Bulletin. Kiosque*, a French monthly listing, is also a must. National newspapers run listings [→xx]. For English theatre information try: www.theatrefactory.com.

the **Théâtre Royal du Parc** looks like a real theatre, with its glass doors and balconies. It produces the most trad French fare – Molière *et al* – whilst its sister, **Théâtre Royal des Galeries** offers a mix of modern French drama and camp revue. The Théâtre du Rideau, based at the **Palais des Beaux-Arts**, is an important part of the Brussels scene. British director Adrian Brine resides at the Palais too and shows French translations of West End and Broadway hits. Keep an eye on **Théâtre 140**, run by the indomitable Jo Deckmine, the trendy **Beursschouwburg** and the welcoming **Théâtre de Poche** in the Bois de la Cambre. All three run seasons of visiting Belgian and international work – very avant-garde.

There aren't any venues devoted entirely to English-language professional theatre. Most of the above venues integrate English work into the overall season, with local producers Theatre Factory Europe organizing incoming tours of major English-language productions. Some theatres, like KVS, are now subtitling plays to attract a more international audience.

Theatres generally run seasons in repertory, with short runs. This means there is a constant change of programme, making the theatre scene as varied as that of any other major city. Added to this is the frisson of French and Flemish theatre traditions: the French promoting its classical heritage, the Flemish embracing the new and experimental. The scene also cuts across the accepted norms of mainstream and fringe, creating a melange of innovative theatrical activity.

puppet theatre

The **Théâtre de Toone** [→70] presents trad puppet plays in old Brussels dialect; don't worry, not many understand it but it's a visual treat. The **Peruchet** also runs a season of modern and classic tales told in puppetry.

cabaret

On the cabaret circuit, **Le Jardin de ma Soeur** is an atmospheric bar with seasons of cabaret, revue and song. The bigger venues, such as **Cirque Royal** and **Forest-National**, host star singers, mainly from France. For alternative revue, **Chez Flo** is a local institution with a varied programme and *travestie*, a spectacular drag show.

→directory 117

festivals

The **KunstenFESTIVALdes Arts** (☎ 02.219.07.07), Brussels biggest international festival, is held every May. The **Euro-** **Theater** festival (☎ 02. 412.70.70), in spring, showcases the biggest and best from a different EU country each year (all performances subtitled). The **Festival des** **Brigittines** (☎ 02. 279.64.36), with its emphasis on dance, physical, and music theatre, is in August, with other events happening through the year.

↓ footloose

dance

Brussels has one of Europe's most vibrant dance scenes. In the last decade, innovative choreographers have put the city firmly on the dance map. Established companies have residencies at theatres around town, affording them a base and a forum for premieres. Smaller experimental groups also find Brussels a great base from which to develop new work.

tickets & reviews

Tickets for major productions are often available from **FNAC** ☎ 02. 209.22.39, or direct from venue box offices; most take credit cards. Places are often limited at smaller venues, so it's best to book; few take credit cards but you can usually phone ahead and reserve.

☾ Shows usually start at 8 or 8.30pm. Smaller venues close Jul–Aug, but the majors stay open.

🄱🄵 Expect to pay 500BF–1000BF for tickets at larger theatres; smaller venues in the region of 300BF–500BF.

❶ For reviews and listings try: *The Ticket* (monthly cultural guide), *MAD Agenda* (Wednesday supplement in *Le Soir*), the Flemish press, and the English-language *Bulletin*. For info on contemporary dance in Brussels see www.users.skynet.be/sky80013/dance.

modern dance

The growing reputation of the dance-oriented performing arts school PARTS (Performing Arts Research & Training Studio) bolsters a steady flow of new talent. The founder, Anna Teresa de Keersmaeker has been at the forefront of European contemporary dance for well over a decade. Her company, Rosas, perform at the **Lunatheater** and **La Monnaie** but are making more use of their new custom-built **Rosas** theatre. Based in Charleroi, but with an increasing presence in the capital, is Frédéric Flamand and his company Charleroi/ Danses-Plan K. When in Brussels, Flamand usually performs in the historic **Halles de Schaerbeek**. Wim Vandekeybus' raw, physical style won him a prestigious Bessie award, and his company, Ultima Vez, are in permanent residence at the **KVS**. American choreographer Meg Stuart arrived in Brussels in 1991 to perform at the Klapstuk Festival and has been here ever since – check out the **Kaaitheater** for performances, and expect the unexpected.

In residence at the **Théâtre Les Tanneurs** is the Compagnie Tandem, run by two of Brussels' most innovative choreographers, Bud Blumenthal and Michèle Noiret, while Thierry Smits' dynamic Compagnie Thor perform regularly at the **Théâtre Varia**. The **Église des Brigittines** is home to a wide variety of local and international artists.

Brussels is on the circuit for larger touring groups, such as Stomp, although these tend to show at the cavernous **Forest-National**. The **Cirque Royal** and the **Palais des Beaux-Arts** are home to occasional dance troupes, whilst a myriad of smaller venues supports a lively programme of experimental performances and mini-festivals.

dance theatre

Belgium has an emerging tradition of what is loosely categorized as 'dance-theatre'. Les Ballets C de la B is a collective of artists at the forefront of this movement. The company runs out of Ghent, but often performs at **Théâtre 140** in Brussels.

classical dance

For a classical fix, Antwerpen is best. See the Royal Flanders Ballet, a well-established, traditional company who put on old favourites like *Swan Lake* at their home base, the **Theater 't Eilandje**. Unfortunately, Brussels' most famous classical dance ambassador, Maurice Bejart, decamped with the renowned Ballet of the 20th Century, to Lausanne in 1987, leaving Brussels without an internationally recognized *corps de ballet*. David Sonnenbluck is one of the few choreographers creating new balletic works in Brussels, and his company is resident at the **Centre Culturel de Woluwe-St-Pierre**.

festivals

The Klapstuk Festival (Oct/Nov) www.stuc.ku leuven.ac.be, in Leuven, is a well-established bi-annual event which has a knack of showcasing up-coming movers and shakers, while the **KunstenFESTIVALdesArts** (☎ 02.219.07.07), held in May, also has a strong dance component.

Actor's Studio
16 petite rue des
Bouchers, Central
☎ 0900.278.54
Ⓜ Bourse

Ancienne Belgique
114 boulevard
Anspach, Central
☎ 02.548.24.24
Ⓜ Bourse

L'Archiduc
6 rue Antoine Dan-
saert, Ste-Catherine
☎ 02.512.06.52
Ⓜ Bourse

Galeries Arenberg
26 Galerie de la
Reine, Central
☎ 0900.278.65
Ⓜ Centrale

Beursschouwburg
20–28 rue August
Orts, Ste-Catherine
☎ 02.513.82.90
w www.beurss
chouwburg.vgc.be
Ⓜ De Brouckère

Le Botanique
236 rue Royale,
St-Josse &
Schaerbeek
☎ 02.226.12.11
☎ 02.218.37.32 (jazz)
Ⓜ Botanique

**Cathédrale de St-
Michel & St-Gudule**
place St-Gudule,
Central
☎ 02.217.83.45
Ⓜ Centrale

**Centre Culturel de
Woluwe-St-Pierre**
9 ave Charles Thiele-
mans, Woluwe-St-
Pierre
☎ 02.773.05.88
🚌 36, 39, 44

Chapelle Royale
5 rue Coudenberg,
Le Sablon
☎ 02.673.05.81
Ⓜ Centrale

Chez Flo
25 rue au Beurre,
Central
☎ 02.513.31.52
Ⓜ Bourse

Cirque Royal
81 rue de l'Enseigne-
ment, Central
☎ 02.218.20.15
Ⓜ Madou

**Conservatoire Royal
de Musique**
30 rue de la
Régence, Le Sablon
☎ 02.513.45.87
Ⓜ Louise

Dolma
331 chaussée
d'Ixelles, Ixelles
(East)
☎ 02.649.89.81
🚌 54, 71

Église des Brigittines
1 petite rue des
Brigittines, Les
Marolles
☎ 02.506.43.00
Ⓜ Anneessens

Espace Catastrophe
18 rue de la Glacière,
St-Gilles
☎ 02.542.54.15
🚌18,81,82

Espace Senghor
366 chaussée de
Wavre, Etterbeek
☎ 02.230.31.40
🚌 34

Forest-National
36 avenue du Globe,
Forest
☎ 02.340.22.11
🚌 48, 54

**Halles de
Schaerbeek**
32 rue Royale Ste-
Marie, St-Josse &
Schaerbeek
☎ 02.218.21.07
🚌 92, 93, 94

Hôtel de Ville
Grand' Place, Central
☎ 02.279.22.11
Ⓜ De Brouckère

**Le Jardin de ma
Soeur**
54 rue du Grand
Hospice, Ste-
Catherine
☎ 02.217.65.82
Ⓜ Ste-Catherine

Kaaitheater
20 place Saincte-
lette, Ste-Catherine
☎ 02.201.59.59
w www.kaaitheater.
vgc.be Ⓜ Yser

Kinepolis
Heysel Bruparck,
20 boulevard du
Centenaire, Heysel
☎ 02.474.26.04
Ⓜ Heysel

**King Baudouin
Stadium**
21 rue Brederode,
Heysel
☎ 02.511.18.40
Ⓜ Trône

KVS
58 rue Delaunoy,
Molenbeek
☎ 02.412.70.70
w www.kvs.be
Ⓜ Beekkant

Lunatheater
20 place
Sainctelette, Ste-
Catherine
☎ 02.201.59.59
Ⓜ Yser

Magasin 4
4 rue du Magasin,
Ste-Catherine
☎ 02.223.34.74
Ⓜ Yser

Marcus Mingus
17–19 rue de la
Fourche, Central
☎ 02.514.16.15
Ⓜ Bourse

La Monnaie
place de la Monnaie,
Central
☎ 02.218.35.27
Ⓜ De Brouckère

Movy Club
21 rue des Moines,
St-Gilles
☎ 02.537.69.54
Ⓜ Étangs Noirs

Musée du Cinéma
9 rue Baron Horta,
Le Sablon
☎ 02.507.83.70
Ⓜ Centrale

Music Village
50 rue des Pierres,
Central
☎ 02.513.13.45
Ⓜ Centrale

**Palais des Beaux-
Arts**
23 rue Ravenstein,
Le Sablon
☎ 02.507.82.50
Ⓜ Centrale

Peruchet
50 avenue de la
Forêt, Boondael
☎ 02.673.87.30
Ⓣ Boondael

Rosas
164 ave Van Volxem,
Forest
☎ 02.340.83.12
🚆 Gare du Midi
then 🚌52

**Sts Jean-et-Étienne
des Minimes**
62 rue des Minimes,
Le Sablon
☎ 02.511.93.84
🚌 20, 48

Sounds
28 rue de la Tulipe,
Ixelles (East)
☎ 02.512.92.50
Ⓜ Porte de Namur

Styx
72 rue de l'Arbre
Bénit, Ixelles (East)
☎ 0900.278.54
Ⓜ Louise

Théâtre 140
140 avenue E Plasky,
St-Josse &
Schaerbeek
☎ 02.733.97.08
🚌 29, 63

**Théâtre de la place
des Martyrs**
9 place des Martyrs,
Central
☎ 02.223.32.08
Ⓜ Rogier; De
Brouckère

Théâtre de Poche
Le chemin du
Gymnase, Bois de
la Cambre
☎ 02.649.17.27
🚌23,90 🚌 38

Théâtre de Toone
6 petite rue des
Bouchers, Central
☎ 02.511.71.37
Ⓜ Bourse

Théâtre les Tanneurs
75 rue des Tanneurs,
Les Marolles
☎ 02.512.17.84
Ⓜ Porte de Hal

Théâtre National
Centre Rogier
rue Neuve, Central
☎ 02.203.41.55
w www.theatre
national.be
Ⓜ Rogier

**Théâtre Royal des
Galeries**
32 Galerie du Roi,
Central
☎ 02.512.04.07
Ⓜ De Brouckère

**Théâtre Royal
du Parc**
3 rue de la Loi,
Central
☎ 02.505.30.30
Ⓜ Arts-Loi

Théâtre 't Eilandje
16 Kattendijkdok-
Westkaj, Antwerpen
☎ 07.815.55.57

Théâtre Varia
rue du Sceptre
Quartier Européen
☎ 02.640.8258
Ⓜ Trône

UGC De Brouckère
38 place de
Brouckère, Central
☎ 0900.104.40 (Fr)
☎ 0900.104.50 (Fl)
Ⓜ De Brouckère

UGC Toison d'Or
8 avenue de la
Toison d'Or,
Ixelles (East)
☎ 0900.104.40 (Fr)
☎ 0900.104.50 (Fl)
Ⓜ Toison d'Or

Vaartkapoen (VK)
76 rue de l'École,
Molenbeek
☎ 02.414.29.07
Ⓜ Comte de Flandre

Vendôme
18 chaussée de
Wavre, Ixelles (East)
☎ 02.502.37.00
Ⓜ 34,38, 60,80, 95,96

117

brussels agenda

What's on when in Europe's adopted capital...

↓ summer

La Bataille de Waterloo (Slag Bij Waterloo)

Spectacular re-enactment of the battle between Wellington's and Napoleon's armies is fought by military enthusiasts.

❶ *Jun (every five years; next one 2001)* @ Waterloo (Wallonia) ☎ 02.352.98.82 [transport →49] 🆓 free

Fête de la Musique

The French-speaking community celebrates the arrival of summer with a three-day multicultural musical event.

❶ *21 Jun & nearest weekend* @ various Brussels locations ☎ 02.209.10.90 🆓 free

Couleur Café

A multicultural world music event [→113].

❶ *end Jun* @ Tour & Taxis, 5–7 rue Picard, Molenbeek ☎ 02.672.49.12 🚇 Ribaucourt 🆓 700BF–1600BF

Ecran Total

A mix of international film classics, documentaries, recent releases, and new movies are shown at this annual festival.

❶ *end Jun–beg Sep* @ Arenberg-Galeries Cinema, 26 Galerie de la Reine, Central ☎ 02.512.80.63 🚇 Centrale 🆓 260BF

Festival de Wallonie

This Francophone extravaganza is a staggered series of classical music events in castles, abbeys, and churches.

❶ *Jun–Oct* @ various locations in Brussels & Wallonia ☎ 08.173.37.81 🆓 300BF–850BF

Brosella

A small, but established, outdoor folk and jazz festival [→113].

❶ *beg Jul* @ Théâtre de Verdure, Parc Osseghem, Heysel ☎ 02.548.04.54 🚇 Heysel 🆓 free

Klinkende Munt

Avant-garde series of pop/jazz/world/rock festival of concerts. And the best thing is it's free.

❶ *6 days beg Jul* @ various locations, including Beursschouwburg [→113] ☎ 02.513.82.90 🚇 Bourse 🆓 free

Ommegang

Medieval pageant re-creating a 16th-century celebration in honour of Emperor Charles V and his son Philip II; people parade with giant effigies on their shoulders and there's a mock battle fought on stilts.

❶ *1st Thu Jul & preceding Tue* @ Grand' Place, Central ☎ 02.548.04.54/02.512.19.61 🚇 De Brouckère 🆓 850BF–2550BF

Rock Werchter

Belgium's biggest open-air rock festival [→113].

❶ *1st weekend Jul* @ Werchter festival site, near Leuven, Flanders ☎ 016. 60.04.06 [→transport 127–130] 🆓 1600BF–3100BF

10 Days Off

One of the biggest annual dance festivals in Belgium, this summer fling attracts the very best international DJs and acts.

❶ *beg Jul* @ location varies each year w www.dma.be/p/5voo12/ [→transport 127–130] 🆓 varies

Fête Nationale Belge (Belgische Nationale Feestdag)

Remembering the day in 1830 when Léopold I was crowned first king of the Belgians. A host of events and military parades ending with a spectacular firework display.

❶ *21 Jul* @ various locations around Parc de Bruxelles ☎ 02.511.90.00 🚍 91, 92, 93, 94 🆓 free

Sfinks Festival

A four-day world music festival in a park crammed with exotic food stalls and workshops.

❶ *last weekend Jul* @ Oude Steenweg, Boechout, near Antwerpen (Flanders) ☎ 03.455.69.44 [→transport 127–130] 🆓 1000BF per day

Gentse Feesten

The medieval city of Gent hosts a 10-day festival of music, street theatre, jazz, and dance in its squares and quays.

❶ *end Jul* @ Gent (Flanders) ☎ 09.225.36.76 [transport →54] 🆓 free

Les Dimanches du Bois de la Cambre

Relaxed series of outdoor jazz and classical concerts in the Bois de la Cambre [→76].

❶ *Jul–Aug: every Sun* @ Pélouse des Anglais, Bois de la Cambre, Ixelles (West) ☎ 02.218.40.86 🚍 23, 90, 93, 94 🆓 free

La Foire du Midi (Zuidkermis)

Huge funfair with over 2km of Ferris wheels, merry-go-rounds, and roller coasters. Try local delicacies like the famous *smoutebollen* (a kind of doughnut) or grilled *boudin* sausage.

❶ *mid Jul–end Aug* @ boulevard du Midi, Les Marolles ☎ 02.279.40.76 🚇 Gare du Midi 🆓 100BF per ride

Meyboomplanting

Commemoration of the Brussels bourgeois' win over a challenge by their Leuven counterparts in 1308 with the planting of a Mey boom (May tree) and an afternoon parade on the Grand' Place.

❶ *beg Aug* @ Grand' Place, Central ☎ 02.217.39.43 🚇 De Brouckère 🆓 free

Tapis aux Fleurs (Bloementapijt)

800,000 flowers carpet the Grand' Place in a three-day tribute to Belgium's world famous begonias.

❶ *mid Aug every 2 years (even-numbered years)* @ Grand' Place, Central ☎ 02.513.89.40 🚇 De Brouckère 🆓 free

Marktrock

A mixed bag of Belgian and international rock and pop acts plays at this three-day event.

❶ *mid Aug* @ various locations across Leuven, Flanders ☎ 016.29.08.23 [→transport 127–130] 🆓 free–500BF

Recyclart

Cultural and urban-renewal group Recyclart presents a festival of music, painting, sculpture, street theatre, and juggling.

❶ *Aug* @ Chapelle Station, Les Marolles ☎ 02.502.57.34 🚇 Centrale 🆓 free

Memorial Ivo Van Damme

An annual track-and-field meet bringing together internationally renowned athletes.

❶ *end Aug* @ King Baudouin Stadium, Heysel ☎ 02.474.72.30 🚇 Heysel 🆓 500BF–2200BF

Grand Prix de Belgique de Formule I

Formula I Belgian-style on one of the most scenic circuits in the world.

❶ *end Aug* @ Francorchamps, Wallonia ☎ 08.727.51.46 🆓 5000BF–14,000BF

↓ autumn

Les Nuits Botaniques

Rock, pop, *chanson*, and world music in Le Botanique [→60].

❶ *mid Sep* @ Le Botanique, 236 rue Royale, St-Josse & Scharbeek ☎ 02.218.37.32 🚇 Botanique 🆓 250BF–1600BF

Journées du Patrimoine (Open Monumentendag)

Historic buildings, artists' studios, and Art Nouveau gems that are rarely open to the public welcome visitors for the weekend.

◗ *2nd or 3rd weekend Sep* @ various locations across Brussels ☎ 02.204.14.20 Ⓜ Porte de Hal 🎟 free

Brueghel Festival

A celebration of local artist Pieter Brueghel the Elder who lived in the Marolles until his death in 1669. There's a parade, street parties and live music.

◗ *3rd Sun Sep* @ various locations in Les Marolles ☎ 02.512.19.00 Ⓜ Porte de Hal 🎟 free

Fête de la Communauté Française

Walloons and some *Bruxellois* celebrate their Francophony with street parties, music, and free theatre performances.

◗ *27 Sep* @ various locations across Brussels ☎ 02.413.23.11 🎟 free

Festival van Vlaanderen

Classical music marathon held in medieval abbeys, cathedrals, and city halls.

◗ *Mar–Dec* @ various locations in Brussels & Ghent ☎ 02.548.95.95 🎟 600BF–3000BF

Armistice (Wapenstilstand)

The end of WWI is commemorated all over Belgium. Military parades take place at the tomb of the Unknown Soldier [→61].

◗ *11 Nov* @ place Madou, Central Ⓜ Madou; Botanique 🎟 free

↓ winter

St-Nicolas (Sinterklaas)

Belgian children get their pressies for the festive season (it's a much bigger deal than Christmas). They also scoff spicy *speculoos* (gingerbread biscuits) and marzipan.

◗ *6 Dec*

Le Marché de Noël (Kerstmarkt)

International Christmas market, with stalls from many EU countries in a warm and friendly atmosphere. A shopper's delight.

◗ *beg–mid Dec* @ Grand' Place, Central Ⓜ De Brouckère

Brussels on Ice

The Grand' Place is transformed into a huge ice-skating rink. Rent some skates or sit back and watch the professionals (in both sporting and artistic shows).

◗ *end Dec–beg Jan* @ Grand' Place, Central ☎ 02.513.89.40 Ⓜ De Brouckère 🎟 150BF

Fête de la St-Sylvestre (Oudejaarsavond)

Festivities across the capital as New Year is the one time of year Belgians really let rip. Catch the fireworks from place des Palais.

◗ *New Year's Eve* ☎ 02.513.89.40 🎟 free public transport

Brussels International Film Festival

Ten days of international films and documentaries [→112].

◗ *Jan* @ various cinemas ☎ 02.227.39.89 w www.brusselsfilmfest.be 🎟 180BF–280BF

Gay & Lesbian Film Festival

A popular annual event with international long and short films and documentaries.

◗ *mid Jan* @ Le Botanique, 236 rue Royale, St-Josse & Schaerbeek ☎ 02.218.37.32 Ⓜ Botanique 🎟 180BF

Carnaval à Binche

A world-famous lenten carnival in Binche, highlighted by Mardi Gras (Shrove Tuesday) with *gilles* (giants) in fancy-dress costumes. It ends in the square with *gilles* throwing oranges at the crowds.

◗ *Shrove Tuesday* @ Binche, Wallonia ☎ 06.433.68.96 [transport →48] 🎟 free

Ars Musica

Inventive, contemporary classical music festival with lots of premieres [→114].

◗ *mid Mar–beg Apr* @ various locations in Brussels & Antwerpen ☎ 02.219.26.60 🎟 prices vary

↓ spring

Musique et Lumière (Muziek- & Lichtshow)

Sound and light show in the wonderful Grand' Place. Sit and sip a beer as the Hôtel de Ville is magnificently illuminated.

◗ *Easter–Sep: daily* @ Grand' Place, Central Ⓜ De Brouckère 🎟 free

Printemps Baroque du Sablon (Barokke Lente van de Zavel)

Music, theatre and festivities in the finest Sablon settings.

◗ *mid Apr* @ various locations in Le Sablon ☎ 02.507.82.00 🚍 91, 92, 93, 94 🎟 free

Foire du Livre Antique (Beurs van het Oude Boek)

An international event for book enthusiasts, particularly those who love old maps, first editions, and secondhand books.

◗ *end Apr* @ Salle de la Madeleine, 14 rue Duquesnoy, Central ☎ 02.512.44.472 Ⓜ De Brouckère 🎟 200BF

Serres Royales de Laeken (Kon Serres van Laken)

The spectacular royal glasshouses are open for a few weeks so the public can admire exotic tropical plants, azaleas, and fuchsias. One day is reserved for the disabled.

◗ *end Apr–beg May* @ ave du Parc Royal, Laeken ☎ 02.551.20.20 🚍 53 🎟 50BF–100BF

Queen Elisabeth Music Competition

A landmark event in Belgium's classical music scene that is now a musical institution. It's the most gruelling classical competition in the world; only the very best make it through.

◗ *May* @ Palais des Beaux-Arts, 5–7 rue Ravenstein, Le Sablon ☎ 02.513.00.99 Ⓜ Central 🎟 prices vary

Dring Dring Festival

A week-long celebration of cycling in Brussels. On the first Sunday, avenue Tervuren is car free. There are guided tours and sales of new and old bikes.

◗ *beg May* @ Parc du Cinquantenaire, Quartier Européen ☎ 02.502.73.55 Ⓜ Schuman 🎟 bike hire varies

Fête du Port (Havenfeesten)

Festivities in Brussels' port, with a display of sailing boats and warships. Lots of activities including water-skiing, tours of the harbour in riverboats, concerts, and fireworks.

◗ *beg May* @ quai de Heembeek & Brussels, Royal Yacht Club, 1 chaussée de Vilvoorde, Voorhaven ☎ 02.421.66.51 Ⓜ Yser 🎟 free

KunstenFESTIVALdesArts

Avant-garde dance, music, theatre, and films [→116].

◗ *May* @ various Brussels locations ☎ 070.22.21.99 w www.kunstenfestivaldesarts.be 🎟 prices vary

Fête de l'Iris (Irisfeest)

Multicultural outdoor event with activities for all age groups. Make-up workshops for children and European food specialities followed by an evening concert and a fireworks display. It's the official Brussels Region festival.

◗ *mid May* @ Parc du Cinquantenaire, Quartier Européen Ⓜ Schuman 🎟 free

Bruxelles (Brussel) 20km

The capital's most important road race attracts runners from all over the world.

◗ *end May* @ Parc du Cinquantenaire, Quartier Européen ☎ 02.511.90.00 Ⓜ Schuman 🎟 free

Jazz Marathon

The capital's famous annual jazz jamboree [→114].

◗ *last weekend May* @ various locations in Brussels ☎ 02.456.04.86 🎟 450BF

events

As Brussels has seized the seat of Euro power, its hotel sector has grown almost exponentially. Prices are lower than in many capitals and the quality of accommodation is excellent, if sometimes short on charm.

But competition is fierce – prices at top places are often slashed at weekends and during holiday periods to attract those not on expense accounts.

heads down
what's where

↓ do it in style

Astoria 103 rue Royale, Central

The Aga Khan's wife once had her bath filled with asses' milk in this historic Belle Epoque hotel. You may not get the same treatment, but it's still like stepping back in time: staff push brass luggage trolleys, the Pullman bar is modelled on an old Orient-Express carriage, and weekly classical concerts are held in the Waldorf Room. The huge bedrooms are awash with antiques, potted palms, and period features; modern touches like air-conditioning have been seamlessly added.

☎ 02.227.05.05 **F** 02.217.11.50 **W** www.sofitel.com **Ⓜ** Botanique ◆ 125 ▣ 🄬 ↔ 🖉 ℘
▯ **Ⓟ** ♿ 🍽 all **ⒷⒻ Ⓖⓕ Ⓖⓟ Ⓖⓑ** doubles: from 10,000BF (w/e rates available)

Crowne Plaza 3 rue Gineste, St-Josse & Schaerbeek

Grace Kelly had an apartment decorated to her liking (for her Brussels visits) at this turn-of-the-century hotel. Now it's a suite, and on a quiet weekend you may be able to stay in it for a song. Like many old hotels in the city, this was occupied by the Germans in WWII – the theories flow about their use of the now-defunct lower-ground floors. Many rooms contain original Art Deco beds and wardrobes with gilt Egyptian motifs. The amenities and service are top class. Drop into the art gallery on the eighth floor.

☎ 02.203.62.00 **F** 02.203.55.55 **W** www.crowneplaza.com **Ⓜ** Rogier ◆ 358 ▭ ▣
🄬 ↔ 🖉 🍸 ℘ ▯ **Ⓟ** ♿ 🍽 all **ⒷⒻ Ⓖⓕ Ⓖⓟ Ⓖⓑ** doubles: from 12,000BF (w/e & business rates available)

Hôtel Métropole 31 place de Brouckère, Central

A landmark *belle époque* hotel with an incredible 19th-century-style foyer: all marble columns, glittering chandeliers, wood panelling, and stained glass. It's cherished by French actors, and some guests come back time and again to revel in its opulence. Rooms along the 9 km of corridors are spacious and varied, with fine examples of Art Deco and Art Nouveau furniture. The interior of the café is magnificent [→105], but the terrace looks out on a busy intersection, and the Alban Chambon restaurant has an excellent reputation and decor to match. Put relaxation first at the Bio Etna health suite with a hammam and beauty treatments.

☎ 02.217.23.00 **F** 02.218.02.20 **W** www.metropolehotel.be **Ⓜ** De Brouckère ◆ 303 ▭ ▣
↔ 🖉 🍸 ℘ ▯ **Ⓟ** ♿ 🍽 all **ⒷⒻ Ⓖⓕ Ⓖⓟ Ⓖⓑ** doubles: from 12,500BF (w/e rates available)

Le Plaza 118–126 boulevard Adolphe Max, Central

There's nothing dated about this magnificent 1930s hotel that reopened in 1996 after a 20-year closure. No expense was spared to preserve the cachet of the original – prized by legends of cinema and entertainment such as Brigitte Bardot and Joséphine Baker – and to meet modern needs. Enormous china sinks, framed illustrations, and comfortable armchairs distinguish the traditional-style rooms. The domed dining room is equally impressive. But for the real cherry, sneak a look at the hotel's incredible listed theatre, now used for fashion and media events.

☎ 02.227.67.00 **F** 02.227.67.20 **W** www.leplaza-brussels.be **Ⓜ** Rogier ◆ 193 ▭ ▣ 🄬 ↔ 🖉
℘ ▯ **Ⓟ** ♿ 🍽 all **ⒷⒻ Ⓖⓕ Ⓖⓟ Ⓖⓑ** doubles: from 10,900BF (w/e & business rates available)

↓ luxury

Amigo 1–3 rue d'Amigo, Central

Potted palms and black flagstones strewn with rugs give a Spanish colonial tone to the lobby of this glamorous hotel. And though it looks like it's been here for centuries, the Amigo was only built in 1958. Flagstones, tiling and furniture are as old as the 16th century, and there are 16th-century Flemish paintings by the likes of Courters and Bastien too. Rooms are decorated in classic blue and cream; and the uniformed staff are so polite they seem to come from another age. Bought by Sir Rocco Forte in 2000, word has it that further embellishments are on the way.

☎ 02.547.47.07 **F** 02.502.28.05 **W** www.hotelamigo.com **Ⓜ** Centrale ◆ 170 ▭ ▣ 🄬 🖉 🍸
℘ ▯ **Ⓟ** ♿ 🍽 all **ⒷⒻ Ⓖⓕ Ⓖⓟ Ⓖⓑ** doubles: from 9500BF (w/e & business rates available)

Prices include all taxes

top hotels

Conrad 71 avenue Louise, Ixelles (West)

Lou Reed, Bill Clinton and other big names have stayed at this luxurious hotel, enhanced in 2000 by the addition of Champney's health club (open to hotel guests only), with dance studio, pool, and beauty treatments. Service and accommodation meet the needs of exacting guests: rooms are a good size with sofas; pricier ones have enormous oval bathtubs; and there's even a 'cyber concierge' to help with computer problems. Money can't buy love, but it can sure as hell buy luxury.

☎ 02.542.48.00 **F** 02.542.42.00 **w** www.brussels.conradinternational.com **M** Louise
♦ 269 ▤ 🅲 ⇆ ↔ 🖊 🕭 🌂 🛏 🅿 ♿ 🖃 all ⓌⓌⓌⓌ doubles: from 16,000BF
(w/e & business rates available)

↓ discreet charm

Bedford 135 rue du Midi, Central

A family-run luxury hotel with a marble lobby, thick carpeting, and friendly service. The manager, who knows everything there is to know about the history of the city's hotels, tells how the Bedford is on the site of a hotel where WWII pilots came for romantic rendezvous. The rooms, some for families, are pink with red-wood furniture; the bathrooms are smallish but sparkling.

☎ 02.512.78.40 **F** 02.514.17.59 **w** www.hotelbedford.com **M** Anneessens ♦ 321 🖳 ▤ 🅲
🖊 🕭 🌂 🅿 ♿ 🖃 all ⓌⓌⓌⓌ doubles: from 9400BF (w/e rates available)

Le Dixseptième 25 rue de la Madeleine, Central

This elegant house was the residence of the Spanish ambassador in the 17th century. The enormous rooms of the old house – with original oak beams, some with four-poster beds and antiques – look onto an interior courtyard. The modern rooms have been converted from the former stables, many with terraces and kitchenettes. All rooms are named after Belgian painters, copies of whose works adorn the walls; and there's an art gallery in the lounge.

☎ 02.502.57.44 **F** 02.502.64.24 **w** www.ledixseptieme.be **M** Centrale ♦ 24 🖳 ▤ 🖊 🕭
🌂 🛏 🖃 all ⓌⓌⓌ doubles: from 7100BF (w/e & business rates available)

Manos Stéphanie 28 chaussée de Charleroi, St-Gilles

You can't help but feel decadent amid the Louis XVI splendour of this hotel, with its marble hallway lined with giant gilt plant-stands. Antiques are dotted all over; red and gold upholstery, and tasteful prints make for an opulent stay. The interior courtyard has tasteful wooden loungers to top off the elegance. There's no restaurant, but an in-house chef caters for room service until 11pm.

☎ 02.539.02.50 **F** 02.537.57.29 **w** www.manoshotel.com **M** Louise ♦ 55 🖳 ▤ 🅲 ↔ 🖊
🕭 🛏 🌂 ♿ 🖃 all ⓌⓌⓌⓌ doubles: from 8250BF (w/e rates available)

Montgomery 134 avenue de Tervuren, Woluwe-St-Lambert

Choose from an Oriental, Laura Ashley, or Ralph Lauren room in this classy joint near the Cinquantenaire. None will disappoint: fittings are top quality and the taste impeccable. Although only built in the 1990s, the Montgomery manages a suave, gentleman's-club feel, with Chesterfield sofas, wood panelling, and a library in the lounge-bar area. La Duchesse restaurant's French chef does sunny Med (and veggie fare) very well.

☎ 02.741.85.11 **F** 02.741.85.00 **w** www.montgomery.be **M** Montgomery ♦ 63 ▤ 🅲 ↔ 🖊
🌂 🛏 🖃 ♿ 🖃 all ⓌⓌⓌⓌⓌ doubles: from 12,500BF (w/e & business rates available)

Royal Windsor 5 rue Duquesnoy, Central

An English-style luxury hotel that appeals to visiting rock stars and statesmen alike. Rooms, though not enormous, are superbly equipped, with bright, marble bathrooms, dark-wood parquet, and elegant upholstery. There are floors with no-smoking rooms, and those on the Godiva floor (which are sponsored and decorated by the chocolate company) come with complimentary choccies too. The only hotel in the city to have its own nightclub, Griffin's.

☎ 02.505.55.55 **F** 02.505.55.00 **w** www.warwickhotels.com/brussels **M** Centrale
♦ 266 ▤ 🅲 ↔ ↔ 🖊 🌂 🛏 🅿 ♿ 🖃 all ⓌⓌⓌⓌⓌ doubles: from 14,119BF

Stanhope 9 rue du Commerce, Quartier Européen

A veritable jewel, this former convent is the choice residence of diplomats and politicians. The compact rooms are individually decorated in English stately-home style: the adorable two-floored Goodwood suite overlooks the shady garden, whilst the Linley is kitted out with the Viscount's own furniture. Oozing good taste and attentive service, this hotel's charm is irresistible.

☎ 02.506.91.11 F 02.512.17.08 W www.summithotels.com Ⓜ Trône ♦ 50 ▤ ⓧ⊷ ⌀
◐ ℘ 🖵 🅿 ♿ ⊟ all ⓜⓜⓜⓜ doubles: from 8900BF (business rates available)

↓ big business

Dorint 11–19 boulevard Charlemagne, Quartier Européen

This area isn't usually known for its style, but the Dorint is an exception – sleek and modern, with lots of black, chrome, and spotlights. The rooms are smart (but not large) and each one is decorated with a different local photographer's work. It's a fave with journalists (as it's next to the International Press Centre, has ISDN lines, translation rooms, and a Reuters terminal). Hit the fitness club (with Turkish bath), or chill out in the palm-tree garden.

☎ 02.231.09.09 F 02.231.33.71 W www.dorint.be Ⓜ Schuman ♦ 212 ▤ ⓧ⊷ ⌀ ◐ ℘ 🖵
🅿 ♿ ⊟ all ⓜⓜⓜⓜⓜ doubles: from 12,500BF (w/e & business rates available)

Radisson SAS 47 rue du Fossé aux Loups, Central

Zip up in the glass elevator of this sleek Scandinavian hotel and look down on the central atrium's winter garden, complete with greenery, burbling brook, and the remains of the 12th-century city wall. Room decor depends on the theme of the floor – Italian, Oriental, Scandinavian (with parquet floors for allergy sufferers), and the swish Royal Club. The top floor has a superbly equipped gym. Check out the renowned Sea Grill restaurant [→102].

☎ 02.219.28.28 F 02.219.62.62 W www.radisson.com/brussels.be Ⓜ De Brouckère
♦ 281 ▤ ⓧ⊷ ⌀ ◐ ℘ 🖵 🅿 ♿ ⊟ all ⓜⓜⓜⓜⓜ doubles: from 13,000BF (w/e & business rates available)

Sheraton Brussels Hotel & Towers 3 place Rogier, St-Josse & Schaerbeek

Whisk through the revolving doors and exchange a busy intersection for some serious pampering. Exceptionally spacious rooms, huge beds, and Playstations to boot: this is where the big boys kick back and chill out. Six floors are dedicated to business travellers (with receptionists and video conference facilities), whilst some rooms keep the offspring happy with toys. The fitness centre has a good-sized indoor pool, with loungers on the outside terrace.

☎ 02.224.31.11 F 02.224.34.56 W www.sheraton.com/Brussels Ⓜ Rogier ♦ 533 ▤ ⓧ ≋
⊷ ⌀ ◐ ℘ 🖵 🅿 ♿ ⊟ all ⓜⓜⓜⓜⓜ doubles: from 13,000BF (w/e rates available)

Swissôtel 19 rue du Parnasse, Quartier Européen

The choice pad of lobbyists, politicians, and consultants with business at the nearby European Parliament [→62]. Swish and modern, it caters for the business traveller, with espresso machines and large desks in the navy and yellow executive rooms. There's an apartment block for long-stay guests. The gym and indoor pool are fab, and the Nico Central restaurant pulls a smart crowd.

☎ 02.505.29.29 F 02.505.25.55 W www.swissotel.com Ⓜ Trône ♦ 257 ▭ ▤ ⓧ ≋ ⊷ ⌀
℘ 🖵 🅿 ♿ ⊟ all ⓜⓜⓜⓜⓜ doubles: from 12,800BF (w/e & business rates available)

↓ personal touch

À la Grande Cloche 10 place Rouppe, Central

A white façade and green awning fronts this family-run hotel. It's just across the square from the best restaurant in town, Comme Chez Soi [→97], but a meal there is a week's stay here. The bright rooms have green carpets that reach halfway up the walls in true Continental style. Some have bathrooms, some toilets, some neither. There's a 1am curfew.

☎ 02.512.61.40 F 02.512.65.91 W www.hotelgrandecloche.com Ⓜ Anneessens ♦ 37 ▭
🅿 ♿ ⊟ AE/MC/V ⓜ doubles: from 1750BF

Prices include all taxes

Bed & Brussels Office: 9 rue Kindermans, Ixelles (West)

Fancy staying with real *Bruxellois*? This not-for-profit organization can sort it out, fixing up rooms in private homes, the majority in the more affluent suburbs south and east of the centre. Breakfast is included, and there are three categories of accommodation, depending on facilities. The longer you stay, the better the deal. Call in advance with what you're after, and they'll send a list of options. Language immersion courses can also be arranged.

☎ 02.646.07.37 **F** 02.644.01.14 **w** www.bnb-brussels.be **M** Louise ✦ 255 beds in 105 homes ⬜ 🖃 all ⓦ doubles: from 1695BF

Les Ecrins 15 rue du Rouleau, Ste-Catherine

Following a change of ownership, this small, gay-friendly hotel was entirely re-fitted in 2000 in sunny colours. The well-lit green and yellow rooms are very comfortable, with white duvet covers, double-glazing, and gleaming white bathrooms. The jolly, globe-trotting owner is charming and loquacious. Breakfast is served in an equally green and yellow room that looks out onto a tiny garden. Highly recommended for its warm welcome and good value.

☎ 02.219.36.57 **F** 02.223.57.40 **w** www.lesecrins.com **M** Ste-Catherine ✦ 11 ⬜ 🖥 📧 🕭 🅿 ♿ 🖃 MC/V ⓦ doubles: from 1900BF

Hôtel Welcome quai au Bois à Brûler, Ste-Catherine

This tiny hotel, self-proclaimed as the 'smallest hotel in Brussels', is run by the charming couple who manage the fish restaurant in the same building. The six rooms are all quite different in style and price: one is blue with white wicker furniture; another warm pinks with a comfy sofa. Guests get a special deal at the restaurant and can be served informal meals in the retro-tiled breakfast room. An airport limousine service is available.

☎ 02.219.95.46 **F** 02.217.18.87 **w** www.hotelwelcome.com **M** Ste-Catherine ✦ 6 📧 🕭 ⓦ 📺 🅿 🖃 all ⓦⓦ doubles: from 2600BF

Noga 38 rue du Béguinage, Ste-Catherine

This charming hotel blends good taste and comfort with crazy objects: enormous bellows, a waist-high statue, and various maritime curios. The result is cozy rather than cluttered, and there's always a friendly welcome. The spacious rooms are individually decorated, but only some have showers. The bright breakfast room/bar is flooded with daylight.

☎ 02.218.67.63 **F** 02.218.16.03 **w** www.nogahotel.com **M** Ste-Catherine; De Brouckère ✦ 19 ⬜ 🖊 📺 🅿 🖃 all ⓦⓦ doubles: from 3300BF (w/e rates available)

↓ quirky

Les Bluets 124 rue Berckmans, St-Gilles

Window boxes and a pretty façade welcome you to this highly individual family-run hotel, crammed with charming antiques and other rarities the owners have picked up on their travels. An English grandfather clock chimes in the hall, while a tropical bird twitters in the dining room. The rooms vary in style, most have antique beds, some of which seem a little cramped. The house has strict rules about silence (no noise after 10pm) and is non-smoking throughout.

☎ 02.534.39.83 **F** 02.543.09.70 **M** Hôtel des Monnaies ✦ 10 ⬜ 🕭 🖃 AE/MC/V ⓦ doubles: from 2000BF

Comfort Art Hotel Siru 1 place Rogier, St-Josse & Schaerbeek

What could have been a bland hotel (albeit an Art Deco one) has been transformed into an aesthetic curiosity. An original work of art was commissioned from a different Belgian artist for each of the 101 rooms, making the place one big gallery. The results vary from the sexy to the kitsch. Check out the folder with details of each artist and choose your decor, from fake rocks above the bed to brightly coloured nudes lounging on the bedstead. Ask for a room with a No. 8 at the end – these are in the octagonal tower.

☎ 02.203.35.80 **F** 02.203.33.03 **M** Rogier; Gare du Nord ✦ 101 ⬜ 🖊 🕭 📺 🅿 🖃 all ⓦⓦⓦ doubles: from 6200BF (w/e rates available)

Pacific Sleeping 27 rue Antoine Dansaert, Ste-Catherine

Old professors and hard-up students gather in this institution. A zebra skin in the breakfast room looks like it's been here since the days of Léopold's Congo, and the the elderly Monsieur Pauwels is a mine of information on all things Brussels. Works of art, lino-covered floors, wallpapered ceilings, hospital beds, and enormous china sinks give the place true character. Facilities are minimal: no rooms have en suite bathrooms and you have to pay to use the shower. Also, disappointingly, there's a midnight curfew. Such individualism at such a great price is a very rare thing in Brussels.

☎ 02.511.84.59 Ⓜ Bourse; Ste-Catherine ♦ 15 ⌂ ▭ none ⊛ doubles: from 1800BF

↓ leafy retreats

Château du Lac avenue du Lac, Genval

This luxury, out-of-town hotel is the retreat for the likes of Boyzone on tour and France's victorious Euro 2000 football team. An ivy-clad, turret-ed hotel, built in 1904 in the style of a Cistercian abbey, it's half an hour from the centre of Brussels and overlooks lush surroundings, a bowling green, and a croquet lawn. Benefits include special deals with 11 nearby golf courses, a business centre, and residential team-building courses. A gastronomic restaurant and superb fitness centre with pool and tennis courts help make it a resort in itself.

☎ 02.655.71.11 F 02.655.74.44 w www.martins-hotels.com ▤ Genval ♦ 121 ⌂ ▤ ㉔ ≋ ↔ 𝒫 ① ℘ ▯ Ⓟ ♿ ▭ all ⊛⊛⊛⊛⊛ doubles: from 12,600BF (w/e & business rates available)

Royal Crown Grand Mercure 250 rue Royale, St-Josse & Schaerbeek

It doesn't look much from the outside, but this 1970s luxury hotel offers an exceptionally friendly welcome, floors of no-smoking rooms, and a view over the Jardin Botanique [→117] for those lucky enough to get a room on that side. All renovated recently, the good-sized rooms are decorated in one of three colour schemes: pink, honey, or green. There's a valet parking service, and a cozy cocktail bar with cream club chairs and wood panelling.

☎ 02.220.66.11 F 02.217.84.44 Ⓜ Botanique ♦ 315 ▤ ㉔ ↔ 𝒫 ℘ ▯ Ⓟ ♿ ▭ all ⊛⊛⊛⊛ doubles: from 8500BF (w/e rates available)

Les Tourelles 135 avenue Winston Churchill, Uccle

On a leafy, suburban avenue in bourgeois Uccle, this family-run hotel is something of a folly – with its gables and turrets, it looks more like an antique hunting lodge, and the interior is decorated to match. Rooms are of different shapes and sizes, with traditional furnishings and decor. The breakfast is generous; the service courteous. Rooms at the back overlook the interior courtyard and are quieter. Great for some respite from the city crowds.

☎ 02.344.95.73 F 02.346.42.70 🛏23, 90 ♦ 22 ⌂ 𝒫 ① Ⓟ ▭ AE/MC/V ⊛⊛ doubles: from 4627BF (w/e rates available)

↓ on location

Arlequin 17–19 rue de la Fourche, Central

Tucked between two cobbled streets, this bright, modern hotel is blessed with two cultural venues practically on its premises: the cool basement bar with its enticing red-velvet sofas hosts regular live jazz concerts; and the tiny Actor's Studio cinema [→117], in the same arcade, shows second-run and art-house movies. The restful rooms in pastel shades are comfortable, while the breakfast room on the top floor has stunning panoramas of the city centre.

☎ 02.514.16.15 F 02.514.22.02 Ⓜ Bourse; Centrale ♦ 92 ⌂ 𝒫 ℘ ▯ ▭ all ⊛⊛ doubles: from 3950BF (w/e rates available)

Galia 15–16 place du Jeu de Balle, Les Marolles

On the sunny side of a cobbled square, and close to an Art Deco swimming pool [→81], this place is ideal for early risers and bargain-hunters, as the excellent daily flea market on place du Jeu de Balles [→87] is right outside. The sturdy doors and double-glazing in the simply furnished, parquet-floored rooms help dampen the 6am sounds of the market set-up.

☎ 02.502.42.43 **F** 02.502.76.19 **w** www.hotelgalia.com **M** Porte de Hal; Gare du Midi ◆ 24 ♨ ◑ ● 🅿 ▤ all ⓦ doubles: from 2200BF

Hôtel Saint-Michel 15 Grand' Place, Central

This tall, skinny hotel, on one of the world's most picturesque squares, the Grand' Place, is sure to make for an unforgettable stay. Remarkably discreet given its location, it's comfortable and unpretentious, with bright, spacious rooms and amazing views onto the Grand' Place (the best of which is from room 22). Those at the front are pricier, but don't count on a quiet night's sleep. And those at the back can be disappointing. Breakfast is served in the rooms.

☎ 02.511.09.56 **F** 02.511.46.00 **M** Centrale ◆ 15 ♨ ▤ 🖉 ▤ all ⓦⓦ doubles: from 3950BF (w/e rates available)

La Madeleine 20–22 rue de la Montagne, Central

Very good value for money, this simple hotel, behind a listed façade, is deservedly popular. All the rooms are different in size and style, but all freshly decorated in green and yellow, with white bathrooms. Rooms at the front overlook bustling place de l'Albertine with craft stalls and buskers; those at the back have no view but are quieter. An absolutely fantastic location.

☎ 02.513.29.73 **F** 02.502.13.50 **M** Centrale ◆ 52 ♨ ▤ all ⓦⓦ doubles: from 3295BF

↓ budget beds

Les Éperonniers 1 rue des Éperonniers, Central

A backpacking clientele stop at this friendly, family-run hotel – economic for groups. All rooms have toilet or shower (some both), plus TVs. The best have varnished floorboards and bright decor. Try breakfast in the café (300BF).

☎ 02.513.53.66 **F** 02.511.32.30 **M** Centrale ◆ 30 ▤ AE/MC/V ⓦ beds: from 2095BF (in a room of six)

Sleep Well 23 rue du Damier, Central

It calls itself a 'youth hotel' and rightly so. With comic strip murals and a games room, this place is fab for the budget-conscious. Rooms are bright and clean; all have sinks, some showers. There's a 3am curfew.

☎ 02.218.50.50 **F** 02.218.13.13 **w** www.sleepwell.be **M** Rogier ◆ 172 (beds) ♨ 🖉 ⌨ 🖳 ♿ ▤ MC/V ⓦ beds: from 350BF (in a room of eight); twins: 570BF per person (+ sheet hire)

↓ aparthotels

Agenda Louise 6 rue de Florence, Ixelles (West)

This discreet hotel offers a friendly reception with a less corporate feel. Rooms decorated in jade, russet, and gold tones have little kitchenettes. A buffet breakfast is served in an attractive navy and yellow room.

☎ 02.539.00.31 **F** 02.539.00.63 **w** www.hotel-agenda.com **M** Louise ◆ 38 ♨ 🖉 🅿 ♿ ▤ all ⓦⓦ doubles: from 4500BF (w/e rates available)

Cascade 128 rue Berckmans, St-Gilles

Built around an interior courtyard, which doubles as a breakfast patio in the summer, this modern hotel has 70 studios and apartment. The two-bed flats have the added attraction of washing machines.

☎ 02.538.88.30 **F** 02.538.92.79 **M** Hôtel des Monnaies ◆ 80 ♨ ▤ ↔ 🖉 ◑ ⌨ 🅿 ▤ all ⓦⓦⓦ doubles: from 20,500BF per week (w/e rates available)

↓ arriving & departing

Brussels' central role in Europe has made it a hub for continent-wide transport networks. Trains from around Europe converge in the central Gare du Midi (Zuidstation), and two airports provide international entry points.

by air

Brussels National Airport (Zaventem)

Located 15km northeast of Brussels, Zaventem Airport is the city's main airport, handling international flights operated by Sabena, the Belgian airline, and other major carriers like Virgin Express.

transport options: Zaventem to central Brussels

🚊 Airport City Express

20 mins to/from Gare Centrale (also stops at Gare du Nord & Gare du Midi).

🕐 four times an hour from 6am–midnight daily.

BF 90BF (tickets from the desk before boarding)

♿ 1| It's quick, cheap and efficient. 2| The train station is underground in the airport, easily accessible by lift.

SNCB ☎ 02.555.25.25

🚌 bus

35 mins to/from Gare du Nord.

🕐 hourly from 6.20am–11.05pm daily.

BF 70BF (tickets on board from the driver)

♿ The cheapest way of getting into central Brussels.

De Lijn ☎ 02.526.28.28

🚕 taxis

15–20 mins to/from city centre.

🕐 24 hours daily

BF 800BF–1000BF

♿ 1| Wheelchair access for foldable chairs. 2| Lots available outside arrivals hall.

👁 1| Watch out for unlicensed taxi drivers in the arrivals hall.

limos & cars

20–30 mins to/from city centre.

🕐 24 hours daily.

BF 2000BF–2385BF

♿ Wheelchair access for foldable chairs.

👁 Most expensive option.

Europcar Limo: ☎ 02.348.92.12
Avis Limo: ☎ 02.504.10.30
Modern Car Limousine:
☎ 02.420.10.00
Belgian Limo: ☎ 02.753.63.73

Airportstop

Internet service where a driver offers a lift to/from the airport or a passenger looks for a lift to/from Zaventem.

BF 10BF/km (divided between number of people in the car).

♿ Very quick and cheap.

BIAC ☎ 02.753.42.28
Taxistop ☎ 09.223.23.10
w www.airportstop.org

☎ useful numbers

General enquiries:
0900.70000/02.753.21.11
Arrivals/departures: 02.753.39.13
Lost property: 02.753.68.20
First aid: 02.753.69.69
Airport security: 02.753.70.00
Customs: 02.753.48.30
w www.brusselsairport.be
🛏 **Sheraton:** 02.725.10.00
🛏 **Holiday Inn:** 02.720.58.65
🛏 **Mercure:** 02.726.73.35

Brussels South-Charleroi Airport

Brussels South-Charleroi is a small, privately owned airport 55km from the centre of Brussels. It deals mostly with holiday charter traffic, but also scheduled flights from Ryanair.

transport options: South-Charleroi to central Brussels

🚌 bus, then 🚊 train

Catch a bus to Charleroi train station (takes 10 mins), then connect onto a Belgian Railways (SNCB/NMBS) train (45 mins to/from Gare du Midi).

🕐 **Shuttle bus:** timed to connect with flight arrivals and departures; 6.50am–8.30pm Mon–Sat (to 2pm Sat); 2.45–7.55pm Sun. **Train:** approx. 7 and 34 mins past every hour 4.31am–11.07pm Mon–Fri; approx. 27 mins past every hour 5.27am–11.27pm Sat–Sun.

BF 300BF to/from anywhere in Brussels

👁 The lack of regularity in this service can make it a slow journey.

☎ 07.160.22.94

🚌 shuttle bus

45 mins to/from the Wild Geese pub [→106] on avenue Livingstone, Brussels, for Ryanair passengers only.

🕐 **Wild Geese–Charleroi:**
7.50am, 2.30pm, 6.20pm Mon–Fri; 7.50am, 11.40am Sat; 1.50pm, 5.40pm Sun.

Charleroi–Wild Geese:
9.50am, 4.40pm, 8.30pm Mon–Fri; 9.50am, 1.45pm Sat; 7.40pm Sun.

BF 250BF

Ryanair ☎ UK: 08701.569.569; Belgium: 07.123.41.15

☎ useful numbers

Enquiries: 07.125.12.11 (all enquiries, including flight info, lost property, customs and lost luggage)
w www.charleroi-airport.com
🛏 **Holiday Inn Garden Court:** 07.130.24.24

all prices single unless otherwise stated

by train

High-speed services on Eurostar, Thalys and other European rail services have opened up a world of inter-Europe travel. Gare du Midi lies at the heart of the network, creating easy access to and from Brussels.

▌▌▌ Eurostar

Eurostar is the high-speed train linking London Waterloo and Ashford International to the Gare du Midi in Brussels. The journey from London takes 2 hrs 40 mins.

🕐 6.14am–7.27pm daily (approx. 14 times a day Mon–Sat; 8 times a day Sun).

🎫 from 6500BF (from £70) return.

Tickets can be bought on the internet, over the phone, at train stations in Brussels, and in travel agencies. Booked tickets can be picked up at the Railtour desk at Gare du Midi up until 30 mins before departure.

♿ 1| Children under 4 travel free. 2| Eurostar trains are well set up for disabled travellers, with toilets designed for wheelchair-users and low-level flooring at train doors.

⚠ While the interior of Gare du Midi is safe, care should be taken if walking around the surrounding area.

❶ 1| Check in 20 mins before departure. 2| You need your passport even if you are an EU citizen travelling from within the EU.

☎ UK: 0870.160.66.00; Belgium: 0900.101.77
w www.eurostar.com

▌▌▌ Thalys

Thalys is a network of high-speed trains connecting Brussels (Gare du Midi) with Amsterdam, Cologne, Paris, Lyons and Geneva. It takes 1 hr 25 mins to Paris and 2 hrs 38 mins to Amsterdam (with a stop-off at Schiphol Airport, Amsterdam).

🕐 There are 22 trains each way per day between Brussels and Paris; and five trains each way per day between Brussels and Amsterdam.

🎫 Brussels–Paris: 3060BF return; Brussels–Amsterdam: 1860BF return.

Tickets can be bought on the internet, over the phone, at train stations, and in travel agencies. Booked tickets can be picked up at the Railtour desk at Gare du Midi up until 30 mins pre-departure.

♿ 1| Children under 4 travel free. 2| Thalys trains are well set up for disabled travellers, with toilets designed for wheelchair-users.

☎ Bookings: 0900.101.77/07.066.77.88 w www.thalys.com

le shuttle

Instead of taking the car over sea, take it underground. Cars go through the Channel Tunnel on Le Shuttle from Folkestone to Calais. There are approx. 70 crossings per day (four per hour during the day, hourly through the night). The journey takes 35 mins and the drive from Calais to Brussels approx. 2 hrs.

UK: 0870.535.35.35 w www.eurotunnel.co.uk

🎫 £169.50 return

by sea

Competition from Eurostar and Le Shuttle has made crossing the Channel by sea cheaper than ever, with offers on almost year-round.

⛴ P&O North Sea Ferries

P&O North Sea Ferries travel to/from Zeebrugge and Hull every night, taking just over 13 hours.

🕐 6.15pm daily from Hull (arrives Zeebrugge 8.30am); 6.15pm daily from Zeebrugge (arrives Hull 8am).

🎫 Foot passenger: from 3832BF (£38) return; car (including 4 passengers): from 6212BF (£161) return.

❶ Train to Brussels takes between 1 hr 15 mins and 1 hr 30 mins (approx. once an hour from 6.03am–9.35 pm Mon–Fri; approx. every 2 hours 6am–10.02pm Sat–Sun). 🎫 445BF.

☎ UK: 01482.377.177; Belgium: 050.54.34.30
w www.ponsf.com

⛴ Hoverspeed

Hoverspeed's Seacat operates to/from Ostend and Dover and takes just less than two hours.

🕐 Five crossings per day in high season; two or three a day in low season.

🎫 Foot passenger: from 3000BF (£56) return; car (including 2 passengers): from 12,580BF (£218) return.

♿ Train connections to Brussels (4 times hourly, 3.57am–10.38pm, 460BF).

☎ UK: 0870.524.02.41; Belgium: 059.55.99.11
w www.hoverspeed.co.uk

by coach

Eurolines runs direct routes to and from major European destinations and the Gare du Nord in Brussels.

🕐 London: 7 times daily each way, 7 hrs 30 mins; Paris: 8 times daily each way, 3 hrs 45 mins; Amsterdam: 7 times daily each way, 4 hrs; Berlin: once a day each way, 10 hrs 15 mins.

🎫 Single fares: to/from London: 1690BF; to/from Paris: 550BF; to/from Amsterdam: 600BF; to/from Berlin: 2100BF.

♿ The cheapest way to travel.

⚠ The journeys are often long and arduous.

☎ UK: 0870.514.32.19; Belgium: 02.274.13.50/02.538.20.49

↓ getting around

STIB/MIVB is Brussels' city transport authority. It operates the entire metro, bus, and tram network in the Brussels Region.

general information

🎫 tickets & travelcards

The same type of ticket is used on all trams, buses, and on the metro. Tickets can be bought in metro stations and on buses and trams and are valid for one hour once validated in the orange machines. The STIB/MIVB Anspach Agency (31 rue de l'Evêque) – the transport authority office – gives out information and sells tickets.

➰ On-the-spot fines of 2200BF are incurred for not having a valid ticket.

♿ disabled travellers

Most trams and buses, as well as the metro, are not accessible to wheelchair users, apart from the newer T2000 trams, which have wide doors and low floors. STIB/MIVB runs a minibus service for the disabled which operates 6.30am–11pm daily. But it needs to be booked 8 days in advance.

🧒 kids

Children under 6 yrs, accompanied by an adult, travel free (four per paying adult).

maps & leaflets

STIB/MIVB maps are available from Porte de Namur, Rogier and Midi metro stations, as well as the STIB Anspach Agency at 31 rue de l'Evêque.

public transport weekend

Buy a ticket (450BF) and travel as much as you like on the metro, buses, trams, and trains all over Belgium for one weekend in October.
☎ 02.555.25.25

☎ useful numbers

STIB/MIVB: 02.515.20.00
Lost property: 02.515.23.94
Minibus for the disabled: 02.515.23.65
w www.stib.be

types of tickets

Carte d'un voyage
A single journey, for 1 hr after ticket validation.
50BF (from drivers on buses and trams, and metro stations)

Carte STIB + Taxi
A single journey, for 1 hr after validation, plus an 80BF reduction on a return taxi journey.
☎ Taxi Verts: 02.349.49.49
60BF (from metro stations)

Carte d'un jour
Unlimited travel for one day on all buses, trams, metro, De Lijn, and TEC.
140BF (from drivers on buses and trams, and from metro stations)

Carte de 5 voyages
Five single journeys, all for 1 hr after ticket validation.
240BF (from metro stations)

Carte de 10 voyages
Ten single journeys, all for 1 hr after ticket validation.
350BF (from metro stations)

transport

on wheels

🚕 taxis

Officially registered taxis display a yellow and blue emblem with the words Région de Bruxelles. You can hail a taxi, go to a rank (biggest are at mainline train stations), or order one by phone.

🕐 24 hours daily.

🎫 The pick-up rate is 95BF, plus 38BF per km within Brussels. The rate doubles when you leave the city. A tip is included in the fare on the meter. A night tax of 75BF is added from 10pm–6am.

❶ 1| Have 100BF notes ready. 2| They take four passengers only, and mean it. 3| A prix forfaitaire (fixed price fare) can be arranged if booked by phone.

Taxis Verts ☎ 02.349.49.49
Autolux ☎ 02.411.12.21
Taxis Bleus ☎ 02.268.00.00

For complaints about services or drivers, call ☎ 0800.147.95

driving & biking

Driving in Brussels is not for the faint-hearted and is only recommended for getting out

of the city. Walking the centre is easy, and longer distances are quicker by public transport.

rules of the road

1| Drive on the right. 2| Trams have *absolute* priority. 3| The *priorité à droite* rule means you have to yield to the right – if in doubt, stop. 4| Speed limits are 50 km/hr in cities, 90 km/hr on other routes, and 120 km/hr on motorways.

car rental

Most international companies have branches at Zaventem airport and Gare du Midi. Minimum age is usually 23. It's expensive – expect to pay £60 per day and £200 per week.
Avis: ☎ 02.527.17.05
Budget: ☎ 02.527.59.47
Europcar: ☎ 02.522.95.73
Hertz: ☎ 02.524.31.00
National Car Rental:
☎ 02.524.57.38

motorbike/moped rental

Age requirements vary – some companies will hire mopeds to 18 yr olds, others only to the over 21's. Expect to pay 2000BF–5000BF per day as well as helmet hire.

Dockx Motorrental:
☎ 02.245.75.75
Brussels Motor Renting:
☎ 02.725.34.35
Baele & Schmitz Motos:
☎ 02.762.60.27

parking

Parking meters take 5BF, 20BF and 50BF coins. 24-hr car parks cost 70BF–200BF per hr and 500BF–800BF for 24 hrs.
Agora: 104 rue du Marché aux Herbes ☎ 02.513.33.18
Ecuyer: 13 rue de l'Écuyer
☎ 02.219.07.18
Hilton Hotel: 38 boulevard de Waterloo ☎ 02.504.11.11

cycling

Brussels is not a bike-friendly city – bicycle lanes are rare, dodging wet tram lines is like dicing with death, and car drivers are none too helpful. But hiring a bike in the leafy suburbs or outside the city is a joy. You'll pay between 350BF–400BF per day and 1250BF–2000BF per week.
Pro Velo: ☎ 02.502.73.55
Bike Events: ☎ 02.757.94.44
Vélo Cité: ☎ 02.241.36.35

→ back cover for transport map of city centre

public transport options

M metro & pre-metro

Looking at a metro & pre-metro map of Brussels, you'd be forgiven for assuming that there's a large network of underground trains. In actual fact, there are only three routes on the metro; the rest is the underground section of the tram network, known as the pre-metro.

◑	{BF}	☎	❶
5.30am–12.30am daily	single journey: 50BF [→types of tickets 129]	STIB/MIVB: 02.515.20.00	▸ Validate tickets in the orange machines on trams and at underground stations. ▸ To open the doors on a pre-metro tram, press the central green strip. ▸ To request a stop on a pre-metro tram, press the black buttons next to the doors. ▸ Metro stations are identified by a white M on a blue background. ▸ There are three main metro routes – line 1A, line 1B and line 2. ▸ It's a fast, safe and efficient system.

⊟ trams

The distinctive blue-and-yellow trams circulate at street level all over Brussels and the suburbs. Route numbers and final destinations are displayed on the front.

◑	{BF}	☎	❶
5.30am–12.30am daily	single journey: 50BF [→types of tickets 129]	STIB/MIVB: 02.515.20.00	▸ Stops are indicated by red and white signs with the stop name and tram numbers they serve. ▸ Trams don't stop automatically, so raise your hand to attract the driver's attention. ▸ The doors don't automatically open, so press the green strip down the centre. ▸ To request a stop once you're on, press the black button – a light comes on over the door, which opens automatically. ▸ Validate tickets in the orange machines. ▸ Hold on tight as many drivers slam on the brakes at times.

⊟ buses

Buses run in Brussels and the suburbs. To travel out of the city, use De Lijn for Flemish towns (from Gare du Nord) and TEC for places in Walloon (at place Rouppé).

◑	{BF}	☎	❶
5.30am–12.30am daily	single journey: 50BF [→types of tickets 129]	STIB/MIVB: 02.555.25.25 De Lijn: 02.526.28.28 TEC: 01.361.94.44	▸ Validate tickets for inner-city buses in the orange machines on board. ▸ Hold on tight standing up, as buses brake quite hard for the priority to the right rule of driving. ▸ Both De Lijn and TEC offer a limited, rather irregular service.

Ⅲ trains

Belgium's railway network, the SNCB/NMBS, is excellent and the distances between destinations never far. There are frequent trains to all towns in Belgium, as well as Brussels' suburbs.

◑	{BF}	☎	❶
4.30am–midnight daily	Varies depending on journey; see ❶ for details of special tickets. Children under 12 travel free.	SNCB/NMBS: 02.555.25.25 w http://sncb.be	▸ A Billet Weekend is 40% cheaper than a weekday ticket. ▸ The B-Tourrail ticket, at 2200BF, is valid for unlimited travel in Belgium on any five days over a one-month period. ▸ The B-Excursion 'all-in' ticket combines a train fare and entrance fee to a tourist attraction (with over 100 choices) such as zoos, leisure parks and museums. ▸ The train and bike scheme lets you reserve a bike at 35 Belgian destinations when booking a ticket. From 365BF per day.

↓ a–z essentials

admission charges

Charges for museums and sights vary but expect to pay 50BF–150BF. Most are closed on Mondays. Some, including the Musée d'Art Ancien and the Musée d'Art Moderne, are free on the first Wednesday afternoon (1pm–5pm) of each month.

banks

Banks are usually open 9am–4pm Mon–Fri. Various branches close for lunch and some stay open late one day a week. A few banks in the suburbs are open Saturday mornings – but none in the centre. Main banks are the Banque Bruxelles Lambert (BBL), Fortis, and KBC. All major branches have 24-hour cash dispensers. Eurocheques of up to 7000BF can be cashed at any bank showing the Eurocheque sign and cash withdrawals can be made at cash dispensers bearing the Eurocheque logo (Eurocheques can also be used in restaurants and shops). For international money transfers:
Western Union ☎ 0800.990.90;
Goffin, 88 rue du Marché aux Herbes, ☎ 02.502.23.82 ◑ 9am–10pm Mon–Sat; or
Camrail Cash Services at Gare Centrale, ☎ 02.511.43.14 ◑ 7am–9pm Mon–Sat.
The most central banks are:
BBL, 90 rue du Marché aux Herbes ☎ 02.506.42.90 ◑ 9am–4pm Mon–Fri; **Fortis Bank**, 3 boulevard Anspach ☎ 02.212.94.11 ◑ 9am–4pm Mon–Fri; **KBC**, 5 pl de Brouckère ☎ 02.250.09.70 ◑ 9am–4pm Mon–Fri.

bars & cafés

Bars and cafés are usually open throughout the day and since there's no official closing time, some stay open until the early hours, depending on the number of customers. As well as alcohol, bars sell tea and coffee, and usually, light snacks. Cafés serve full menus. Officially, larger cafés are supposed to have a non-smoking area. In reality, only a few bother. Children and pets are usually welcome.

bureaux de change

Expect to pay 25BF on traveller cheques' exchanges. Beware of good rates but high commission. Thomas Cook doesn't charge a commission if you change their own cheques (now issued in euros) at one of their offices. Banks offer a fixed rate of exchange whereas bureaux de change can vary, so do shop around.
Basle, 23 rue au Beurre ☎ 02.511.56.30 ◑ 9am–6pm daily.
Thomas Cook, 4 Grand' Place ☎ 02.513.28.45 ◑ 9am–7pm daily.
Camrail Cash Services, Gare Centrale ☎ 02.511.43.14 ◑ 7am–9pm daily.
Camrail Cash Services, Gare du Midi ☎ 02.556.36.00 ◑ 6.30am–10pm daily.

children

Activities: check the What's On section of The Bulletin [→111], in newsagents every Thursday.
Babysitters: contact Baby Kid Sitting ☎ 02.646.46.11.
Hotels: many hotels allow children to share their parents' room at no extra charge or at a reduced rate per child.
Restaurants, cafés & bars: children are welcomed with open arms in most restaurants,

cafés, and bars. Kids' menus are also common. There aren't many high-chairs or play areas, however, and the only downtown public facility for changing nappies is at the M&S store on rue Neuve.
Transport: children under 6 travel free on STIB buses, trams, and metro – a maximum of four kids is allowed per paying adult. Children under 12 travel free on trains within Belgium.

clubs

Admission: clubs are often free 11pm–midnight, but expect to pay 150BF–400BF thereafter (the price usually includes a drink).
Dress code/door policy: dress codes vary so it's best to check ahead. At most clubs, doormen expect a tip of at least 50BF as you leave.
Opening times: generally 11pm until 5–6am.

conversion chart

Clothing	Women's				Men's			
European	36	40	44	46	46	50	54	56
British	8	12	16	18	36	40	44	46
US	6	10	14	16	36	40	44	46

Shoes	Women's				Men's			
European	37	38	39	40	40	42	43	44
British	4	5	6	7	6	7	8	9
US	5	6	7	8	7	8	9	10

courier services

National services within Belgium:
EMS Transport ☎ 078.15.33.43
Taxi verts ☎ 02.349.46.46
BCC ☎ 02.463.44.99
International services:
DHL ☎ 02.715.50.50
FedEx ☎ 0800.135.55
UPS ☎ 0800.128.28

credit & debit cards

The most widely accepted cards are American Express, MasterCard/EuroCard, and Visa. All major credit cards can be used in restaurants, hotels, and some taxis. As long as you have a PIN number, you can withdraw cash with your debit or credit card at one of the many ATMs in the city displaying the Eurocheque or Visa logos. Remember there's an extra charge for credit card withdrawals. Cards carrying the Cirrus logo can only be used at ATMs displaying the same logo.
For lost or stolen cards call:
American Express ☎ 02.676.26.26
MasterCard/EuroCard ☎ 070.34.43.44
Visa ☎ 070.344.344

currency

Belgium's currency is the Belgian franc, usually referred to as FB or BF. Coins come in 0.5BF, 1BF, 5BF, 20BF, and 50BF. Notes come in denominations of 100BF, 500BF, 1000BF, 5000BF, and 10,000BF.
On 1st January 2002 the euro will become the official currency of Belgium and on 1st July 2002, the Belgian franc will disappear altogether. Until then prices are given in both Belgian francs and euros (1 euro = 39.2501BF).

customs & quarantine

Brussels customs (douane) has 'a goods to declare' exit and a 'no goods to declare' exit. There are no quarantine laws in existence but certain endangered species are prohibited. Meat, flowers, and plants are also prohibited.
Customs ☎ 02.753.48.30

practical information

dentists

For urgent dental care: Service de Garde Dentaire, 107 avenue Jacques Sermon ☎ 02.426.10.26 or 02.428.58.88
St-Pierre hospital: ☎ 02.535.40.55 (for emergency treatment at weekends).

disabled visitors

The Grand Place and the surrounding streets have cobbled stones making life difficult for wheelchair users. Furthermore, the city's trams, buses, and the metro are not easily accessible for disabled visitors – the exceptions are the T2000 trams which have wide doors and low floors. Contact the TIB ☎ 02.513.89.40 for information on disabled access to hotels, museums, and restaurants in Brussels.

driving

Driving in the capital is difficult as the *Bruxellois* tend to drive fast and aggressively. The public transport system, however, is efficient and distances are short, so it's only worth driving for days out of the city.

duty free

Duty-free goods are still available to non-EU nationals and usual restrictions apply. Visitors are allowed a maximum of 200 cigarettes, 1 litre of spirits or 2 litres of wine. EU nationals can still benefit from reductions on clothes, cosmetics, and perfumes. (**Customs** ☎ 02.753.48.30).

electricity

Electrical supply is 220 volts and sockets are the standard European two-pronged type. British appliances need an adaptor; US ones need a transformer and an adaptor. These can be purchased at main airports.

email & internet

You can surf the net in:
Cyberb@r 185 chaussée d'Ixelles
☎ 02.502.51.25 📠 250BF/hour ◐ 12pm–midnight Mon–Sat.
Internet Center 182 chaussée de Charleroi
☎ 02.534.61.41 📠 3000BF/hour
◐ 9am–7pm daily.
Pointnet Surf Center 16 Petite rue des Bouchers ☎ 02.513.14.15 📠 200BF/hour (unlimited access over one week for 2000BF)
◐ 10am–10pm Mon–Sat (to 6pm Sat).
Sport Avenue 4–5 avenue de la Toison d'Or
☎ 02.500.78.78 📠 250BF/hour (50-hour pass costs 5000BF) ◐ 10am–11pm Mon–Sat. To locate other cyber cafés go to http://cyber café.potaulait.be or www.netcafes.com

embassies & consulates

American Embassy: 27 boulevard du Régent
☎ 02.508.21.11
Australian Embassy: 6–8 rue Guimard
☎ 02.286.05.00
British Embassy: 85 rue d'Arlon
☎ 02.287.62.11
Canadian Embassy: 2 avenue de Tervuren
☎ 02.741.06.11
Irish Embassy: 98 rue Froissart
☎ 02.230.53.37
New Zealand Embassy: 47–48 boulevard du Régent ☎ 02.512.10.40

emergencies

For emergency ambulance, fire brigade, or medical service call 100 or go to one of the following major hospitals:
Hôpital St-Pierre, 322 rue Haute
☎ 02.535.40.51 (emergencies)

Clinique St-Luc, 10 avenue Hippocrate
☎ 02.764.16.02 (emergencies)
Centre Hospitalier Brugmann, 4 place Van Gehuchten ☎ 02.477.20.01 (emergencies)

help & advice lines

Alcoholics Anonymous ☎ 02.513.23.36
Aids ☎ 02.511.45.29 ☎ 078.15.15.15
Community Help Service (CHS) ☎ 02.648.40.14
(24-hr telephone helpline in English)
Télé Accueil ☎ 107 (24-hr Samaritan-type line)

hotels

Charges: Surprisingly, low season in Brussels is Jul–Aug and during the end-of-year festivities. This is because Brussels attracts such a large number of business people on weekdays during the rest of the year. Cheap hotel rates are available during these periods and you can book a five-star hotel at a reasonable price. Low rates operate during weekends all year round and there are reductions for children who share their parents' room. Some hotels will charge a cancellation fee if you cancel after 6pm. Check-out time is usually 11am.
Useful contacts: A free hotel reservation service is operated by **Belgium Tourist Reservations** ☎ 02.513.74.84 ◐ 9am–5pm Mon–Fri. For home-swaps and a bed and breakfast guide, call Taxistop ☎ 02.223.23.10.

immigration

If you're planning to stay more than 3 months, you have to report to the town hall of the commune where you plan to live (there are 19 communes or districts in Brussels). Telephone in advance for opening hours and the documents you may need as they vary between communes. Most communes will require a passport, 2 passport photos, and either your lease on accommodation or a letter from your employer stating that you are in full-time employment. A fee will be charged to cover administrative costs. For the number of your local town hall look under 'Administrations communales' in the white pages telephone directory (*Les Pages Blanches/De Witte Gids*). Central Brussels (1000), ☎ 02.279.22.11

insurance

Comprehensive travel and medical insurance is recommended, particularly for non-EU citizens. EU nationals should be in possession of an E111, which covers basic medical treatment. Keep all receipts as you have to pay on the spot and be reimbursed on your return.

left luggage

24-hour access lockers are available at Gare du Midi and Gare Centrale. Manual lockers cost 60BF for 24 hours. Electronic lockers cost between 60BF–100BF (depending on the volume) for 24 hours.

lost property

Report all lost property to the police (☎ 02.279.79.79 for central Brussels) to substantiate insurance claims. If you lose your passport you will also need to report it to your embassy [→132]. For lost property on public transport contact the public transport authority (STIB) ☎ 02.515.23.94; at Brussels Zaventem airport ☎ 02.753.68.20.

maps

De Rouck maps (www.de-rouck.be) are readily available at newsagents, bookshops, and supermarkets. The Tourist Information Brussels (TIB) on the Grand Place also has city maps for sale.

measurements

As a rule, metric measures are used.

metric : imperial	imperial : metric
1 mm = 0.04 inch	1 inch = 2.5 cm
1 cm = 0.4 inch	1 foot = 30 cm
1 m = 3.3 ft	1 mile = 1.6 km
1 km = 0.6 mile	1 ounce = 28 g
1 g = 0.04 oz	1 pound = 454 g
1 l = 0.6 (US) gallon	1 pint = 0.6 l
	1 (US) gallon = 3.8 l

medical matters

Go to the outpatients department of one of the hospitals listed [→emergencies] or call the CHS helpline ☎ 02.648.40.14 for advice if you need an English-speaking doctor. For abortion and contraception advice call La Famille Heureuse, 4 place Quetelet ☎ 02.217.44.50 or ☎ 02.217.46.02.

medicine & chemists

A *pharmacie* (in French) or *apotheek* (in Flemish) sells everything from over-the-counter medicines to prescription drugs, as well as everyday toiletries. An extra charge of 158BF is added to the price of your prescription if you go to chemists outside normal hours. A list of the *pharmaciens de garde* (chemists open at night and at weekends) is posted on chemists' windows. You can also check the *Le Soir* newspaper or call ☎ 0900.105.00 for a list of them. ◐ generally 9am–6pm. Some open until 7pm and a few open on Saturday mornings.

office & business services

Faxing, colour copying and binding services are available at:
Business Copy 6a rue Volta ☎ 02.649.76.97
Chasse Copy & Multimedia 16 avenue Pirmez ☎ 02.644.06.34 (also offers use of its computer terminals).
Mister Copy 117–123 boulevard Général Jacques ☎ 02.640.94.21
The **NCI Business Center** offers fully equipped offices, multilingual secretarial and translation services, and personalized answering services: 149 avenue Louise ☎ 02.535.75.11; 50 rue Wiertz ☎ 02.401.68.11.
For stationery, call into the **Inno** department store, 111 rue Neuve ☎ 02.211.21.11.

opticians

The following branches of Optic City offer free eye-tests on condition you buy a pair of glasses from them:
Optic City City 2 Shopping Centre, 123 rue Neuve ☎ 02.218.11.55; 30 boulevard Anspach ☎ 02.218.71.97

parking

(→transport)

photography

For a one-hour developing service try:
Flash One City 2, 123 rue Neuve ☎ 02.217.05.15 ◐ 9am–7pm daily.
For cheaper, three-day options try:
Di stores City 2, 123 rue Neuve ☎ 02.218.01.90 ◐ 10am–7pm daily. (other branches)
FNAC City 2, 123 rue Neuve ☎ 02.275.11.11 ◐ 10am–7pm (to 8pm Fri). This is the largest FNAC store and also offers a one-hour development service.
For camera repairs try:
Campion 13 rue St-Boniface ☎ 02.512.13.31 ◐ 10am–7pm Mon–Sat.
Lontie 1528 chaussée de Wavre ☎ 02.672.30.80 ◐ 10am–7pm Mon–Sat.

police

Only use ☎ 101 in emergencies. Otherwise call the police station in central Brussels, 30 rue du Marché au Charbon ☎ 02.279.79.79 to find out the nearest station.

postal services

Post offices ◐ 9am–5pm Mon–Fri. Most post offices are closed at weekends and on public holidays. The central post office is in the Centre Monnaie, place de Brouckère ☎ 02.226.21.11 ◐ 8am–7pm Mon–Fri (9.30am–3pm Sat). There's also a post office at 48 avenue Fonsny ☎ 02.538.33.98 ◐ 24 hours daily.
Stamps: To send letters and cards within Belgium costs 17BF and 21BF for other EU countries. The post office on rue Cortenberg (near Schuman) has a stamp machine if you want to avoid the queues.
Poste restante: the post office at the Centre Monnaie in central Brussels accepts mail for collection. You will need your passport to claim your poste restante.
Info poste ☎ 02.226.23.10

public holidays

New Year's Day – 1st January
Easter Monday – March/April (variable)
Labour Day – 1st May
Ascension – 6th Thursday after Easter
Whit Monday – 7th Monday after Easter
National Day – 21st July
Assumption – 15th August
All Saints' Day – 1st November
Armistice – 11th November
Christmas Day – 25th December

religion

For information on religious services and places of worship contact:
Catholic ☎ 02.511.81.78
Jewish ☎ 02.512.43.34
Muslim ☎ 02.735.21.73
For further information call:
Bruxelles-Accueil 6 rue de Tabora ☎ 02.511.81.78 ◐ 10am–6pm Mon–Sat.

restaurants

Reservations: it's advisable to make a reservation for the more up-market restaurants, particularly at weekends.
Opening times: restaurants usually serve lunch 12–2.30pm and dinner 6–10.30pm. Many close for either the whole of July or August so call in advance if you're going around this time.
Prices: vary enormously but on the whole, eating out is cheaper than in other major cities.
Tipping: is usually left to the discretion of the customer as service is included in the bill.
Smoking: non-smoking sections are rare and Belgians don't mind nearby patrons lighting up.
Moules: Watch out for *moules*, which can be unsafe if eaten out of season. Most restaurants will only serve them August–April.

safety

Take the usual precautions that you would in any major city. Avoid walking alone late at night in poorly lit, isolated areas. In particular, be wary of the areas around the Gare du Nord and the Gare du Midi. Public transport is pretty safe, but women travelling alone should be cautious in underground stations off the beaten track late at night. As ID is compulsory, it's preferable to have a photocopy of your passport in your possession.

practical information

shopping

Export: some shops offer VAT discounts to non-EU nationals [→VAT]
Opening times: generally from 9/9.30am–6/6.30pm. Supermarkets are open longer.
Payment: can be made by cash or credit card.
Returns: should be made as soon as possible. You will need your receipt in order to exchange goods or get a refund. Note that sales goods are non-refundable.
Guarantees: are available on larger goods and equipment. Keep your receipt and ensure the guarantee is stamped before leaving the shop.
Sales: The winter sale starts in January and lasts the whole month. The summer sale takes place during the whole month of July.

smoking

Belgians tend to smoke in restaurants, bars, and cafés, but public buildings such as banks and post offices are no-smoking areas, as is public transport.

students

USIT Connections ☎ 02.550.01.00 and Acotra World ☎ 02.289.78.00 offer discounts for students under 26 who carry an International Student Identity Card (ISIC). ISIC cards are available at **USIT Connections** – you will need proof you are still a student plus 350BF.

telephoning

Phone sounds: repeated short beeps = engaged; long beeps = ringing.
Local codes: numbers within Brussels use the prefix ☎ 02.
International codes: to call Belgium from the UK and Ireland dial ☎ 0032; from the US ☎ 01132; from Australia ☎ 001132. To call from Belgium dial ☎ 00 plus the country code: UK ☎ 44; US ☎ 1; Australia ☎ 61; Ireland ☎ 353. Complete international numbers to Belgium by removing the first 0 from the regional code.
Directory enquiries & operator: for numbers within Belgium dial ☎ 1405 (English), ☎ 1307 (French), ☎ 1207 (Dutch), and ☎ 1407 (German).
International directory enquiries: dial ☎ 1304 (French), ☎ 1204 (Dutch), and ☎ 1404 (German).
International prefix information: dial ☎ 1324 (French), ☎ 1224 (Dutch), and ☎ 1424 (German).
Phone directories: the official directory is *Les Pages Blanches/De Witte Gids*. There are two volumes of *Les Pages d'Or/De Gouden Gids* (yellow pages).
Phone rates: standard local rate 8am–7pm weekdays is 2BF/min; evening local rate 7pm–8am weekdays, and all day on weekends and public holidays is 1BF/min. There is a basic connection charge of 2BF per local call within Belgium and 4BF for an international call. 0900 numbers cost 18BF/min while calls to GSMs (mobile phones) cost 13BF/min during peak hours. The same rates apply throughout Belgium.
Freephone numbers: numbers preceded with ☎ 0800 are free of charge.
Phone boxes: most public phone boxes are phone card- or credit card-operated.
Phone cards: *Télécards* come in units of 200BF or 1000BF and are available from newsagents, supermarkets, and post offices. Scratch the surface of the *télécard* to reveal a PIN code, dial the local number given on the card, then dial your PIN number.

A pre-recorded voice tells you how much credit you have on the card before you dial.
Mobile phone hire: try Locaphone at Zaventem airport ☎ 02.652.14.14 who rent mobiles at 365BF per day (for the first 5 days). Insurance costs 430BF and calls are paid by credit card.

time

Belgium is on Central European Time which is one hour ahead of GMT. Clocks go forward one hour in spring (end of March) and back one hour in autumn (end of October).
Dial ☎ 1300 for the 24-hour speaking clock.

tipping

Tipping isn't expected in cafés, restaurants, and hotels, as service is included in the bill – it is left entirely to the discretion of the customer. If you do wish to leave a tip in a restaurant, it's usual to give about 10% of the total bill. In hotels you can choose to tip the chambermaid or porter. Hairdressers expect a tip of at least 100BF.

toilets

There are few public toilets so pop into a railway station or a fast-food chain where you'll pay a 10BF fee. Some bars charge a fee even if you are a customer.

tourist information

Tourist Information Brussels (TIB) offers information on restaurants, museums, car hire, and events, and stocks maps and brochures.
TIB Hôtel de Ville, Grand' Place
☎ 02.513.89.40 ◑ *9am–6pm daily*.
Belgium tourist centre, 63 rue du Marché aux Herbes ☎ 02.504.03.90 ◑ *9am–6pm daily (to 1pm Sun)*.

transport

[→127–130]

travel agents

Travel agents offering cheap flights include:
Acotra World ☎ 02.289.78.00
USIT Connections ☎ 02.550.01.00
Last-minute cheap flights are on offer at
Nouvelles Frontières ☎ 02.547.44.44
w www.nouvelles-frontieres.

travellers' cheques

This is still the safest way to carry money. The most widely accepted currencies are pounds sterling and US dollars. The best places to change travellers' cheques are bank-operated bureaux de change or Thomas Cook [→bureaux de change].

VAT (Value Added Tax)

Goods in shops are taxed at 21% and non-EU citizens are entitled to a VAT refund on purchases. Take the relevant forms (a receipt and certified VAT form from the shop where you bought the goods), ID proof of non-EU citizenship, and your unopened goods to the VAT/Customs desk at the airport for refunds.

visas & entry requirements

All nationalities must carry a valid passport (or ID for EU citizens). For most non-EU citizens, a visa is not required but check with the Belgium Embassy or Consulate before leaving.

weather

Brussels' weather is very changeable. You can experience all four seasons in one day. Check the local press for the weather forecast or see w www.weather.com for daily reports.

↓ general index

135

index

137

index

↓ where to shop

139

↓ where to eat

↓ acknowledgements

Conceived, edited & designed by
Virgin Publishing Ltd
London W6 9HA
Tel: 020-7386 3300

Project Editors: Georgina Matthews, Clare Tomlinson
Project Designer: Gadi Farfour, Trond Wilhelmsen
Designer/DTP Designer: Jane Webber
Main Consultants: Clare Thomson, Matthew Davis
Consultants: Pieter van Doveren (restaurants), Michael Leahy (bars & cafés), An Mertens (languages) Sarah Wolff (shopping)
Researchers: Julie Coppock, Bess Stonehouse, Sarah Wolff

Design & editorial assistance: Alexandra Arfi, Carolyn Hewitson, Tony Limerick, Naomi Peck, Marianne Petrou, Ingrid Vienings, Sylvia Tombesi-Walton
Series Editor: Georgina Matthews
Proof Reader: Felicity Laughton
Index: Hilary Bird
Design concept: Paul Williams
Jacket concept: Debi Ani
Jacket design: Gadi Farfour

Maps:
Cartographic Editor: Dominic Beddow
Cartographers: Jethro Lennox, Simonetta Giori
Draughtsman Ltd, London
Tel: 020-8960 1602
maps@magneticnorth.net

Photography:
Photographers:
Peter de Bruyne: cover image; Le Sablon; Les Marolles; St-Gilles; Quartier Européen; St-Josse & Scharbeek; Antwerp; top restaurants; top bars; top clubs.
Matthew Lea: Ste-Catherine; Central; Ixelles (West); Ixelles (East); landmarks; sights, museums and galleries; parks & gardens; kids; game for a laugh; body & soul; hotels.

Reproduced by Colourwise
Printed by Proost, Belgium

Features were written and researched by the following:
Getting your bearings areas: Clare Thomson, Matthew Davis | **Area introductions**: Clare Thomson, Matthew Davis | **Ste-Catherine**: Steven Tate | **Central**: Steven Tate | **Le Sablon**: Steven Tate | **Les Marolles**: Steven Tate | **St-Gilles**: Michelle Carlile, Sarah Wolff | **Ixelles (East)**: Gareth Harding, Sarah Wolff | **Ixelles (West)**: Gareth Harding, Sarah Wolff | **Quartier Européen**: Renée Cordes, Gary Hills | **St-Josse & Scharbeek**: Steven Tate | **Getting your bearings out of town**: Clare Thomson, Matthew Davis | **Antwerpen**: Shaheda Ishaque | **Gent**: Shaheda Ishaque | **Brugge**: Shaheda Ishaque | **Leuven**: Shaheda Ishaque | **Sights, museums & galleries**: Clare Thomson, Matthew Davis, Renée Cordes, Dave Cronin | **Parks & gardens**: Clare Thomson, Matthew Davis | **Children**: Dave Cronin | **Game for a Laugh**: Bess Stonehouse | **Football**: Matthew Davis | **Body & Soul**: Bess Stonehouse | **Getting your bearings shopping**: Sarah Wolff | **Top shops**: Sarah Wolff | **Restaurants**: Gary Hills, Tricia Sheeky-Skeffington, Shaheda Ishaque, Michelle Carlile, Renée Cordes, Dave Cronin | **Bars & Cafés**: Gareth Harding, Michelle Carlile | **Clubs**: Steven Tate | **Media**: Michelle Carlile | **Cinema**: Gareth Harding | **Music and Classical Music & Opera**: Dave Cronin | **Theatre**: Gary Hills | **Dance**: James Lehmann | **Events**: Kathleen Cagney | **Hotels**: Katherine Mill | **Transport**: Kathleen Cagney | **Practical**: Kathleen Cagney | **Phrasebook**: An Mertens

Acknowledgements:
Virgin Publishing Ltd would like to thank all galleries, museums, shops, restaurants, bars, and other establishments who provided photographs.

Virgin Publishing Ltd is grateful to the following for permission to reproduce their photographs.
(t=top, b=bottom, c=centre):
Musée d'Art Modern (66b): *Des caresses* by Fernand Knopff © Musées Royaux des Beaux-Arts; CCNOA (75t): Transforms & Constellations by Pierre Vanderbrecht © CCNOA Brussels 1999; Ghent (54t), Brugge (56t, 56b), Leuven (57t, 57c): © Tourism Flanders-Brussels.

Please write to: Virgin Travel Guides
Virgin Publishing Ltd
Thames Wharf Studios
Rainville Road
London W6 9HA
Fax: 020-7386 3360
Email: travel@virgin-pub.co.uk

↓ get the lingo

Brussels is the bilingual capital of a trilingual country with a Flemish, Walloon, and German community. Although Brussels is geographically situated in the Flemish area, you cannot speak of its inhabitants as Flemish or Walloons. The majority speaks French, a minority speaks Flemish, and a bunch of people use both languages miscellaneously. Since a third of Brussels' population consists of immigrants, the safest language to use is French.

When you make the effort in French, you'll easily pick out the Eurocrats and the Dutch-speakers. They will immediately switch languages and explain everything in fluent English.

phrasebook

Dutch pronunciation

Consonants

ch	as in loch (coming from your throat)
g	as in loch (never pronounce it as the English g, except when words end in ing)
j	as in yes
k	as in cat
p	as in a short English t
sch	a combination of s and ch (as above)

Short vowel sounds

a	as in card
e	as in lazy
i	as in thin
o	as in dot
u	as in hurt

Long vowel sounds

aa	as in flat but longer
ee	as in same or fail
eu	sounds similar to flirt, but with rounded lips
ie	as in eat
oe	as in look
oo	as in goat
uu	sounds similar to good/übermensch

Vowel combinations

au/ou	as in loud
aai	as in bye
eeuw	as in fail (but a much longer vowel sound)
ei/ij	as in fight
ieuw	as in feel
ooi	as in oi, but with a much longer o
uw	as in phew
ui	similar to house (but say with rounded lips)
oei	pronounced oo-ee (as one long sound)

French pronunciation

Consonants

ce/ci/ça	as in centre
ca/co/qu	as in catch
ge/gi/j	as in Zhivago
ga/go/gu	as in game
r	as in lair
t/th	as in table
w	as in vanilla

i	as in tick
oi	as in one
ou	as in book
u/ue	as in übermensch

Vowel sounds

a	as in hat
ai/è/ei/er	as in bay
au	as in boat
e	as in bay (if followed by a double consonant); as in fur (in any other case)
eau/o	as in Omagh
é	as in neigh
eu/oeu	as in fur

Combinations

aile/el/elle	as in L
ain/ein/in/un	ahn
on	ohn
an/en	on (with a shortened, nasal n)
ette	as in let
euil(le)/oeil	as in oi-ye (with a shortened oi)
ien	as in yen, but more nasal
ière	as in as in premiere
ill	as in year
oin	as in one, but more nasal

Essentials

hello/hi	bonjour/salut	bon-zhoor/sa-lü	hallo/dag	hu-llo/duch
bye	au revoir	o rev-wahr	tot ziens	tot-seens
yes	oui	wi	ja	yaah
no	non	nohn	nee	nay
thank you/thanks	merci	mair-si	dank u wel/bedankt	dank i wel/be-dankt
please	s'il vous plaît	seel voo play	alstublieft	als-too-bleeft
sorry	désolé	day-zo-lay	sorry	sorry
excuse me	pardon	par-dohn	párdon	pardon
How are you?	Comment allez-vous?	Co-mon-tallay-voo?	Hoe gaat hét?	Who chaaht et?
good	bon	bon	goed	chood
bad	mal	mal	slecht	slecht
open	ouvert	oo-vair	open	o-pen
closed	fermé	fair-may	gesloten	che-sloaw-ten
entrance	entrée	on-tray	ingang	in-chang
exit	sortie	sor-tee	uitgang	owt-chang
toilet	toilettes	twa-lett	wc	vha-say
left	gauche	goash	links	links
right	droite	drwat	rechts	rechts
what?	quoi?	kwa?	wat?	what?
when?	quand?	kahn?	wanneer?	whan-eer
where?	où?	oo?	waar?	whaar?
how?	comment?	co-mon?	hoe?	hoo?
how much?	combien?	com-byan?	hoeveel	hoo-vay
Do you speak English?	Parlez-vous anglais?	Par-lay-voo on-glay?	Spréek jij Engels?	Sprayk yiy Engels?
I don't speak French/Dutch	Je ne parle pas français/néerlandais	Zhe ne parl pa fran-say/nay-air-lahnday	Het spijt me, ik spreek geen Frans/ Nederlands	Et spight meh, ik sprayk chane frans/Na-der-lands
Could you repeat that please?	Pouvez-vous répéter s'il vous plaît?	Poo-vay-voo ray-pay-tay seel voo play?	Wilt u dit een keer herhálen?	wilt oo dit an kayr her-ha-len?
Do you take credit cards/traveller's cheques?	Acceptez-vous les cartes de crédit/ traveller's chèques?	Accept-ay-voo lay kart de kray-dee/ traveller's shek?	Accepteert u credit cards/traveller's cheques?	Ack-cep-tiert oo cred-it cards/traveller's cheques?
help	à l'aide	a led	help	help
emergency	urgence	ühr-zhonse	noodgeval	nowt-ge-fall
police	police	po-leese	politie	pow-leet-see
ambulance	ambulance	ahn-bü-lahnse	politie	ahm-boo-lans-e
fire brigade	pompiers	pom-piay	brandweer	brahnt-wir
doctor	docteur	doc-ter	dokter	doc-tur
hospital	hôpital	o-pi-tahl	ziekenhuis	seek-en-howse

phrasebook

Numbers

1	*un*	eun	*een*	ayn
2	*deux*	deu	*twee*	tway
3	*trois*	twra	*drie*	dree
4	*quatre*	**kat**-re	*vier*	veer
5	*cinq*	sank	*vijf*	fayve
6	*six*	sees	*zes*	zehs
7	*sept*	set	*zeven*	**safe**-en
8	*huit*	wheat	*acht*	ackt
9	*neuf*	neuf	*negen*	**nay**-gen
10	*dix*	dees	*tien*	teen
11	*onze*	ohns	*elf*	alf
12	*douze*	doos	*twaalf*	twahlf
13	*treize*	trays	*dertien*	**der**-teen
14	*quatorze*	kat-**ohrs**	*veertien*	**veer**-teen
15	*quinze*	kahns	*vijftien*	**fayve**-teen
16	*seize*	sez	*zestien*	**zehs**-teen
17	*dix-sept*	dees-**set**	*zeventien*	**safe**-en-teen
18	*dix-huit*	dees-**wheat**	*achttien*	**acht**-teen
19	*dix-neuf*	dees-**neuf**	*negentien*	**nay**-gen-teen
20	*vingt*	vahn	*twintig*	**twin**-tich
21	*vingt-et-un*	vahn-tay-**eun**	*eenentwintig*	**ayn**-en-twin-tich
30	*trente*	trohnt	*dertig*	**der**-tich
40	*quarante*	karohnt	*veertig*	**veer**-tich
50	*cinquante*	sank-**ohnt**	*vijftig*	**fayve**-tich
60	*soixante*	swas-**ohnt**	*zestig*	**zehs**-tich
70	*septante*	set-**ohnt**	*zeventig*	**safe**-en-tich
80	*quatre-vingts*	kat-re-**vahn**	*tachtig*	**tach**-tich
90	*novante*	nov-**ohnt**	*negentig*	**nay**-gen-tich
100	*cent*	sohn	*honderd*	**hohn**-derd

Days & months

Monday	*lundi*	lurn-**dee**	*maandag*	**maahn**-darg
Tuesday	*mardi*	maar-**dee**	*dinsdag*	**dins**-darg
Wednesday	*mercredi*	mair-cray-**dee**	*woensdag*	**woo**-ns-darg
Thursday	*jeudi*	zheu-**dee**	*donderdag*	**don**-dehr-darg
Friday	*vendredi*	vondre-**dee**	*vrijdag*	**frei**-darg
Saturday	*samedi*	sam-**dee**	*zaterdag*	**sat**-er-darg
Sunday	*dimanche*	dee-**monsh**	*zondag*	**son**-darg
January	*janvier*	zhon-vee-**ai**	*januari*	**jan**-oo-ar-ee
February	*février*	fev-ree-**ai**	*februari*	fe-broo-ar-ee
March	*mars*	mahrs	*maart*	maahrt
April	*avril*	avril	*april*	a-**pril**
May	*mai*	mai	*mei*	my
June	*juin*	zhü-ahn	*juni*	**ju**-nee
July	*juillet*	zhwee-**yeigh**	*juli*	**ju**-lee
August	*août*	oot	*augustus*	**ouw**-gus-tus
September	*septembre*	sept-**om**-br	*september*	**sep**-tem-ber
October	*octobre*	octo-br	*oktober*	**ok**-too-ber
November	*novembre*	no-**vohm**-br	*november*	**no**-vem-behr
December	*décembre*	day-**som**-br	*december*	**day**-cem-behr

Hotels

I have a reservation	*J'ai une réservation*	**Zhay** ühne raysayr-vaziohn	*Ik heb gereserveerd*	Ik heb chu-ra-zur-**vayrd**
Do you have any vacancies?	*Avez-vous des chambres libres?*	Avay-**voo** day shambre lee-bre?	*Heeft u een kamer?*	Hayft oo an **kah**-mer?
single	*simple*	**sahm**-ple	*eenpersoons*	**ayn**-per-soans
double	*double*	**doo**-bleu	*tweepersoons*	**tway**-per-sowns
with bath/ shower/toilet	*avec baignoir/ douche/toilettes*	avec **bay**-nwar/ doosh/twa-**lett**	*met bad/douche/ toilet*	mit baht/doosh/ **twa**-let
half/full board	*demi-pension/ pension complète*	deu-**mi** pon-**sion**/ pon-**sion** com-**play**-te	*half/vol pension*	holf/vol **pen**-syon

Shopping

antiques shop	*antiquaire*	ahn-tee-**kayr**	*antiekwinkel*	an-**tick**-winck-el
bakery	*boulangerie*	boo-lan-**zheree**	*bakker*	**back**-er
bookshop	*librairie*	lee-brai-**ree**	*boekwinkel*	**book**-en-winck-el
chocolate shop	*chocolaterie*	sho-ko-la-te-**ree**	*chocolatier*	shocko-la-**tyay**
chemist	*pharmacie*	far-ma-**see**	*apotheek*	a-po-**tayk**
delicatessen	*traiteur*	tray-**tehr**	*delicatessenwinkel*	delicatessen vinck-el
newsagent	*tabac*	ta-**ba**	*krantenwinkel*	**kran**-tun winck-ul
supermarket	*supermarché*	su-pair-mar-**shay**	*supermarkt*	**soup**-er-markt
price	*prix*	pri	*prijs*	priys
sale	*solde*	**sol**-de	*uitverkoop*	**owt**-ver-coup
special offer	*offre spéciale*	ofre spayciale	*aanbieding*	**arn**-bee-ding
secondhand	*d'occasion*	do-ka-**ziohn**	*tweedehands*	**tway**-deh-**honts**

Transport

I want to go to...	*Je veux aller à...*	Zhe **veu** allez a ...	*Ik wil naar .... gaan*	Ik wil **naahr** ... daahn
How much is the fare to...?	*Combien coûte un billet pour...?*	Com-**byan** cooht ahn bee-**yay** por...?	*Hoeveel kost het naar...?*	Hoo-**yail** cost et nahr?
bus	*bus*	büs	*bus*	buzz
tram	*tram*	trahm	*tram*	trom
train	*train*	trahn	*trein*	trayn
metro	*métro*	may-**tro**	*metro*	**ma**-tro
bicycle	*vélo*	vay-**low**	*fiets*	**feet**-s
platform	*quai*	kay	*perron*	**pur**-ron
ticket	*billet*	bee-**yay**	*kaartje*	**kaahrt**-ye
airport	*aéroport*	a-eigh-ro-**por**	*vliegveld*	**vleeg**-velt
arrivals	*arrivées*	a-ree-**vay**	*aankomst*	**aahn**-cumst
departures	*départs*	day-**par**	*vertrek*	**vur**-trek
customs	*douane*	doo-**ane**	*douane*	**doo**-ahn-e
baggage-claim	*consigne*	cohn-**seegne**	*baggage claim*	baggage claim
check-in	*enregistrement*	on-reg-eestre-**mon**	*check-in*	check-in
delay	*retard*	ray-**tard**	*vertraging*	**vur**-trah-ging
single/return ticket	*aller simple/aller retour*	allez sahmple/ allez retoor	*enkele reis/ retour*	**ankel**-e reys/ re-toor
first/second class	*première/seconde classe*	pre-**miayr**/se-**gohnd** clas-se	*eerste/tweede klasse*	**ar**-ste/tway-deh **clas**-se

Telephoning & posting

telephone	téléphone	tay-**lay**-phone	telefoon	ta-la-**phone**
telephone box	cabine téléphonique	ca-been-tay-**lay**-phone-eek	telefooncel	ta-la-**phone** cell
telephone directory	annuaire	an-**nu**-**air**	telefoonboek	ta-la-**phone**-book
phonecard	télécarte	tay-lay-**kart**	telefoonkaart	ta-la-**phone**-caahrd
out of order	en dérangement	on day-ronzhe-mon	buiten dienst	**bowten** deenst
post office	poste	**poh**ste	postkantoor	**post**-khan-toar
postcard	carte postale	kart post-**al**	ansichtkaart	**ahn**-sickt-karht
stamp	timbre	**tahm**-bre	postzegel	**post**-za-gel

Eating & drinking

bill/check	l'addition	la-di-**siohn**	rekening	**ray**-ke-ning
menu	menu	me-**nü**	menukaart	menu **carht**
service included	service compris	sair-vees com-**pree**	bediening	be-**dee**-ning
			inbegrepen	in-**bhe**-grayp-en
service not included	service non compris	sair-vees **nohn** com-pree	exclusief	ex-cloo-ceive
			bediening	be-**dee**-ning
breakfast	petit-déjeuner	pay-**tit** day-zhay-**ner**	ontbijt	**ont**-bite
speciality of the day	plat du jour	pla dü **zhoor**	dagschotel	**dach**-schoa-tul
starter	entrée	on-**tray**	voorgerecht	**fohr**-ge-reckt
main course	plat de résistance	pla de ray-zistohns	hoofdgerecht	**howft**-ge-reckt
dessert	dessert	day-**sayr**	dessert	da-**surt**
wine list	carte des vins	kart day van	wijnkaart	**wine**-cahrt
cheers	santé/tchin	sohn-**tay**/chin	proost	prowst
vegetarian	végétarien	ve-zhay-tah-**ryahn**	vegetarisch	vay-ge-**tah**-ris
glass	verre	**vair**	glas	glas
bottle	bouteille/carafe	boo-**tayeu**/ca-**raff**	fles	fles
bread	pain	**pahn**	brood	browd
sugar	sucre	**sü**-kr	suiker	**souw**-ker
tea	thé	**teigh**	thee	tay
coffee	café	ca-**feigh**	koffie	**cough**-fee
orange juice	jus d'orange	zhü do-ranzh	jus d'orange	shoo-d'orange
red/white wine	vin rouge/blanc	van rouzh/**blon**	rode/witte wijn	**roa**-der/wit-eh wine
beer	bière	bi-**yair**	bier	**bee**-ehr
blonde/brown	blonde/brune	**blohnd**/brün	blond/bruin	blond/brown
draught beer	demi pression	**dum-my** pre-**syohn**	bier van 't vat	beer van **tvat**
gin	genièvre	zhun-yay-**vruh**	jenever	**zhu**-na-vur
mineral water	eau minérale	o mee-ney-**rahl**	mineraal water	**mi**-nehr-al **wah**-ter
salt & pepper	sel & poivre	sel ay **pwavre**	peper en zout	**pay**-per en **sowt**
garlic	ail	**eye**	knoflook	**knof**-lowk
eggs	oeufs	**urfs**	eieren	**ay**-r-en
cheese	fromage	fro-**mazh**	kaas	kaars
milk	lait	**lay**	melk	melck
french fries	frites	**freet**	frieten	**free**-tun
crisps	chips	**sheeps**	chips	chips
I have a reservation for..	J'ai une réservation pour..	zhay ün ray-sayr-va-**siohn** poor..	Ik heb gereserveerd voor..	ik eb ge-**res**-ser-veehrd
Have you got a table for...?	Avez-vous une table pour..?	avay-**voo** ün **tab**-le poor..?	Heeft u een tafel voor..?	**hayft** oo ayn **tarf**-el for..?

menu guide

mussels with chips	moules-frites	mool-**freet**	mosselen met friet	mos-sel-lun met freet
eel stewed in sorrel, chervil and citronelle	anguille au vert	ahn-**gueeye** o vare	paling in 't groen	**paah**-ling int **chroon**
veal stew	blanquette de veau	blahn-**kett** de vo	kalfszwezerik	**calfs**-zwa-zurick
venison	chevreuil	she-**vroïye**	wild gebraad	wild chah-**braahd**
rabbit with prunes	lapin aux prunes	lap-ahn o **prüne**	konijn met pruimen	co-**nayn** met **proy**-mun
wild boar	marcassin	mar-ca-**sahn**	wild zwijn	wild zweyn
chunks of chicken in pastry with creamy sauce	bouchée à la reine	boo-**shay** ah lah **rahn**	koninginnehapje	koan-**ing**-ginna-hapya
lean chunks of beef simmered in beer	carbonnades	car-bo-**na**-der	carbonnaden	car-bo-**naah**-der
endives wrapped in ham with cheese	chicon au gratin	shick-**ohn** o grat-**ahn**	witloof met kaas en hesp	**wit**-loaf met **kaahs** en hesp
Flemish stew with oxtail, pigs trotters	hochepot	osh-**po**	hutsepot	**hut**-sah-pot
sprouts with bacon and goose fat	choux de Bruxelles	shoe de brü-**sell**	Brusselse spruitjes	**brus**-sels-e **sproyt**-yus
white asparagus dressed with melted butter and crumbled hard-boiled egg	asperges de Malines	as-**perzhe** de ma-**leen**	Mechelse asperges	**mech**-chals-e as-**per**-zhes
red cabbage cooked with apples, onions, red wine, and vinegar	chou rouge à la flamande	shoe **roo**-zhe allah fla-**mond**	Vlaamse rode kool	**Vlaahm**-se **roa**-de koal
white and black sausages	boudin blanc/noir	boo-dan **blon**/**nwar**	witte en zwarte pensen	**wit**-te en **zwar**-te **pen**-zun
mashed potatoes & vegetables	purée	pür-**ay**	stoemp	stoomp
tomatoes stuffed with boiled fish	tomates garnies	to-**matt** gar-**nee**	gevulde tomaten	chu-**vul**-de **tom**-aah-tun
chicken or fish stew with vegetables	waterzooi	**waah**-ter-soy	waterzooi	**waah**-ter-soy
raw minced beef with chopped onions and mayonaise	filet américain préparé	filay ah-**ma**-ri-ckahn pra-pa-**reigh**	filet américain préparé	filay ah-**ma**-rick-ahn pra-pa-**reigh**
onion soup	soupe à l'oignon	soop a lon-**yon**	ajuinsoep	ah-**yoyn**-soop
open sandwich with soft white cheese and chopped radishes	tartine au fromage blanc	tar-**tin** o fro-**mazh** blon	boterham met plattekaas	**boat**-er-ham met **plat**-te kaahs
grilled ham & cheese sandwich	croque-monsieur	crock me-**syur**	croque-monsieur	crock me-**syur**
Brussels waffles	gaufres de Bruxelles	gow-fre de brü-**sell**	Brusselse wafels	**Brüs**-sels-e **waah**-fuls
Luikse waffles (with crumbled sugar)	gaufre de Liège	gow-fre de lee-**ayzh**	Luikse wafels	**Loyck**-se **waah**-fuls
pancakes	crêpes	**crayp**	pannenkoeken	**pah**-ne-cooker
fried doughnuts	beignets	bay-**nyah**	smoutebollen	**smaw**-tu-bowler
brown spicy biscuits	spéculoos	spay-cü-**loas**	speculoos	**spa**-cu-loas

⬇ key to symbols

symbols

☎ telephone number
f fax
e email
w worldwide web
❶ hot tips
🖒 good points
◐ opening times
♿ wheelchair access
(phone to check details)
🎁 shop
☜ restaurant/café *or* food available
🖵 bar
☆ entertainment
● club
☞ hotel
[BF] (admission) price
◷ frequency/times
► picture arrow
✍ map reference
🖃 credit cards are accepted
★ recommended (featured in listings section)

transport

Ⓜ metro & pre-metro/ metro & pre-metro station
🚊 tram/tram stop
🚌 bus/bus station
🚗 taxi/car
✕ airport
🛥 ferry
🅿 parking available

sights, museums, galleries & parks

☎ recorded information line
☞ guided tours
🎧 audio guides
🧒 kids/age group

key to area maps

white streets = streets with lots of shops, restaurants, bars, etc

black block = important building

restaurants, bars & cafés, & clubs

🍴 seating capacity
▤ air conditioning
🌿 outdoor area/garden
♪ live music
Ⓥ good vegetarian selection
Ⓡ reservation recommended
BF set menu available
● DJs
📺 satellite/cable TV
👔 dress code
🍸 queues possible
👫 gay/lesbian crowd
◻ small venue
⬜ mid-sized venue
⬜ large venue

🇧🇫 main courses under 400BF
🇧🇫🇧🇫 main courses from 400BF–800BF
🇧🇫🇧🇫🇧🇫 main courses over 800BF

hotels

◆ number of bedrooms
☕ breakfast included
▤ air conditioning
24 24-hour room service
〰 swimming pool
↔ facilities
✐ business facilities
🌿 outdoor area/garden
🚬 smoking allowed

🇧🇫 double room under 2500BF
🇧🇫🇧🇫 double room from 2500BF–5000BF
🇧🇫🇧🇫🇧🇫 double room from 5000BF–75000BF
🇧🇫🇧🇫🇧🇫🇧🇫 double room from 7500BF–10,000BF
🇧🇫🇧🇫🇧🇫🇧🇫🇧🇫 double room over 10,000BF